CW00687740

THE ROMANTIC NATIONAL TALE AND THE QUESTION OF IRELAND

In *The Romantic National Tale and the Question of Ireland*, Ina Ferris examines the way in which the problem of "incomplete union" generated by the formation of the United Kingdom in 1800 destabilized British public discourse in the early decades of the nineteenth century. Ferris offers the first full-length study of the main genre to emerge out of the political problem of Union: the national tale, an intercultural and mostly female-authored fictional mode that articulated Irish grievances to English readers. Ferris draws on current theory and archival research to show how the national tale crucially intersected with other public genres such as travel narratives, critical reviews, and political discourse. In this fascinating study, Ferris shows how the national tales of Morgan, Edgeworth, Maturin, and the Banim brothers dislodged key British assumptions and foundational narratives of history, family, and gender in the period.

INA FERRIS is Professor of English at the University of Ottawa. She is the author of *The Achievement of Literary Authority: Gender, History, and the Waverley Novels* (1991) and *William Makepeace Thackeray* (1983). Her work has also appeared in essay collections and in journals such as *Modern Language Quarterly*, *Nineteenth-Century Literature*, *Studies in Romanticism*, and *Eighteenth-Century Fiction*.

THE ROMANTIC NATIONAL TALE AND THE QUESTION OF IRELAND

INA FERRIS

University of Ottawa

PUBLISHED BY THE PRESS SYNDICATE OF THE UNIVERSITY OF CAMBRIDGE
The Pitt Building, Trumpington Street, Cambridge, United Kingdom

CAMBRIDGE UNIVERSITY PRESS
The Edinburgh Building, Cambridge CB2 2RU, UK
40 West 20th Street, New York, NY 10011-4211, USA
477 Williamstown Road, Port Melbourne, VIC 3207, Australia
Ruiz de Alarcón 13, 28014 Madrid, Spain
Dock House, The Waterfront, Cape Town 8001, South Africa

http://www.cambridge.org

First published 2002

Printed in the United Kingdom at the University Press, Cambridge

Typeface Baskerville Monotype 11/12.5 pt *System* LaTeX 2ε [TB]

A catalogue record for this book is available from the British Library

ISBN 0 521 81460 x hardback

for Stephen
and
in memory of my mother, Grazina Balciunas

John remarked upon the misnomer of *settlers* applied to the Irish, who are always un-settling both at home and abroad.

Journal of Thomas Moore (3 August 1823)

Contents

Acknowledgments

This book has benefited enormously from the generosity of friends and colleagues, who shared information, resources, and suggestions as it made its (slow) way toward completion. My thanks in the first instance to Anne Mellor, whose panel on Gender and Genre for the inaugural NASSR conference occasioned the paper that proved to be the start of the book; to Tillotama Rajan and Julia Wright for important interventions that helped make my work more visible; and to Jim Buzard, Claire Connolly, Laura Doyle, Ian Duncan, Peter Garside, Sonia Hofkosh, Ann Rowland, and Ruth Yeazell for opportunities to try out my ideas in congenial and stimulating settings. I was fortunate in finding responsive audiences while my work was in progress, and this book has been reshaped in fruitful ways by their questions and comments. Particular thanks to Marshall Brown, Jill Campbell, Julie Carlson, Stephanie Friedman, Leah Price, David Skilton, Alexander Welsh, and Judith Wilt. I owe a special debt to James Chandler and Katie Trumpener, who provided support for the book at critical moments and whose own work has done so much to prompt a rethinking of questions of nations, novels, and literary history in the Romantic period. I am also grateful to Gary Kelly and Jane Millgate for early and substantial encouragement; to Stuart Curran for keeping this project in mind; to Cormac Ó Grada for a magnanimous spirit that defines collegiality; and to Linda Bree for her smooth steering of the manuscript.

Closer to home, I have been equally fortunate in my students and colleagues. Esther Wohlgemut served as a superb research assistant, bringing to bear on her research tasks the resources of an especially fine and alert mind. It has been an enormous pleasure to work with her. My thanks as well to Keith Wilson, exemplary Chair, whose unstinting support of his colleagues and their research facilitated my work in countless ways. As always, I am indebted to April London, who shared her formidable knowledge of the period with me and whose high intelligence and warm humour have long animated my own scholarly life. For a generous grant that enabled research in Ireland and Great Britain I am grateful to the Social Sciences and Humanities Research Council of Canada.

The book is dedicated to the two people who are most deeply entwined in its pages. My mother, Grazina Balciunas, died while I was completing the final draft, but it was her life as an exile from a beloved small nation that inspired much of my thinking about female patriotism and "minor" nationalism. Stephen walked and talked each chapter with me, and he remains, as ever, the best of my readers in every sense. This Irish tour has been a memorable one for us both.

Portions of Chapters 3 and 4 rework material from "Narrating Cultural Encounter: Lady Morgan and the Irish National Tale," *Nineteenth-Century Literature* (1996) and "Writing on the Border: The National Tale, Female Writing, and the Public Sphere," *Romanticism, History and the Possibilities of Genre*, edited by Tillotama Rajan and Julia Wright (Cambridge: Cambridge University Press, 1998). Some pages in Chapter 2 draw on "Mobile Words: Romantic Travel Writing and Print Anxiety," *Modern Language Quarterly* (1999). My thanks in all three instances for permission to reuse material.

INTRODUCTION

The awkward space of Union

Politics is, essentially, a matter of words.
Pierre Bourdieu *In Other Words*

This book came out of thinking about the awkwardness of a particular phrase, the lumbering "United Kingdom of Great Britain and Ireland," which names the equally awkward new polity that came into being on 1 January 1801. Oddly enough, neither the phrase nor the reconfigured polity has received a great deal of attention in British Romantic studies despite ongoing interest in the construction of a new national consciousness around the turn of the century, when the imperial nation-state was at once expanding and defending itself. Whereas "Great Britain" and "Britishness" feature prominently in recent work, "United Kingdom" rarely surfaces, in part perhaps because the term refers not to a national identity but to a political unit. It names no "imagined community" (in Benedict Anderson's influential formulation) to command affection or allegiance, while its cumbersome articulation testifies to its provenance in the musty and dubious sphere of parliamentary legislation.[1] The United Kingdom thus invokes an outmoded and narrow "politics" rather than the more current and capacious notion of "the political" with its ability to yield witty analogies and surprising intimacies across cultural zones. But both the politics and the awkward phrase are worth taking seriously, for "the United Kingdom of Great Britain and Ireland" defines the new state as less a solution than a problem from the start. The very name adumbrates a dilemma: Ireland is at once a part of the kingdom (a political subject) but not a part of Great Britain (not a national subject). Where the names of Scotland and England have been resolved into the larger unity of Great Britain, holding out the possibility of both preserving and assimilating national difference, Ireland stands within the union but outside the unity, ambiguously attached through vague coordination: "and

Ireland." Is it an afterthought? An equivocal supplement? A singular difference? Perhaps even the start of a series?

Such ambiguities of political discourse did, of course, tend to be rapidly clarified in the immediate context of the Union by the power of state violence on the one hand (the "white terror" following the United Irishmen rebellion of 1798, along with the continuing presence of almost 60,000 troops in Ireland) and British wealth and the requirements of its imperial economy on the other. But at the same time the political and discursive energies released by the Act of Union continued to generate instability on both sides of the Irish Sea, as the Union lurched from crisis to crisis over the next one hundred and twenty years. If the 1707 union of England and Scotland, as Clifford Siskin has argued, constituted a historically significant effort to produce a new national whole by articulating rather than erasing difference – Scotland was politically and economically integrated but remained distinct in law, religion, and education – the incorporation of Ireland introduced a difference that disarticulated and scrambled political and cultural energies held together, albeit not without difficulty, in the compound of "Great Britain."[2] Unlike the Presbyterians of Scotland, the Catholics of Ireland were granted neither full political integration nor autonomous civil institutions (their own "culture," as Siskin has it), and this, combined with the bitter history of their relations with England, meant that their entry into the polity served to unbalance rather than to establish British bearings. More radically than Scotland, early nineteenth-century Ireland marks a vulnerability in the British body politic, one of which it was itself acutely aware, so that the question of Ireland draws particular attention to the workings of political consciousness in Romantic-era Britain as much as to that of the political unconscious with which recent criticism has made us perhaps more familiar.[3]

The literary implications of this consciousness form the subject of this book, which argues that the whole matter of post-Union Ireland bears in significant and insufficiently recognized ways on what Paul Magnuson has called "public Romanticism," the thick and interwoven realm of publication and publicity that forms the matrix of "public cultural consciousness" in the period. Magnuson emphasizes that in early nineteenth-century Britain this matrix was a wide and loose "public discourse" rather than the more limited eighteenth-century "public sphere" posited by Habermas, and he underscores the degree to which the civic culture of writing and reading in Britain during this period operated in openly rhetorical and combative terms rather than in those of an ideal rational consensus.[4] This does not mean that the notion of the public sphere loses either historical or analytic pertinence. Discussion of the Irish question consistently invoked – and manipulated – the authority of reason and the role of consensus stressed by Habermas, while the critical self-understanding of periodicals like the *Edinburgh Review* remained very much tied to Enlightenment models of rationality and discipline. But in the aftermath of the French Revolution and in the context of domestic unrest and foreign war not only was there an acute sense of different "publics" to be addressed but politics had converged with sentiment in new ways, and public debate increasingly become a matter less of discursive reasoning than of performance. In placing Ireland within this public discourse, I want to focus on it as an actor within the domestic literary field and hence to shift the scene of analysis from the imperial stage, which has been garnering most of the attention in the last decade, to a more strictly civic forum.

Ireland is undeniably part of what we now call colonial or imperial Romanticism, and my study owes a great deal to the postcolonial inflection that has brought Ireland a heightened, if still wavering, visibility in English studies of the period. In particular it follows on the important reshaping of Romantic fiction undertaken by Katie Trumpener's *Bardic Nationalism: The Romantic Novel and the British Empire*, which not only gives prominence to Irish genres but recasts literary history in terms of intersecting networks of discourses rather than chronological lines of influence.[5] And it shares with Mary Jean Corbett's recent *Allegories of Union in Irish and English Writing, 1790–1870* a conviction that the matter of Ireland played a crucial role, generally overlooked by English studies, in the discursive formation of the imperial English nation in the nineteenth century.[6] But my interest lies more particularly in the fact that the specificity of Ireland as a problem for the empire in the early decades of the century derived from its incorporation into the British body politic. To put the problem this way – to think about the question of Ireland via civic rather than imperial or colonial discourse – is to highlight the gesture of bringing in rather than the gesture of moving out. To be sure, the imperial nation moves out in order to bring in (e.g., raw materials, capital, profits), but it maintains all the more strenuously a line of demarcation between it and its colonial possessions. The doubleness of Ireland after the formation of the United Kingdom – at once part of the scattered colonial body and of the (ideally) compact domestic body – confounded such demarcations, and placed special pressure on the state in which it was so ambiguously located.

The point is nicely underlined by Byron in his speech on Ireland to the House of Lords in 1812:

> If it must be called an Union, it is the union of the shark with his prey, the spoiler swallows up his victim, and thus they become one and indivisible. Thus has Great Britain swallowed up the parliament, the constitution, the independence of Ireland, and refuses to disgorge even a single privilege, although for the relief of her swollen and distempered body politic.[7]

Voicing a standard critique of the Union, Byron infuses the political figure of incorporation with a literal charge, defining it as a devouring that produces a "swollen and distempered body politic," which refuses to give itself relief by granting the measures commonly known as Catholic Relief (by 1812 the Catholic question had led to the downfall of two ministries and been raised in parliament on at least five prominent occasions). By conflating the idealized British body politic with the grotesque Irish body of English imaginings, Byron produces the engorged body of a United Kingdom stubbornly feeding the distemper that is destroying it. Even if for most English subjects Ireland continued to be placed outside home space and the Irish remained foreign objects "over there," it nonetheless was the case, as Byron's image emphasizes, that Ireland threatened the new body politic as an internal and implosive force. The "sister-kingdom" and "sister-island" (phrases insistently repeated in writing on Ireland) was now part of the body of the nation, but this "sister" strained the body politic and made it ill, proving herself a sister who was somehow not kin. This disconcerting situation – what we might call the reversed uncanny of the stranger-become-family – motivates troubled post-Union genres like the Irish tour, which search for terms in which the United Kingdom might in fact come to mirror what was widely regarded in middle-class public discourse as the more successful union of Scotland and England in Great Britain.

Byron's speech usefully recalls two further points about the institution of the United Kingdom. First, it underlines how quickly the Union changed its meaning, especially on the whiggish side of the British political spectrum; second, it testifies to the way in which the moment of Union was incomplete from the outset because of the outstanding question of Catholic civil rights. It is often forgotten – indeed, the meaning of the Union itself changed so quickly that the participants themselves seemed to forget – that the most bitter opponents of the measure were the privileged Protestants of the Ascendancy, anxious to maintain their local power base, and the fiercely Protestant Orange order which had come into existence in the turbulence of the late 1790s.[8] "The Union,"

Kevin Whelan has bluntly stated, "was a devastating defeat for Irish Protestants."[9] There was certainly some popular and nationalist opposition in Ireland, but by and large, the measure was supported by reformers on both sides of the Irish Sea and accepted (without much enthusiasm) by most Irish Catholics.

While clearly an English cause in the sense of being a security measure against France precipitated by the 1798 United Irishmen rebellion (which was both ideologically inspired and materially supported by republican France[10]), the Union also appeared a more strictly liberal political cause, for it proposed not only to abolish an Irish parliament widely regarded as corrupt but to institute a far-reaching reform of the borough system that would move Ireland far in advance of the British mainland. The Irish "oligarchy" (as journals like the Foxite *Critical Review* liked to call it) was perceived as an obstacle to such reform, and the more liberal English press regularly targeted and vilified members of the Irish Parliament as (in the words of the young Coleridge) a set of "[j]obbers, place-hunters, unconditional hirelings." To have such a "faction" opposed to the measure of Union, Coleridge declared, "we cannot but consider as a species of presumptive argument in its favour."[11] It is worth recalling such language, for within a few years the Union was increasingly seen by liberal-minded English commentators as a cynical exercise of imperial power (as in Byron), while on the other side of the Irish Sea it was quickly rewritten into a nationalist narrative that turned all opposition to it into a sign of patriotism and political virtue.[12] Benefiting from such recoding, the exclusively Protestant Irish Parliament was soon transformed (to cite a Catholic Irish character in John Banim's *The Anglo-Irish of the Nineteenth Century*) into "our own parliament."[13]

The changing meanings of Union had a great deal to do in turn with the second point highlighted by the passage from Byron: the vexed entanglement of the question of Catholic rights with the question of Union. When it was proposed, the Union was generally understood, especially but not only by Catholic Ireland, as a double moment of which political incorporation was simply the first moment, to be followed by the removal of the remaining legal disabilities of Irish Catholics. Coleridge, for example (like most commentators for and against the Act of Union) assumed that emancipation would follow its passage, assuring readers that in an "Imperial Legislature" such civil rights could be "safely conceded, and indefinitely extended."[14] Although emancipation was never explicitly promised (at least in public), its expectation was explicitly encouraged, so that it attained what Thomas Bartlett calls "the status of an union engagement."[15] This "engagement" remained unfulfilled for almost three decades, and during that period Catholic petitions and Catholic Relief bills were repeatedly rejected. The failure of the British state to grant Catholic relief meant that it lost any residual political authority it may have had with Irish Catholics, and this loss of authority was not only very public but also a trigger for the emergence of alternative forms of authority "out of doors." It is not that the Irish (whether Catholic like Daniel O'Connell or Protestant like Henry Grattan) gave up on official politics but that the campaign for emancipation simultaneously mobilized forces on unofficial territory. Activating for themselves the properly political power Hannah Arendt has identified with the pledge, Irish agitators banded together to form rival or resistant organizations to act as levers in the official sphere.[16] Daniel O'Connell's Catholic Association of the 1820s (discussed in Chapter 6) is the best-known instance of such banding together in the period, but it had been occurring on a smaller scale, especially among Catholic gentry and merchants, since soon after Union. In the same year that Byron spoke on the Irish question, for example, Irish Catholics from different counties held meetings in which they pledged to vote only for those parliamentary candidates willing to support emancipation. Repeatedly, the British government attempted to snuff out such efforts, invoking or threatening to invoke the 1793 Convention Act which forbad setting up a rival public body to parliament. Suggestively, the granting of emancipation coincided with the spectacular achievement of precisely such a body through the groundbreaking and formidable experiment in mass politics spearheaded by O'Connell in the late 1820s.

From the start, then, the Union was an unstable and incomplete moment – indeed the motif of "incomplete Union" became something of a mantra in the period. Thus cast in terms of lack, it served as an incitement to intervention and discourse, promoting a re-accentuation of established discursive forms (e.g., travel writing, periodical reviews, lyric poetry, memoirs) along with the production of new ones, notably the national tale that is my focus. What largely motivated all this activity was desire to "secure" the Union, a desire predicated on the alarm generated by the incomplete first moment. So Francis Jeffrey and his allies mounted a vigorous emancipation campaign in the pages of the *Edinburgh Review*, urging parallels between the Irish Catholics and the excluded and degraded *roturier* before the French Revolution: "What the Roturier was in France, the Catholic is in Ireland: – and, if his conduct should ultimately be the same, it will not be without a precedent, nor those who provoke it, without a warning."[17] A year later his colleague Sydney Smith (indefatigable campaigner for emancipation) put it more directly, declaring that it was "by no means improbable, that the country may be, ere long, placed in a situation where its safety or ruin will depend upon its conduct towards Catholics."[18] The alarmist language of such statements is more than simply a rhetorical tactic in the emancipation debate; it points to a sense of the volatility of the political space whose bounds were threatened by the "leftover" of Catholic claims. What threatened in Ireland at this point, however, was never revolution, despite spurts of militancy such as Robert Emmet's rising of 1803. The real risk implicit in the Union was not that the Irish masses would take to violence but that they would begin to understand themselves as a public and hence take to politics.

The potential emergence of a new public is what was at stake in the long frustrated campaign for emancipation, a campaign that might otherwise seem to have been much ado about rather little. It is not that there was massive British interest in the Catholic question – the *Monthly Review* commented in 1812 that Irish affairs generally drew "the thinnest houses" in parliament – although there was a continuing marked interest at the highest official levels.[19] It is rather that a constitutional measure making a difference to only a few privileged persons generated such strong response (both for and against) and – even more – succeeded in mobilizing the Irish masses within so short a period of time. Catholic emancipation basically meant only the right to sit in parliament, along with access to the most senior political and judicial offices, so that radicals and conservatives alike often dismissed the constitutional matter as "mere politics," an irrelevant formal concern and distraction from real, material evils. But such criticisms, James MacIntosh argued in the *Edinburgh Review*, missed the point. To dismiss the emancipation question as "the repeal of a few remaining disabilities" was to overlook that the exclusion of Irish Catholics from full constitutional privileges was (as he put it) "a fact of a very peculiar nature." Unlike similar religious exclusions by dominant sects in other countries brought in to ensure a "monopoly of profit and power," the exclusion of Irish Catholics, MacIntosh explained, was "not directed against a sect – it was directed against a nation. It was the proscription of a people, under the name of a religion." The exclusionary laws were promulgated by a "conquering colony" against a "conquered nation," and no matter the specific names they used for those excluded (Irish, Papists, Rebels), their target was always the "same body of men."[20] Such reiteration had inevitably produced a powerfully negative climate of hatred, fear, and contempt, and it was this amorphous and emotive level of "discontent" that had to be addressed if the Union was to hold.

MacIntosh's point is not just that under the conditions of colonization the law partakes of the original violence of conquest but that because it does so, it achieves a peculiarly affective and representative power. There is always more at stake than seems to be the case, so that when it comes to law (or, for that matter, to politics), the situation tends always to exceed both the text and the standard parameters of interpretation. Specific laws are immediately generalized, for both sides read the law as a doubled synecdoche: a particular law implies the entire polity from which it emerges; particular exclusions imply the whole social body even as they name only a part.[21] Through this slippage from part to whole and back again, the law gains its affective power, especially in relation to the subjected group, for every subject therein feels "named" in the law and hence insulted or degraded by it. This is why those not directly affected by laws nonetheless become heavily invested in them, a point made by Francis Jeffrey in accounting for the puzzling fact that so many Irish felt so strongly about legal exclusions which made a difference to only a few: "the sense of injustice and partiality communicated itself to the whole body." It is this phenomenon, he says, that accounts for general Catholic "disaffection" and for "that impatience for the removal of their remaining badges of inferiority, which has sometimes appeared more turbulent than the object could justify."[22] In appearing "more turbulent than the object could justify," Irish response testifies to the troubling asymmetries of signification and interpretation on Irish ground. British public discourse generally located the whole question of representation in relation to Ireland (whether political, legal, or literary) in a slippery realm where the conventional relations governing signs and their interpretation gave way. Irish terrain was perceived as equivocal and conflictual, and on such terrain, as the editors of a recent volume on nineteenth-century Ireland have noted, ideology was "unable to 'naturalize' itself."[23] When it came to Ireland, that is, very little could go without saying.

The matter of saying (directed words rather than transparent truths) is very much to my point. To think about Ireland via the question of incomplete Union is to think about words that draw attention to themselves as performative instead of effacing themselves in the act of signification: words that *do* something (to recall J. L. Austin's famous title). It is thus to move into the foreground a sense of language and public discourse as a mobile scene of agitation and agency (rather than impersonal system and containment) and hence to understand a cultural field in terms of friction as much as analogy or homology. As political topos, early nineteenth-century Ireland marks the intersection of different discursive spheres: the official realm of high politics; the semi-official realm of public discourse (many of whose writers were not infrequently also participants in the official political realm); and the unofficial realm of "out of doors" pamphlets, speeches, caricatures, assemblies, and so on. At a certain level of historical analysis the differentiations of this field may dissolve, absorbed into the larger unity of bourgeois culture or imperialism or patriarchal law, and there are good analytic reasons for performing this kind of positive reduction. But it is equally important to recall the particular discursive processes and practices that shape the specificity of topics and the making of publics within a cultural or political field. At this level, the pragmatics of language move into sharp relief; at the same time so does a more dynamic notion of culture as encounter, often of an abrasive kind. More precisely, the discourse on Ireland helps to underline that if, as Bourdieu argues, politics is basically a struggle over access to the symbolic power of constitutive naming, the authority of political words to name depends in a fundamental way on the fact that they are in the first instance modes of address, activators of an interlocutory encounter in which the lines of influence may move in uncertain directions.[24]

Percy Shelley's early foray into the question of Ireland helps to make the case. In February 1812, nineteen-year-old Percy and his even younger wife, Harriet, landed in Dublin to print and distribute copies of a pamphlet (written by Percy in England the previous month) in which he addressed Irish Catholics, and presented Catholic emancipation and repeal of the Union as "rational means of remedy" for the evils of their state. Cast in the imperative mood ("O Irishmen, REFORM YOURSELVES"), the pamphlet spends most of its time urging the importance of politics (discussion, assembly, union) and discouraging revolutionary violence: "Think, read, and talk . . . disclaim all manner of alliance with violence, meet together if you will, but do not meet in a mob."[25] To this text, Shelley appended a present-tense Postscript, in which he announces that having now been in Dublin for a week, he has made himself "more accurately acquainted with the state of the public mind on those great topics of grievances which induced me to select Ireland as a theatre, the widest and fairest, for the operations of the determined friend of religious and political freedom."[26] The result of these observations on the spot has been a conviction of the need for an association to obtain emancipation and repeal, and so he writes another pamphlet directed to very different readers, the young men of Dublin College.[27] This pamphlet drops the imperative mood, replacing it with a more philosophical tone (gentleman-to-gentleman), but makes essentially the same political point. In the event, neither class of reader was impressed; Shelley's pamphlets were massively ignored (nor was his attempt at oral address to an assembly of middle-class Catholics any more successful). Urged by Godwin, he withdrew both texts and, in short order, himself from Ireland as well.

My point is not that Shelley's words lacked authority in Dublin nor that he, like many other civic-minded English visitors of the period, arrived in the country with ideas for its improvement firmly in tow, a prescriptive text already written. What makes the Shelley incident particularly telling is that even so limited an encounter with the subject of his discourse occasioned a new text and a change of genre. Shelley altered neither his political model nor his basic approach to the question of Ireland. On the contrary. But he did alter his perception of the problem, and registered this shift, notably, as a change in his sense of his addressee. "These were the persons to whom in my fancy I had addressed myself," he writes from Dublin, referring to the urban poor of Ireland; "how quickly were my views on this subject changed! yet how deeply has this very change rooted the conviction on which I came hither."[28] Contact with the Irish has reinforced his political stand, but it has also dispelled his "fancy" about becoming Tom Paine in Ireland; more particularly, it has dispelled his a priori understanding of what constitutes the proper genre of intervention.[29] Shelley shifts from the genre of address – "An Address, To the Irish People" – to that of the proposal – "Proposals For an Association of Those Philanthropists, etc." – directing himself to a different audience and hence framing the question of Ireland in a quite different way.

Even as public discourse enacts the systemic and regulative functions with which we have become familiar (words as symptomatic effects), it at the same time operates more dynamically as the making of utterances (words as intersubjective events). The matter of utterance is crucial to an understanding of public discourse and its literary genres not only because, as Mikhail Bakhtin insists, "[u]tterances are not indifferent to one another" but because they pivot on the situation of the enunciation. What Bakhtin observes about speech genres applies equally to the public genres of print culture: "Each speech genre in each area of speech communication has its own typical conception of the addressee, and this defines it as a genre."[30] Especially in those genres that Paul Magnuson has termed "genres of public utterance," sites of enunciation and modes of address move directly into the foreground.[31] The pamphlet debate preceding Union, for instance, featured countless titles such as "An

Appeal to the Sober Understanding of Englishmen, on the Present State of Ireland" (1797); "A View of the Present State of Ireland . . . addressed to the People of England" (1798); "A Letter Addressed to the Gentlemen of England and Ireland on the Inexpediency of a Federal Union Between the Two Kingdoms" (1798); "An Address to the People of Ireland, on the Present State of Public Affairs" (1798); and so forth. Titles like these remind us of the often obscured performative notion of representation itself: representation as less a portrayal *of* something than a presentation *to* someone.[32] The shift of preposition from the ostensive "of" (of something) to the pragmatic "to" (to someone) involves a shift, usefully defined by Merleau-Ponty, from first-order to second-order language. In first-order language, he remarks, we speak of events, ideas, and objects in order to point to them; but in second-order language, we speak of these things primarily "to reach some person."[33] Genres with a distinct set to an addressee can be understood as second-order genres, necessarily possessing an ostensive dimension but generically motivated by the interlocutory occasion. This means that such genres always – and importantly – keep in play what we might call a sense of the preposition: a sense of discourse as the activation of specific relations (a speaking before, to, on behalf of, against, etc.). Given the dominance of the idea of representation as duplication of a given, however, the *pre*positional space of discourse can always dissolve and transform itself (or be transformed into) *pro*positional space, so that a speaking "of" or "to" becomes the assertion "that." Herein lies the importance of second-order genres, for their rhetoricity makes such a move difficult by reminding us of the *directed* nature of writing and of language as a social and intertextual field in which words respond to words as much as they point to things.

The innovative power of the national tale, the most important literary form emerging out of the debate on Ireland and a female-authored genre only beginning to move back into critical purview, lies precisely in its status as such a second-order genre.[34] Named by Sydney Owenson (later Lady Morgan) in her pioneering *The Wild Irish Girl: A National Tale* (1806) but shaped as well by the better known Maria Edgeworth in *Ennui* (1809) and *The Absentee* (1812), the national tale was an explicit response to the civic and English genre of the Irish tour. As such it not only placed itself directly inside properly public discourse but did so at a critical angle, at once complementing and targeting the travel-text and its civic assumptions. Although it maintained the liberal politics of the tour, in particular its commitment to the cause of Catholic Emancipation, the national tale rewrote the metropolitan traveler-figure by mobilizing the old romance plot of encounter to subject this figure to a disorientation that altered his (more rarely her) center of both personal and national being. The implications of such displacement have only recently begun to be pursued, however, primarily because the national tale's address to an English reader led to its being routinely dismissed as a suspect or, at best, naive colonialist genre.

Historicist and feminist analysis of the last decade has done much to obviate this kind of dismissal, most notably in the case of Edgeworth whose critical profile has become markedly more prominent in a very short time.[35] But Morgan has been less fortunate in her relations with the critical field, as was the case in her own lifetime as well. Although she is starting to receive more serious attention and some of her texts are returning to print, her impact remains under-recognized, and part of my purpose in this book is to highlight her significance for Romantic literary history, especially in terms of notions of female patriotism and authorship in the period.[36] Mingling nationalist and cosmopolitan motifs in provocative ways, especially after the success of *The Wild Irish Girl*, Morgan pushed questions of femininity and the nation beyond the prevailing domestic model into speculative and improvisational terrain that confounded standard analogical conflations of the female and national body. Herself an actor's daughter (as contemporary reviews liked to remind their readers), she also exploited and experimented with her dubious status in the literary field in ways not open to the more respectable Edgeworth, writing female authorship itself in a more aggressive and performative register than Edgeworth was willing to do. Accordingly, she receives more attention in the book than does her more prestigious compatriot. This is not to minimize Edgeworth's achievement either in establishing a distinctive strand of Irish fiction or, more generally, in bringing the novel as a form into literary respectability in Great Britain.[37] Rather, it is to bring to notice less familiar and rational forms of female literary intervention, ones whose authority does not mesh quite so readily as does that of Edgeworth with the model of the "mother–teacher" to whose centrality within public discourse Anne Mellor and other feminist historians have been drawing attention.[38]

Both Edgeworth and Morgan, however, understood the national tale as the same kind of novelistic project within post-Union public discourse. Walter Scott summed up this project in the very year of Catholic Emancipation when, in an often cited remark, he declared that the novels of Maria Edgeworth had done more "towards completing the Union, than perhaps all the legislative enactments by which it has been followed up."[39] For Scott, the key to this completion of Union (whose announcement, as always, was premature) lay in Edgeworth's ability to mobilize the affective resources available to fictional, as opposed to legal, language in order to generate sympathy for Ireland in English readers. This is so widely conventional a view of the power of fiction that we tend to overlook the degree to which it gives priority to the readerly rather than referential pole of Edgeworth's Irish fiction: it is always possible, after all, that Edgeworth's Ireland might not be true even though it is sympathetic. Scott and other contemporary readers may have deployed a normative vocabulary of representation in their assessments – there was much praise for the "accuracy" of Edgeworth's Irish portraits – but at the same time they assumed that the national tale as a genre was primarily motivated less by mimetic than pragmatic impulses, its representational ambitions subordinated to its desire to produce sympathy. Morgan made the point even more clearly when explaining why she turned to fiction to promulgate a political argument: "A novel is especially adapted to enable the advocate of any cause to steal upon the public, through the by-ways of the imagination, and to win from its sympathies what its reason so often refuses to yield to undeniable demonstration."[40]

Worth notice is Morgan's metaphor of fiction's furtive movement ("to steal upon the public"), for it illuminates the particular dynamic of sympathy structuring the national tale. As fiction steals up on the public, it induces inner agitation in the reader, animating the sympathetic faculties against a recalcitrant reason that refuses (rather like the engorged body of the United Kingdom in Byron) to be reasonable. Importantly, emphasis thus falls not on the sense of sympathy as a bridging or mediating emotion between separate entities, but on sympathy as the activation of internal disequilibrium. In contrast to Adam Smith's well-known model of sympathy, which posits a ready alignment of the affective and the rational in a moment of stabilizing self-reproduction, the national tale operates out of a more Humean model in which sympathy insinuates itself into and disturbs the regular flow of one's consciousness.[41] It makes pivotal the initial moment of internal estrangement and dislodgment on which the subsequent outward flow of feeling depends. In its scenario, then, cultural sympathy depends on an initial discomfort, on a certain unhinging of a consciousness from its familiar place.

This dynamic within the national tale points to the way in which the entire discourse on Ireland in the early decades of the nineteenth century in Britain was marked by a persistent and profound discomfort. As a literary and, more generally, a cultural motor in the period, discomfort has not received the attention of more glamorous motors like desire or the sublime. Although, like them, discomfort is the register of disequilibrium, it pertains to those more mundane and everyday matters that are part of our existence as conditional beings in a world where relations to others are inescapable and not always easy. An indistinct threshold state involving both body and mind (a sensation-emotion), discomfort lacks the drama of the limit attached to other sensation-emotions such as panic or terror; nor is it to be understood in terms of interiority like the more familiar romantic moods of melancholy, nostalgia, or yearning. Two analytic points are central: first, discomfort belongs to consciousness, for it is consciousness that registers discomfort (we are aware of ourselves as uncomfortable); second, discomfort foregrounds the unsettling side of sociability and hence of cultural being and beings. What it marks are those moments when individuals experience the pressure of something outside themselves as a rubbing up against something that makes them feel not-at-home rather than, say, as moments of transport or coercion or some other affective modality of encounter. Significantly, what generally produces such a sense is not so much a confrontation with alterity as a coming up against indeterminacy, an encounter with forms of in-betweenness that elude familiar categories and do not occupy a fixed place (as "the other" usually does).[42]

Ireland was precisely such a form in British public discourse in the Romantic period, and its persistent irritation of that discourse draws attention to the often overlooked level of culture that we might call the subsurface. This area just below the surface is the sensitive edge of cultural consciousness where minds, bodies, and social rule chafe against one another, operating neither in the coherence of unconscious forces (deep structure, dialectics) nor in the randomness and disjunction of the surfaces marking modern cultures. It is at this level of subsurface that the Anglo-Irish enunciation (which was to have so profound an impact on the formation of "English literature" later in the century) had its peculiar effect. The term "Anglo-Irish" itself, in fact, seems to have taken hold in the decades immediately after Union. Rarely appearing in 1800, when terms like "English-Irish" or "Anglo-Hibernian" or, simply, "Irish" were more common, it was sufficiently established by 1828 to enter the title of John Banim's bitter *The Anglo-Irish of the Nineteenth Century*, a national tale that essentially undoes the genre as it mounts a fierce assault on the very possibility of being Anglo-Irish. Increasingly aware of themselves in the wake of Union as an "embattled minority,"[43] Irish Protestants lived out this minority status in different ways, as the careers of Edgeworth and Morgan themselves sufficiently indicate. But all shared a certain insecurity and fearfulness that came from belonging neither to England (which found them a nuisance) nor to Ireland (which was coming to define itself as a Catholic nation), members of a cultural formation that made everyone uncomfortable.

As Patrick O'Farrell has observed, theirs was essentially a negative rather than syncretic identity: "neither Irish nor English. (The negative catches this situation better than the positive form – *both* Irish and English)."[44] So caught in the negative, Anglo-Irish writers like Sydney Morgan and Charles Robert Maturin came to live the hyphen of their existence not so much as a bridge between names as a slipping out of the name altogether. "I am an Irishman, unnoticed and unknown," declared Charles Robert Maturin in the Dedicatory Letter to *The Wild Irish Boy*, and his privatives ("unnoticed," "unknown") point to more than his own eccentric personal condition.[45] As the Connellite John Banim was to put it in the 1820s, when the campaign for Catholic emancipation was in its heated final stages, in terms of "national name" the Anglo-Irish were in fact "nothing": "They are unknown to the world; and, even by their connexions in other lands, unrecognized as a people."[46] To stand outside the recognition of a name in this way is to stand outside history and its narratives of national memory. If individual Anglo-Irish sought terms of entry into the historical narrative, whether of Britain or Ireland, the group itself presented a distinctive case within the polity. Unlike groups within Scotland or England, it was cut off from the appeal to and authority of history at the very moment when the turn to history began to assume definitive status across a wide range of cultural and cognitive spheres. In an important sense, this book suggests, forms like Maturin's Irish Gothic or Morgan's later national tales constitute a writing *around* rather than within history, and it is precisely because of this position of not-quite-belonging that they estrange foundational narratives of history and gender. It is no accident that contemporary English reviewers consistently aligned both writers with foreign rather than domestic genres.

In arguing for the question of Ireland as a lever in early nineteenth-century British public discourse, I concentrate on modalities of motion, on the agitations of discourse, and on the changing relations (rather than changing representations) of cultural discussion. Chapter 1 focuses on travel narratives by civic-minded travelers, which emerged out of anxieties over the state of the Union. The post-Union Irish tour, setting out to resolve the problem of "incomplete Union," presented Ireland as a "case" to be addressed through liberal reason and sentiment, but it found itself at once stymied in Irish home space and caught up in a repetitive, non-progressive temporality discomfitingly like – but also importantly unlike – that to which it routinely confined the Irish. If the traveler-narrator's enunciation was discomfited, however, it was not really altered, and the project of the national tale was to bring the traveler-narrator figure inside the travel narrative, a narrative now governed by a different site and gender of enunciation. Chapter 2 thus reads the national tale as a migratory genre that foregrounded the narrative pragmatics of enunciation and address as it sought to gain Ireland a new kind of hearing on the metropolitan stage. It concentrates on *The Wild Irish Girl* but makes reference to novels by Edgeworth and Maturin in stressing the degree to which the political project of the national tale was crucially dependent on a narrative act of dislocation – an unbalancing of the traveler/reader – and an exploitation of the position of the stranger. This was a deeply equivocal position in Ireland, as the national tale well understood, but the genre nonetheless made this liminal social role the hinge that allowed for the possibility of movement between cultures and for a certain transformation of subjectivity. In Morgan's first national tale such transformation is effected by erotic encounter with a pastorally inflected national heroine, but her later national tales dramatically rewrite this heroine and the notion of the nation associated with her. Chapter 3 argues that in novels like *Florence Macarthy* and *The O'Briens and the O'Flahertys*, Morgan rethinks the question of femininity and national-political agency in an increasingly feminist key, bypassing the family as the affective and theoretical basis of national order. In these texts, Morgan rejects the aesthetics of intimacy and interiority shaping domestic genres to experiment with an aesthetic of estrangement attached to an unconjugal and performative heroine. Operating in a strikingly mobile way, this heroine is linked to informal and tenuous forms of sociality at once local and cosmopolitan as well as ambiguously Catholic.

Turning to Maturin's little-read *The Milesian Chief*, Chapter 4 considers another modulation of the national tale, as Maturin pushes the travel plot of Morgan's political romance into a limit-zone and invents Irish Gothic in the process. Placing Maturin's text in relation to Romantic ruin genres, the chapter argues that Irish Gothic, generally read in psychological terms of fantasy and displacement, was at the same time an intervention in period debates over history and culture. As *The Milesian Chief* negotiates different forms of ruin writing, the novel activates the gothic "shudder" of the ruin (a nihilist moment) to undo late Enlightenment forms of history from cosmopolitan humanism to romantic and revolutionary nationalism. Maturin thus releases a negativity which was inherent in the national tale from the outset as a consequence of its Anglo-Irish enunciation, and it was precisely this enunciation that came under attack when a newly confident Catholic nationalism began to move onto the literary scene in the 1820s. Chapter 5 foregrounds this volatile decade, when Daniel O'Connell and his Catholic Association forged a new Irish public and a new hybrid politics of demand, bringing Ireland into the modern political arena. Actively participating in this process, the national tale became the novel of insurgency, as writers deliberately summoned rankling memories of the 1798 rising as part of the emancipation campaign. Taking the form of engaged "recollection," such novels underline that on Irish ground the writing of history typically blocked both nostalgic "memorial" and impersonal "knowledge," so throwing off balance a British discourse that sought to sustain itself on an ethos of distance, moderation and impersonality. But if the O'Connellite ethos of immediacy and embodiment acted on the one hand to dislodge the consolidations of British discourse, on the other it functioned on Irish soil itself as a demand for consolidation and identification. Under the pressure of such demand, the chapter concludes, interstitial and equivocal forms like the national tale were inevitably dissolved.

In highlighting notions of mobility, transfer, and modulation, this book stresses that literary history is as much about movements and shifts, if not necessarily radical ruptures, as about systematic and spatial relations. In general, the historical turn of recent decades has tended to downplay the temporal in favour of the spatial, producing an outpouring of literary histories governed by geographical metaphors of historical understanding: maps, topographies, geologies, and so on. These have been enormously productive, but at the same time, they tend to skirt the issue of what Michel de Certeau calls cultural operations. "Today we have a surfeit of knowledge and methods as far as structures are concerned," Certeau writes, "and we are impoverished as soon as we have to study operations, transformations, in short, movement."[47] For Certeau cultural operations are performed far inside the interstices of official structures, but the question of Ireland in the early nineteenth century points to mobilities and aggravations at the more visible subsurface of official structures that may equally displace its equilibrium. If the structure recovers, at least for a time, the point is that it is never quite so secure as it seems. To recognize its discomfort while not forgetting its reach is the aim of the chapters that follow.

CHAPTER I

Civic travels: the Irish tour and the new United Kingdom

"What can possess you to go to Ireland?" exclaimed a friend of mine, "where the hedges are lined with pikes and blunderbusses?"

John Carr *The Stranger in Ireland* (1806)

The roads in Ireland, even those called post-roads, are often in the very worst line of direction, and not unfrequently go zig-zag and round about, when there is no occasion for it.

The Reverend James Hall *Tour Through Ireland* (1813)

To travel in Ireland in the early nineteenth century, these British tour-texts suggest, was not to know quite where you were. It was not just the propensity of Irish roads to become parodies of the very idea of a road, as in the Reverend Hall's account, nor the way in which boundary lines threatened to turn into screens for those bent on erasing those very lines, as in John Carr's not entirely serious evocation of the standard English motif of Irish insurgency.[1] The problem was one of specifying the location. Officially, British visitors were simply moving about in another part of the single polity known as the United Kingdom, but Ireland continued to feel (as it long had in English eyes) remote and peculiar. Its incorporation into Great Britain in 1801 thus generated for the English the disconcerting situation nicely summed up by Seamus Deane: "They see Ireland in conventional terms as a foreign place much given to rebellion; whereas in fact it is home."[2] As Deane's formulation suggests, Ireland was disquieting less because it was "strange" (its strangeness was a well-established trope in British discourse) than because its radical ambiguity after Union – the foreign place that was also home – estranged home space itself. The question of Ireland kept intruding on British culture in this period, for the alterity of Ireland now lay inside that culture, and the problems it raised were precisely those that bore on notions of the interior, the home, the domestic. This is not to downplay the urgency of its status as an "internal colony" nor to suggest that other internal colonies like Scotland did not destabilize home space, but it is to argue that the "incomplete Union" of the United Kingdom exerted a particular and powerful pressure on metropolitan discourse in the period, complicating the colonial paradigm and rewriting some of the basic oppositions (internal and external, literary and political, public and private) structuring the Romantic literary field.[3]

A liberal and English genre (even when written by Scots or Anglo-Irish), the Irish tour makes especially clear the degree to which Ireland was understood in post-Union British public discourse as a domestic and civic issue.[4] The "safety of empire" at stake in the tour was primarily that of the "home" empire of the United Kingdom, so that in a very real sense what the post-Union Irish tour sought to domesticate (to bring home) was not so much the Irish as the unhomely Union itself. This process certainly involved domesticating the Irish; indeed, the Union itself was an attempt to pacify Ireland so as to secure the internal boundaries of Britain against the threat of both external (French) enemies and internal (Irish and English) agitators. But from the start it was mired in contradictions and shot through with instabilities, so that it came into being, as the previous chapter suggested, not so much as a solution as a new problem. To understand and help resolve this problem was the civic ambition of the early nineteenth-century Irish tour, a genre practiced mostly by male writers drawn from the professional and gentry classes: landowners, clergymen, educationists, social reformers, and lawyers, along with a sprinkling of leisured gentlemen and professional travel writers.[5] Motivated by its civic concern, the tour was anxious in particular both to conciliate the Irish and to convince English policy makers to remove the discriminatory political and economic measures that obstructed full union. "The union of Ireland will ever want a cordial cement," declared John Carr, striking the generic keynote, "as long as political distinctions that degrade her are permitted to exist."[6] Advocating legislative measures like Catholic emancipation and economic measures like free trade or currency reform, the tour typically framed the Irish problem in terms inherited from the rationality of the Enlightenment, looking to its analytic power for ways to extricate the Union from its dilemma. "The union has certainly created a demand for a statistical, economical, moral and political view of Ireland," wrote Maria and Richard Lovell Edgeworth in their review of Carr's Irish travels for the *Edinburgh Review*, and they sum up the liberal ideology informing the tour in calling for "clear explanation" of the continuing obstacles to "progress" and "improvement," as well as for remedies in line with "sound policy and practical humanity."[7]

But if Ireland enters public discourse in the Romantic period as something to be explained – "an *explicandum*," as Joep Leerssen puts it[8] – the Irish tour, like the national tale that takes off from it, seeks to complete Union by forging ties not only of reason but of sentiment as well. Carr wants a "cordial cement," while an English agriculturalist and former member of parliament named J. C. Curwen sets out to persuade English readers "that nothing can so effectually promote the moral and political improvement of Ireland, and so essentially serve the first and best interests of both contries [*sic*], as a cordial co-operation and union of sentiment."[9] The interest in sentiment and cordiality testifies to the awareness among commentators on Ireland that the Union, while generally regarded as a rational and practical measure for both England and Ireland, was at the same time a murkier and less rational affair. Thus the Reverend James Hall, Scottish chaplain to the earl of Caithness, adds to his account of his 1813 tour an appendix on the Union, declaring his conviction that it will ultimately benefit Ireland but conceding that at the present moment it has thrown "a general damp and discontent over the sister-kingdom."[10] To account for this dissatisfaction, a dissatisfaction that seems to him especially puzzling when found among those outside the political order, he mounts an argument that both individuals and nations are driven by a law of "self-continuation" from which emerges a "consciousness of identity." This consciousness inevitably resists what will bring about its own destruction, so that when a great state proposes an "amalgamation" with a small nation, the small nation instinctively feels "an alarm for self-preservation" and a reluctance to "be swallowed up as a stream in the ocean."[11]

It is not only Ireland Hall has in mind, as becomes apparent when he cites the earlier experience of Scotland at the moment of its union with England. Working with a nationalist model that pits the laws of economic reason against those of national identity, he argues that union with England might bring with it the prospect of greater wealth and comfort for the Scots but at the price of their own identity: "There would be no more genuine Scotsmen."[12] Impelled by this model, he provides a rare reading of the 1798 Irish rebellion as a revolutionary expression of separatist nationalist energies rather than seeing it (as do most travel-texts) as a civil war fuelled by long-standing internal grievances. By now having alarmed even himself, Hall pulls up short: "Having made these observations, it may be proper for me to add that I am very far from thinking that the Union was not a measure advantageous to both countries."[13]

Katie Trumpener has argued that travel writing on Ireland in the Romantic period typically crossed the rational discourse of the

Enlightenment survey with a counter-strain deriving from a "bardic nationalism" developed in the Celtic peripheries, and Hall's is an unusually explicit and conflicted instance of the pressure of those peripheries on an essentially metropolitan genre.[14] But it points as well to the way in which the Union itself operated as a site of unease in the tour. The desirablility of achieving Union was rarely in doubt but neither was the fact that it had not yet been achieved. Moreover, the unsavoury matrix of its passage (rebellion and repression, bribery, deliberately misleading language in relation to the Catholic situation, and so forth) combined with the continuing sense of unrest that I have been calling "incomplete Union" to make the whole subject not just unsettled but unsettling.[15] Anxiety hovers around the term, and its appearance in a travel-text is always highly charged. Even a solid statistician like the English agricultural authority Edward Wakefield moves into excess when Union comes into view. Defending the measure in the preface to *An Account of Ireland, Statistical and Political* (1812), he goes into overdrive: "Connexion with Great Britain – union – inseparable union – the being one and the same empire – one and the same people – to have the same interests – throwing the broad parental shield of the British monarchy over the farthermost parts of Ireland, and over the meanest of her inhabitants, can alone promote the general and individual welfare of both countries." What makes this noteworthy is not just the nervous insistence of the prose but the fact that the previous page includes an odd footnote in which Wakefield retells an anecdote from Boswell's *Life of Johnson*. Johnson tells an Irish gentleman: "Do not make an union with us, Sir; we should unite with you only to rob you. We should have robbed the Scotch, if they had had any thing of which we could have robbed them."[16] Wakefield may simply enjoy the dig at the Scots, but the unresolved juxtaposition of an England that "robs" and an England that acts as "parental shield" renders the act of political amalgamation literally dubious, and establishes the Union as an event inhabited by ambiguity and incoherence.

Other travelers were more direct. "But how can we call this a union between two countries," one writer asks, "where one lost every thing, and the other gave up nothing[?]"[17] "Nearly twenty years of an union has produced nothing," asserts John Bernard Trotter, an eccentric Anglo-Irish Whig who had served as private secretary to Charles James Fox. Blaming both the revered Fox and less-revered Pitt for failure to "consolidate" the empire, Trotter presents Ireland as an explosive force waiting for the opportunity to throw off English power. So long as England holds "the great body of the population unredressed in Ireland," he warns, "so long must expence [*sic*], danger, and uncertainty for the future, continue."[18]

Trotter's warning, while clearly tactical, is not simply so; it registers as well an acute sense of the fragility of English power in Ireland, a sense apparent throughout his text. He keeps reiterating that the English have failed in their rule, declaring that "they have made little impression on the language, religion, or mind of the country. Princes, lord-deputies, and armies, have laboured to change them but fruitlessly."[19] Trotter thus calls attention to the obvious but often overlooked point that the equilibrating narratives of empire (such as travel writing) are posited on an initial disequilibrium, on a dissonance that dislodges the confidence of imperial discourse in the first place. The post-Union Irish tour is imbued with the recognition on the part of early nineteenth-century travelers that Ireland testified as much to the failure as to the reach of British power. As they observed the barracks studding the Irish landscape or recalled the origin of picturesque ruins in the cannons of conquest, they recorded the force of an order that had refused to take. And never far in the background was the awareness of recent and perhaps future insurrection.

In their review of John Carr's tour, the Edgeworths castigated travel writers for avoiding the topic of Irish violence, censuring "well-meaning timid persons" who forbore speaking "upon what are called *dangerous subjects*; as if the danger were created by inquiring into the means of defence; or as if it could be dissipated by pretending that it does not exist."[20] But in a sense their charge misses the point. It is true that Carr struck a characteristic note when he told readers in the preface to *The Stranger in Ireland* that he would avoid inflammatory topics: "Upon those unsettled subjects which have too long excited *party animosity*, I have advanced nothing which can have the remotest tendency to inflame the public mind." As here, the Irish tour typically presented itself as a cool genre in a hot zone. All the same, tour-texts are shot through with apprehension, and the 1798 rebellion, which surfaces on several occasions in Carr's own text, remains a point of constant *irritation*, neither fully confronted nor yet completely banished. So the author of a short and very odd tour published in 1806, who hastens to inspect the site of Robert Emmet's 1803 rebellion on arrival in Dublin and remains in a high state of apprehension throughout his journey, makes sure to register the rebel status of towns through which he passes. Carlow is "the seat of rebellion," for example, while Leighlin-bridge is "a nest of rebels."[21] And in a surreal episode that looks forward to the ironic scenes of arrest featuring the beleaguered hero of the Waverley Novels, he finds himself arrested on the suspicion of being a French spy. Less self-dramatizing but equally aware of moving through a volatile landscape, the Reverend Hall suspects that the people of county Kildare will be "ready to rebel again, whenever a favourable opportunity occurs," and notes that in Wexford, the flashpoint of rebellion, he had difficulty persuading interlocutors "that it would not be the duty of the people to rebel, so soon as an opportunity offered." On his visit to the Edgeworths he commends their enlightened social ways (they invite both Catholic priests and Presbyterian ministers to dinner) but also their post-1798 fortifications, "so that there was no fear of being attacked, either by the windows or doors, after these were secured in the evening."[22] As late as twenty years after the rebellion, Curwen articulates the fear never far from the surface of English writing: "Though every thing at present has a tranquil appearance, the calm is not, I fear, accompanied with any confidence in its permanence. Every idle rumor [*sic*] spreads widely, and indicates an apprehension that revolt may again produce its devastating effects."[23]

Wakefield's well-respected *Account of Ireland* provides an especially telling example of how the question of insurrection, stemming from the trauma of 1798, troubles the early nineteenth-century tour. A two-volume work modelled on Arthur Young's foundational *A Tour in Ireland* (1780), most of its chapters are devoted to expected matters like "Rural Economy," "Fuel," "Fisheries," "Money and Circulating Medium," "Weights and Measures," and so forth. But the work includes as well a less predictable chapter titled "Rebellion in 1798: French Invasion in 1798." Wakefield enters upon the subject of the rebellion with great reluctance. Only the apprehension that "the torch of discord is not wholly extinct," he says, has induced him to write of a subject he would prefer to see "consigned to eternal oblivion" (II: 358). His hope is that once the source of danger has been pointed out, "measures of prudence" will be put in place to prevent or counteract "calamity," measures which include the kinds of policies (Catholic emancipation, encouragement of industry, mitigation of "evils") favored by liberal thought of the time. All this is unexceptionable. What makes Wakefield's account notable is what it does not do. He himself, it turns out, was in Ireland during 1798, traveling the very terrain of rebellion as he crossed from Waterford to Sligo. There, he tells us, he saw "many houses in ruins" and "wretched inhabitants . . . wandering about in an extreme state of desolation" (II: 359). But his actual narrative of the events of 1798 not only operates at a high level of generality but draws heavily on textual sources like parliamentary reports and memoirs rather than on his own experience. Having raised the possibility of a certain narration, that is, he then refuses it, telling the reader that although he is "well acquainted" with the sufferings of many individuals and has visited the locations of the conflict, he will go into few details: "I seek not to revive tales of woe, to add to the pangs of misery; many still suffer by horrid recollections, and I should be the last person to tear the bandage from the unhealed wound, when it could not produce a beneficial effect" (II: 358). Representation in both literary and political senses thus remains a charged and painful issue. Wakefield withdraws from the one to give the other a chance, hoping as he does so that the body of the Irish nation is not endemically diseased but simply, as his metaphor has it, suffering a temporary wound.[24] Nonetheless, the last lines of his work deliver a pointed warning to the British public:

> A whole people cannot causelessly be impelled to brave the mouth of the cannon, or rush upon the bayonet against their rulers; and when such events do take place, and when the voice of complaint does arise from a whole people, let their governors attend to the awful warning, and remember, that it will not be necessary to seek a heavenly-gifted interpreter to expound the HAND-WRITING UPON THE WALL! (II: 838).

Writing barely a generation after Arthur Young, Wakefield testifies to the way in which the Irish tour after 1798 replaced the benevolent assurance of the late eighteenth-century tour with a decidedly more agitated and nervous note, reflecting its own specific genesis in a moment of British crisis rather than British confidence. In the early years of the nineteenth century, British liberals tended to be at once ashamed and fearful when it came to Ireland; indeed, even the venerable *Gentleman's Magazine* (no liberal beacon) confessed in 1819 that "the very mention of Ireland conjures up a host of painful recollections and forebodings, from which the mind . . . would willingly escape, seeking refuge from the trouble of devising a present remedy, in the passive hope that future events may, somehow or other, avert the threatened evil."[25] The post-Union Irish tour marks an important faltering in the self-possession of British civic discourse in the period. Its confidence by no means collapsed, but poise was tenuous and the generic mood typically one of discomfort. Witness, for example, a suggestive sequence in one of the few Irish tours written by a woman in the period: Anne Plumptre's account of why she did not see the ruins of Cashel in her *Narrative of a Residence in Ireland During the Summer of 1814, and That of 1815* (1817).

In the summer of 1815, Plumptre (an Englishwoman of letters traveling around Ireland) set out from Limerick to see the famed Rock of Cashel.[26] On the way there, she learned that the Mail had been robbed two nights earlier just past Cashel in an attack that left one soldier dead.

Interestingly, what most disconcerts Plumptre about this news is not the violence of the robbery but the fact that its goal was arms, not money. On hearing this detail, she experienced an emotion she cannot articulate ("a feeling not to be described"), although she is certain it was not fear for her own safety. "I know not what it was," she says, "but my mind was wholly untuned to thinking of anything else" (*Narrative*, 311). Indeed, she was so possessed by this indeterminate emotion that she passed the celebrated monastic ruin without stopping. Now, when she looks back on that day, she cannot quite account for her refusal to stop: "At present my feelings upon this occasion seem strange to me, they seemed so in a few hours after, but at the moment they were irresistible. I have often asked myself since, why I did not see the ruins of Cashel, – I could never answer the question satisfactorily" (312). When her driver pointed out the place where the robbery actually occurred, she was relieved to have passed it, and reports that she "tried to think of the thing no more" (312). But "the thing" lingers in her text for a while longer, as she again thinks back to her journey that day. Then she abruptly dismisses the whole episode: "But enough of it" (313).

With this imperative, Plumptre expels the unsettling moment from her travel-text. But unease persists. Not long after the narration of the Cashel journey, she turns to the general question of the relationship of the Irish and the English, striking a keynote of the post-Union tour when she asserts her belief that the vast majority of Irish wish "to attach themselves warmly to the English" and would even be willing to forget "humiliations" attendant on the Union if only they could feel that it was indeed "an *union*" (337). Plumptre bases this belief on her personal experience during her travels ("my own reception"), but it soon becomes apparent that this is a belief determinedly maintained in the face of a barely suppressed distrust: "I must either think that I saw nothing but hypocrites, or believe that the flattering attentions I experienced were of the heart, not merely of the head; for worlds I would not think the one; I must believe the other; – I must believe that the Irish are a kind and warm-hearted people" (337). The reiterated imperatives ("I must believe") defend against the memory of recent "troubles and commotions," and Plumptre reinforces their import by arguing that only a trifling minority of "troubled spirits" has ever been involved in such commotions. Somewhat surprisingly, she turns to the fierce outbreak of 1798 to support her claim: "This was particularly manifest in the rebellion of 1798; had it not been a very, very small minority of the nation who were engaged in it, never would it have been so easily subdued" (337). Choosing to highlight the brevity rather than ferocity of the rebellion, she once again offers a resolutely optimistic reading. But no amount of adjectival insistence ("very, very small minority") can quite conjure "the thing" away.

This sequence offers an unusually explicit rendition of English discomfort in Ireland as a subsurface phenomenon experienced in – and as – a scene of agitation. Plumptre comes up against something that impinges on her consciousness but cannot be readily absorbed (named) by it, and her whole encounter is cast in terms of energies just below the surface that make surfaces themselves hard to read. At least two meanings of agitation cross in this scene: the traveler herself is disturbed and shaken, internally agitated, at unexpectedly running across agitation in the external, political sense of an ongoing activity seeking to dissolve social equilibrium. Under the influence of this agitation, Plumptre is literally pushed off her course and loses her bearings. Ireland itself splits in two, and she finds herself distracted from the ancient ruins of picturesque rural Ireland by a glimpse of militant rural Ireland and a potentially violent future with its very different kind of ruin. In this compounded moment on the road to Cashel, at once highly concrete and curiously abstract (she only hears about the incident), two forms of Ireland and two forms of history collide. Plumptre, importantly, shuts out both: "But enough of it." Turning and re-turning the topic of Ireland only to reach an impasse, her discomfited consciousness is emblematic of the liberal English anxiety that entered into the public discourse on Ireland in the years after Union and largely determined its contours in the early decades of the nineteenth century.

BAFFLED REASON

Even as the romantic Irish tour was imbued with affective modalities like discomfort and drew on sentimental and antiquarian traditions, however, its official self-understanding highlighted rational affiliations. The genre as a whole participates in the well-known separation of the literary and the political in the period, but it does so from the less familiar side of the duality, at least so far as recent literary history is concerned. In this instance, it is the political that expels the literary rather than the other way around, and it does so to save, precisely, the notion of public genres. Emerging out of late Enlightenment discourses of political economy, moral philosophy, and historiography, the post-Union tour aligned itself with high-minded genres of public and political concern rather than with aesthetic and touristic genres associated with the private pleasures linked to the sentimental and the picturesque. The line between these two modalities of travel was not, of course, very firmly drawn, and in writerly practice they tended to overlap. Even the earnest agrarian Arthur Young, who pioneered the modern Irish tour, peppered his massive survey of rural habits and agricultural statistics with appreciative and stylized accounts of "views" and "prospects." He himself traveled to Killarney and other tourist areas, and public-minded visitors after 1800 likewise followed a well-established itinerary organized around standard sights and must-see spots.

While this itinerary certainly yielded its share of aesthetic travel-texts by painters and leisured gentlemen under titles like *A Picturesque Tour Through Ireland, Illustrated With Numerous Coloured Views of the Most Interesting Scenery* (a volume published by Dennis Sullivan in 1824), the distinctive inflection of the Irish tour as travel writing derived from the long-standing, intensely fraught relationship between England and Ireland which discouraged casual picturesque rambles or proto-ethnographic surveys governed by simple "curiosity." From the outset, as John P. Harrington has pointed out, English writing on Ireland had been governed by the persistent theme of the country as "a problem."[27] All the more so after the Union when British visitors, no matter their specific allegiances and interests, shared a sense of Ireland as a *predicament* for England. The country was never simply a place to be traversed, one land among other lands, so that to write on Ireland, as Anne Plumptre observed, was not at all the same kind of thing as to write on a country like France, for Ireland was a nation that stood in relation to England as a "sister."[28]

This "sister," however, continued to remain strangely unfamiliar despite the outpouring of public writing on Ireland since the late 1790s, and traveler after traveler evokes the motif of Ireland as the close but unknown place. "[T]hough the name of Ireland is most familiar to our ears," George Cooper remarks in the preface to his *Letters on the Irish Nation* (1800), "yet both the kingdom and its inhabitants have been as little described as if the Atlantic had flowed between us";[29] almost twenty years later, Curwen remarks that he is visiting a country that "although almost within our view, and daily in our contemplation, is as little known to me, comparatively speaking, as if it were an island in the remotest part of the globe."[30] Motivated by the desire to direct significant public attention to Ireland – to promote a serious writing and serious reading linked to political power – the early nineteenth-century tour generally defined seriousness (as do Cooper and Curwen) as a function of distance from the literary and aesthetic. So Cooper, for example, reports that the "state of the Irish kingdom had been the great subject of public discussion, ever since its Legislative Union with Great Britain was proposed" by way of explaining his own focus on matters like government, religion, and commerce rather than on the natural scenery that attracts "admirers of picturesque beauty." Establishing his authorial gravitas, he adds: "I could not persuade myself to fill my letters with descriptions of that sort."[31] A similar note, this time more clearly directed at readers, is struck by James Glassford, a Scottish Commissioner of Inquiry into the State of Education in Ireland, who refuses to apologize for the formal imperfections of his text on the grounds that he does not seek "to cater to the literary epicure."[32]

Such disclaimers of the literary were of course a long-standing convention in travel writing. What distinguishes the post-Union Irish tour is that their purpose was less to establish the cognitive authority of the text (as in Arthur Young's late Enlightenment Irish tour or, more generally, in travels of exploration) than to guarantee the ethical authority of the writer as citizen and to emphasize the urgent, problematic status of Ireland. "Accustomed as I have been to have my time and attention directed to useful pursuits," writes the former politician John Curwen, "I should be quite out of my element on a tour exclusively devoted to pleasurable objects."[33] Eschewing the irresponsibility of personal pleasures, the practitioners of the Irish tour identify themselves with the responsible time of a life lived in public, civic space. Thus an expatriate Protestant Irish surgeon named Thomas Reid refuses to "waste" time on picturesque descriptions: "As my visit to Ireland is purely with a view to inquire into some of the evils, both moral and physical, under which, unhappily, it has too long been permitted to labour, I shall not waste my own or my reader's time by attempting to depict the scenery of every place through which I may have occasion to pass."[34] The generic distinction secured by such moves is underwritten by (and in turn underwrites) distinctions of gender and national character. "Waste" belongs to the effeminacy of literary pursuits and to Ireland itself, whose own wastefulness ("luxuriantly fertile" yet desperately poor) must be countered by a masculine and British discursive reason.

The *Edinburgh Review* makes the point in its review of Wakefield's *Account of Ireland*:

> But we should be ashamed to waste our time in literary criticism on an account of Ireland ... published at a moment when that country is the great hinge, on which the whole of our domestic policy turns, and when the speedy as well as the general prevalence of right opinions concerning it may materially affect

the safety of Empire. Whoever at such a moment could measure his attention to this work by its literary merit, must have lost every thing masculine in his understanding, by the process which refined his taste.[35]

Pitting "taste" against "understanding" in this way, the review not only confirms public discourse as the sober space of responsible masculine reason but places it in direct opposition to the distracting and self-indulgent realm of a feminized literary discussion and refinement. This distracting realm of the literary, it should be stressed, appears as *internal* to the male critic and writer (rather like Ireland in the United Kingdom), a potential within male sensibility against which he must defend. James Chandler has noted that the potency of political-historical genres like "the state" (to which travel writing is related) meant that they were fiercely guarded as a male prerogative in the period.[36] The passage from the *Edinburgh Review* suggests further that this called not only for the exclusion of women but for the expulsion from within male discourse of the ambiguity that allows words to be both rational and literary at the same time.

But when it came to Ireland, lines were difficult to draw, not least those of public genres. Travels concerned themselves with "the state" of Ireland, as is apparent in titles such as *A Brief Inquiry into the Present State of Agriculture in the Southern Part of Ireland*, *A Sketch of the State of Ireland, Past and Present*, *Observations on the State of Ireland*, and others. Importantly, the "state" of Ireland at once fit into and eluded the genre of the state, usefully defined by Chandler in his investigation of Romantic historicism. Chandler identifies the genre of the state primarily with the annualized representations of the state of the nation that began to emerge in the eighteenth century (as in the series of *Annual Registers*), and he understands it as a genre that actively participates in the making of national history. The civic tour is more strictly political in that it intervenes in the field of public policy and is only secondarily interested in the construction of national narrative, but the two activities are interdependent, especially in the question of Ireland and the United Kingdom when arguments about national identity buttressed the campaign for specific policies. Both, however, were stymied by the fact of the Irish; hence the need to investigate their state in an analytic performance deploying the even chronological grid Chandler calls "the historian's code" and the notion of uneven development articulated by the philosophical history of the Scottish Enlightenment. Such analysis reveals a telling difference. The state of the (British) nation has a date – "England in 1819," for instance – and this places it within modern history, but the "state of Ireland" typically does not. Suggestively, what corresponds to something like "England in

1819" is not "Ireland in 1819" but "A Journey to Ireland in 1819." Dates pertain to the traveling subject, the visitor from the metropolis, whose journey is usually carefully and prominently dated.[37] By contrast, the traveled subject, Ireland, has no date, generally placed in the notorious ethnographic present with its colonialist denial of coevalness.[38] It is no accident that when the modern editor of the odd 1806 Irish tour noted above reprinted the text in 1980, he also changed the title from *Journal of a Tour in Ireland &c. &c. performed in August 1804* to *Ireland in 1804*.[39]

For early nineteenth-century commentators, however, the problem was precisely how to relate Ireland to 1804 or 1822 or, more generally, to the sense of their own contemporaneity, a sense largely secured by a confidence in their own historicity. Ireland's relation to modern history and to the modernity of Great Britain was the pressing issue and the main puzzle. Ethnographic tropes defined the Irish as outside modern historical time altogether, and travel-texts not only routinely relegated the Irish to "savage" and "barbarous" states of society but described them in the exact same words used by much earlier commentators on Ireland such as Edmund Spenser or (in the conflation characteristic of the comparative analytics of the period) in the even earlier and paradigmatic words of a writer like Tacitus. So an observer like Cooper could declare: "The natives of that country . . . still remain the same rude barbarians that our earliest accounts describe them. I shall have little difficulty in describing this character, as it may be depictured [*sic*] in the same few words with that of all nations who have been in a state of ignorance and barbarity."[40] Most travelers were rather more observant, but they nonetheless tended to place the Irish and their history within repetitive and reproductive modes of time, which did not appear to accumulate in any significant way but simply to return. Ireland thus did not operate in the historical temporality that would allow it to move into the genre of the state, but at the same time it had to be related to that temporality. Herein lay the challenge to the civic tour and the reason for its constant recourse to the coordinating categories of Enlightenment history or to the heartening example of Scotland, generally understood as having made the successful move from pre-modern to modern soon after entering into union with England.

But Ireland confounded in a way that Scotland in general did not. "We all know," declared the *British Review* in 1818, "that Ireland presents an aggregate of paradoxes and anomalies both civil and moral."[41] What "we all know" was reiterated again and again in the reviews and the travel-texts, as the situation of Ireland remained intractable even in light of the most benevolent prescriptions of enlightened reason. Ireland, that is (to draw on another of Chandler's useful genres), was also "a case." A case, as Chandler emphasizes, is an anomaly that presents a problem for a general scheme or system; because it does so, it makes central the act of deliberation: weighing pondering, balancing. Indeed, Chandler writes, the case is "the very form of 'deliberation'."[42] To bring Ireland into the dated historical time of the state (hence to make it a member of the modern nation) first of all required determining the nature of the case. But no matter how much the case of Ireland was deliberated, it yielded neither a precise definition in terms of existing norms ("this is the case") nor a new framework for deliberation (an altering of the case). Rather, it hovered in the indistinct zone between these two possibilities, so that travelers who went out to make sense of the anomaly typically ended up simply reiterating the fact of anomaly. "The state of Ireland is an anomaly among nations," declared Reid, and summed up the standard definition of its case: "Although possessing almost every requisite for making a nation prosperous and happy, still the people are poor though industrious; discontented amidst abundant natural advantages; starving, though surrounded by plenty; and, whilst other nations are progressing in the arts and blessings of civilization, this alone seems to retrograde in every useful improvement."[43] The very reiteration of the point of anomaly, however, underscores that Ireland was never *simply* an anomaly within British order. It was more "peculiar" (a favourite epithet of the period), a peculiarity encapsulated in the ambiguous designation offered by one travel-text when it referred to the "strange anomalous condition" of the country.[44] To be anomalous is to come under the rule of the law even if only to overturn the law (a case to be determined); to be strange is to lie outside the purview of the law. But to be a strange anomaly is to inhabit ambiguity itself (to be at once inside and outside) and hence to disquiet rather than to engage (either in positive or negative terms) the logic of the law.

In its ambiguity, then, Ireland operated less as "other" than as heterogeneous to modern English (i.e., British) reason. This does not mean that the Irish did not continue to be subjected to the familiar move of othering that had shaped English discourse on Ireland from the Elizabethan period onward. The construction of the "wild Irish" persisted, generally re-accentuated through Enlightenment motifs of exoticism and sentimentalism. But the repositioning of the country placed new pressure on the metropolitan subjectivity accustomed to sustaining itself through the axiological distinction of self/other. Moved within national space, the strange anomaly of Ireland became the figure of dissolution itself, a negativity hollowing out the kinds of binary distinctions on which national identity was founded. Over and over again in the travel literature, Ireland is cast in terms of overflow and surplus, manifesting itself as an energy that precedes differentiation and eludes structuration. As puzzled British eyes encountered crowded spaces of intimacy, witnessed the spillover of the faithful at Catholic chapels, or observed baffling limit-rituals like Gaelic funerals, Ireland came to seem the very primal scene of Confusion. In this space, history could run backwards, lines of force be reversed. Wakefield, for instance, fears that Ireland presents a regressive sphere threatening to undo the work of civil government, which is to prevent a return to "a state of nature." Although he claims that any absolute return to such a state is impossible in this enlightened age, he is nonetheless alarmed that events in France and Ireland have demonstrated that a people may "nearly return" to that state.[45]

Behind such anxieties lay not only the memory of recent insurrections but the pressure of the Irish population, whose extremely rapid rate of growth from 1760 to 1840 placed a strain on both the Irish and English economies. Commentator after commentator reports on the large families, crowded cabins, and alarming dependence of the poor on the potato. Debate raged over whether Ireland served to confirm or, by contrast, to refute Malthus' notorious argument in his *Essay on Population* that population tended to outstrip the means of subsistence unless checked by disaster or (preferably) moral reserve, and Malthus himself entered the debate, beginning with a review of Thomas Newenham's *A Statistical and Historical Inquiry into the Progress and Magnitude of the Population of Ireland* in the *Edinburgh Review* in 1808.[46] Suggestively for my purposes, Malthus frames his review as an argument for Catholic emancipation (a point that would not be lost on Daniel O'Connell), and he pursues a line of thought that, somewhat unexpectedly, foregrounds political as much as economic conditions. He expands the argument about reliance on the potato, for example, beyond the usual claims about fertile soil and ease of cultivation to urge that "the political degradation of the Irish poor powerfully contributed to make them adopt potatoes as their principal food" (352). The political argument meshes with the economic argument – a more advanced and just polity develops habits and tastes that retard population – but Malthus' emphasis in this article falls less on the "natural" economic and moral checks that were his hallmark (although these are certainly strongly argued) than on the indirect but crucial role of political legislation. It does so because Malthus' real interest is in Ireland as a member of the United Kingdom, a kingdom of whose population it now formed "above a fourth part" (336). Ireland's population, he notes, had "more than quadrupled" in the last hundred years, and it now formed a "rapidly increasing physical force" that urgently required conciliation: "Every year the proportion of the Catholics to the Protestants is rapidly augmenting, – a circumstance which might be contemplated without fear if they were once conciliated; but, till that time arrives, must be regarded with increasing apprehension, as daily diminishing the prospect of a cordial and permanent union between the two countries" (337, 349).[47]

While Malthus' argument about the need to conciliate this large population is rational enough, he casts the population-fact itself in language that exceeds the rational. Over and over again Malthus stresses "astonishment" and a sense of the "extraordinary" when he contemplates Ireland. In part he is heightening his theory's claim to explanatory power, but there is more to it than that. His imagination reels at the thought of the "prodigious mass of people" the potato-based culture will produce before the economy regulates itself. At the current rate of increase, he predicts, Ireland will contain "*twenty millions* of people in the course of the present century," and again he warns that this huge physical force will not remain united to Great Britain "without sharing, in every respect, the full benefits of its constitution" (343).[48] Quite literally, the margins of the nation begin to press on the center, assuming a frightening gigantism, and the population-fact begins to exceed its strictly economic dimensions. If some Irish tours preferred to confine it to a rational and managerial problem of "unprofitable exuberance,"[49] for others it resonated more obscurely: "The greatness of the population in so small a space as Ireland," mused Trotter, "gives it an extraordinary energy, which, polypus like, seems uninjured by partial cutting, and defies all attempts to chain and enervate it."[50] Ungraspable and uncontrollable, this "extraordinary energy," blocked in one direction, simply runs in another. And running *inside* British power, it disturbs its placement, generating an effect (or affect) that recalls Kristeva's account of the abject as "[w]hat does not respect borders, positions, rules."[51] Pushed out from here, it shifts over there, operating in the motility of the semiotic space of pre-objects and pre-subjects theorized by Kristeva. And as potent unformedness, it threatens less opposition to than erosion of identity and system.

There is an intriguing and emblematic moment of such erosion in Carr's *The Stranger in Ireland* when the normally jovial Carr, visiting the fabled tourist spot of Killarney, enters Muckross Abbey and is horrified to discover recently interred bodies in coffins whose planks have begun to start. The corpses emit a "putrid effluvia," and Carr quickly makes the rational humanitarian case for shutting up the burial spot as a danger to public health. But what fascinates – and unsettles – is the weird contrast that constitutes the gothic scene: "Contrast renders doubly horrible the ghastly contemplation of human dissolution, tainting the surrounding air with pestilence, in a spot which nature has enriched with a profusion of romantic beauty."[52] Horror surfaces not simply because of the presence of death in the heart of "romantic beauty" but because of the way in which the corpses make manifest at the level of the body the fragility and permeability we must forget in order to live as subjects. Kristeva, defining the corpse as the abject, a literal crumbling of signification, stresses that it does not (like a flat encephalograph) "*signify* death," something one can accept or understand. "No," she writes, "as in true theatre . . . refuse and corpses *show me* what I permanently thrust aside in order to live."[53] Amid the seeping coffins, the English traveler finds himself at the border of his condition as a living being (and not just as a national subject), and he immediately pulls back, invoking the rule of the proper: the call to regulate the boundaries that will put a cessation to this unseemly mingling of death in life, and allow him once more to *be* on the other side of a clearly demarcated line.

Such dissolution of lines and boundaries through overflow unhinges, if only temporarily, the Irish tour. It may do so more or less lightly, as in the comically solemn complaint by the Reverend Hall that although "there are acts of parliament against pigs running in the streets, yet this act is daily and hourly broken in Cork, where pigs are sometimes so numerous, that you are not only often impeded in your walking by them, but sometimes likely to be overturned."[54] Or it may surface more seriously, as in Thomas Reid's graphic account of cottiers preparing to plant potatoes by first gathering up the manure (a mixture of "dung and filth of every kind") they have collected in front of their cabins:

> the man is seen up to his ankles, and sometimes nearly to his knees in sludge, scraping up matter, both animal and vegetable, in a state of semi-decomposition, partly in a fluid state, which is called *gullion*. This he fills, heedless of effluvia, into a square wicker basket, called a *kreel* (the interstices being clogged to prevent the contents from running out), which he carried on his back to the "garden," where his wife is employed in spreading this stuff on the ground with her hands, while some of the children, of whom there is seldom any scarcity, are employed in depositing the seed potatoes on the beds.[55]

Thus immersed in fluids and mixtures, working in an indistinct zone where earth and water, waste and nourishment, animal and human intermingle, the image of the cottiers underscores the standard English perception of rural Irish life as a space of crossings and confusion, which generates a way of being that compels but repels understanding.

The Irish cabin is the classic instance, its typically low contours blurring the distinction between earth and habitation, and its rapid proliferation in the late eighteenth-century countryside representing what a recent historian calls a "seeping through the cracks of an otherwise well ordered geographical pattern."[56] By the turn of the nineteenth century, the cabin was already a venerable cliché in travel-texts; nevertheless, it continued to be foregrounded in the Irish tour. This repeated return to the trope, Hadfield and McVeagh argue, had a great deal to do with the way in which the cabin represented a challenge to English notions of domestic space, particularly to English assumptions about "the permanence, comfort and strength required of a family house."[57] Indeed, for most British writers the cabin was inconceivable *as* domestic space. "In hovels, too wretched to deserve the name of houses, or even of pig-styes," wrote James Mill in the *Edinburgh Review*, "mixed at bed and board with the animals whom they rear, more than half naked, with nothing but potatoes to eat . . . they lead the life of beasts rather than of men."[58] Since Mill himself had never visited Ireland, his cabin is an entirely textual construct drawn from the standard repertoire of cultural tropes. But while Mills' cabin is standard, his blunt contempt is unusual in the period, when most travelers tended not so much to dismiss the cabin with disgust as to transform it into a sentimental sign of economic wretchedness and political neglect. Curwen is exemplary, visiting cabins along the way to ascertain the extent of misery, and describing several "heart-rending" scenes. But he soon stops such visits: "I had not courage to explore further, and became impatient to escape from the repetition of scenes too wretched for human nature to endure, and too multiplied to be within my power to relieve."[59] Overwhelmed by such multiplication, he retreats from that which his liberal reason cannot alleviate even as his text continues to search for rational solutions suggested by its paradigms.

In such moments, Curwen constructs himself as a man of sentiment, but he also underlines a split between affect and reason that points to a bafflement of the English mind in Irish home space. The characteristic note of the Irish tour when faced with the Irish cabin is puzzlement. The cabin confounds because it suggests that the Irish live in their bodies and in their families in a very different way.[60] Surrounded by a dung-hill on the outside and mixing sexes and species within, it was generally read as a site of primitive undifferentiation and excess, but at the same time it proved a place of surprising reserve and decorum. The tone is struck by an influential late eighteenth-century tour, Thomas Campbell's *A Philosophical Survey of the South of Ireland* (1777). Campbell, an Anglo-Irish clergyman living in Ireland but assuming the role of Englishman in his text, offers a lengthy description of the stock Irish cabin on which later travelers were repeatedly to draw. In particular, he presents the cabin as a scene of mingling: "upon the same floor, and frequently without any partition, are lodged the husband and wife, the multitudinous brood of children, all huddled together upon straw or rushes, with the cow, the calf, the pig, and the horse, if they are rich enough to have one."[61] What surprises Campbell is that although one would expect incest to be common in such "promiscuous" scenes, he finds no evidence of it. Later travelers reiterate the point, often explicitly citing Campbell, as does Carr when he notes that the crowding together of different sexes in one room does not produce "sensual depravity." Nor, he notes, is the promise of the exterior (with its heaped-up "filth") fulfilled by the interior, where "every degree of decency prevails."[62]

A certain pastoralism is often at work in such commentary, but the perplexity is nonetheless genuine and profound. Travel writers were especially puzzled by how the cabins produced strong bodies and healthy children in defiance of modern reason and prediction. Arthur Young had stressed the point himself in his pioneering *Tour in Ireland*, where he cited the health of the Irish as evidence for the nourishing qualities of the despised potato.[63] But in early nineteenth-century tours such rational explanation tended to drop out and only the unexpected outcome of health remained. Native Irish children, commented Thomas Erlington, former Provost of Trinity College, in 1808, "are generally half, and sometimes altogether naked, living without distinction of sexes in dirt and mire, almost with the cattle. Yet from this nakedness and filth, they grow up to that strength and stature for which they are admirable."[64] Travel writer after travel writer made similar comments, astonished at the way in which an apparently insalubrious environment produced robust and modest beings. Such insistence may work doubly: to domesticate Irish difference on the one hand (the wild are decent after all) and to make it substantial on the other (they really are a different race of beings). By the mid-nineteenth century both readings of the Irish body were to be firmly in place, but in the early years of the century, matters were more fluid, the Irish question itself in uncertain transition. In such an intervalic moment, the persistent return to the cabin attests to a troubled sense of an alterity that cannot quite be turned to account. The Irish cabin keeps obtruding in English discourse, and the note of bafflement lingers: How can Ireland be so fertile and so poor? The people so wretched and so healthy? This cabin a home?

As the post-Union Irish tour keeps coming back again and again to these questions, articulating them through the same tropes and reaching the same bafflement, not only does Ireland emerge as a limit-point of English intelligibility but the travel-text itself begins to take on something of the repetitive, non-progressive temporality in which it routinely confined the native Irish. An odd merging or duplication occurs. The Irish tour – liberal, rational, responsible, and masculine in its official self-understanding – turns out to display at the same time a textual promiscuity and fecklessness that align it with the grotesque female body of the illiberal Ireland it so distrusts. What helps account for this convergence, the last section of the chapter will argue, is that the civic ambition of the tour was unhinged not just by encounter with a baffling referent but by an ambiguity internal to the genre of travel writing itself.

EQUIVOCAL FORM

In the early nineteenth century, travels could be said to constitute less a genre than a generic possibility: a loose discursive field, notoriously diverse and disordered, out of which the new and powerful critical discourse linked to quarterlies like the *Edinburgh Review* sought to carve a normative form, a specific genre. The problem was not simply that travel writing manifested itself in assorted modes – picturesque, sentimental, scientific, philosophic, agricultural, antiquarian, and so forth – but that any volume of travels, no matter its primary mode, generally took the form of what John Gough's *A Tour in Ireland* cheerfully calls a "heterogeneous medley" (239). As a hybrid and uneven writing operating well outside the stabilizing author-function famously defined by Foucault, it was understood as a frontier discourse, a quasi-genre on the edge of the settled literary field. It occupied an ambiguous position, straddling the genres of entertainment on the one hand (e.g., the lounging book) and those of utility on the other (e.g., the statistical treatise); travel books were at once objects of display and repositories of knowledge, serving their middle-class readers as signs of both social status and intellectual capital. And even more unsettling than their generic indeterminacy was their notorious "intertextual plenitude" (to use Frances Bartkowski's phrase[65]),which confounded the distinction between one text and another, between what is properly one's own and what belongs to someone else. Undermining the literary category of authorship through this casual sense of text as private property, travel writers were typically relegated to the commercial category of mere "book-makers," greedy or naive participants in the "mania for book-making" routinely regretted in the periodical press as one of the follies of the age.

John Carr is a primary example. A prolific travel writer, he produced a commonplace European tour almost every year between 1803 and 1811, and by the time *The Stranger in Ireland* appeared in 1806, the *New Annual Register* noted with some regret that the writer had chosen "the secondary praise of being a judicious book-maker to the original merit of being a good author."[66] The *Edinburgh Review* put it less tactfully when discussing Carr's Dutch tour the following year, sardonically observing his habit of taking a trip and routinely producing "a quarto volume, which is in the shops at the proper period of the ensuing book-season."[67] What largely accounts for these charges of book-making is the excessiveness with which Carr deployed the generic licence of citation, filling his volumes with quotations that went on for pages at a time only to be themselves followed by another swatch of lengthy quotation from yet another text.[68] So ingesting and incorporating other texts, travels like his evidenced a careless sense of boundaries and of the provenance of words that discounted not only authorship but the empiricism grounding language in the travel genre. For Walter Scott, for instance, reviewing Carr's Scottish tour in the *Quarterly Review*, the traveler might as well have stayed home in London: "so much of this quarto may be traced to Pennant and his numerous successors, that we are really of opinion it might have been compiled without the author taking the trouble to stir from No.2, Gardencourt Temple; and that the mountains being thus brought to Mahomet, in the shape of quartos and octavos, Mahomet might have dispensed with his personal attendance on the mountains."[69] Viewing Scottish mountains not only through but *as* quartos and octavos, Carr underlines the obsessive intertextuality of travels in general that was always threatening to turn mimesis into semiosis, to cut the referential tie and transform text into a simulacrum formed by the accumulation and ricochet of recycled signs.

To stabilize all this errant wordiness and print, critical discourse effected a clearing by sanctioning a preferred form that would harness the sprawling energies of travel writing for productive use.[70] The early *Edinburgh Review* in particular, as Marilyn Butler has noted, vigorously campaigned on behalf of a utilitarian, scientific model of travels, and other reviews followed suit, promoting the notion of "information" as the key to the positive value of the genre.[71] They thus defined it primarily as a descriptive knowledge genre, one that gave details about how other societies governed themselves, used their resources, and so forth: "A traveller who passes through countries little known, should tell us how such countries are cultivated – how they are governed – what is the face of nature – what is the state of the useful arts – what is the degree of knowledge which exists there."[72] Behind this insistence on restricting and subordinating travels to the pragmatic category of information lies an uneasy recognition of the way in which travel writing represented a fault line in the discourse of knowledge being promulgated by the reviews. Travels were not of course the only genre to make visible a certain vulnerability in this discourse inherited from the Enlightenment, but travels placed the discourse of knowledge under special pressure because they destabilized its form in an acute way. In particular they risked undoing the hinges that linked sign to referent (the conceptual order of language) and word to world (the mimetic order of language), and on their terrain the gestures of order sustaining enterprises like the literary reviews themselves came perilously close to parody. Travels, for example, wielded a familiar analytic apparatus (e.g., maps, lists, charts, footnotes, citations, appendices), but their disjointed and dubious texts also threatened its corrosion. Since this apparatus yields the very category of information, it is not surprising that the reviews were intent on disentangling the bits of information from the wayward texts in which they floated and on picking out any usable data. As the ubiquitous travel reviewer Henry Brougham put it in the *Edinburgh Review*, he carefully sorted through every travel-text, "noting the defects, and separating and preserving the useful parts, even though they should be as two grains of wheat in a bushel of chaff."[73]

But extraction of the useful bits did not alter the wasteful nature of the travel-text as a whole, and travels were typically cast in terms of a garrulity and blowsiness that aligned them with fluid and overblown feminine spaces rather than with those of a bounded and responsible masculinity. Or, more accurately, travels belonged to both genders and at the same time. One sign could frequently point in two directions, as in the travel writer's denial of literary-formal concerns, which (as we saw in the previous section) denoted a male and civic seriousness but could also flip around to signal a nonchalant disregard for discursive regularities and authority. In their loose and informal procedures, travels stood in equivocal relation to the protocols defining domestic and discursive order even when they were harnessed on behalf of that order. Therefore they had to be turned to responsible account, especially when, as with the Irish tour, they dealt with a volatile and domestically pressing issue. Hence the fierceness of the Edgeworths' review of Carr's Irish tour in the *Edinburgh Review*, their attention to a lightweight writing that would otherwise have been most unlikely to stir their concern. In contrast to most travelers to Ireland in this period, Carr was simply making another of many journeys, and although his tour is shaped by the standard liberal and civic concerns of the tour, he was anxious to entertain as much as to inform. His rambling and digressive text is filled with bad jokes, condescending references to the Catholic Irish as "Pat," and quaint anecdotes, along with the massive amounts of quotation to which I have referred. For the Edgeworths, Carr's text – rather like the Irish peasant constructed in English discourse of the period – lives an irresponsible and lazy life in a largely reproductive (as opposed to productive) space. "To save himself the trouble of thought or arrangement," they point out, "he has emptied and overwhelmed us with his common-place book." Moreover, his style is "careless and affected, trivial and inflated," his sentences "sometimes without meaning, and often without grammar." Not only grammatical but generic decorum is repeatedly violated by Carr, whose "high-flown descriptions, which are neither prose nor poetry, frequently terminate in striking instances of the bathos." In fact, the review notes with sarcasm, the only "beauty" he offers is that of contrast: "that species of contrast, which results from want of order, where grave and gay, just and absurd, fine and vulgar, sublime and ludicrous, succeed each other."[74]

At a deeper level than triteness and incompetence, it is this indiscriminate "want of order" that offends the Edgeworths because it points to a cavalier attitude to discursive authority that undermines the seriousness of the question of Ireland. "I write just as my thoughts occur," announces Carr, "without marshalling them with the solemnity of herald, according to their rank and precedence," thereby casually dismissing the categories of subordination and coordination on which meaningful organization depends.[75] His remark is generically representative, echoed in travel-text after travel-text, as the writers make a special point of placing their travels outside not only literary decorum but also the more highly organized knowledge genres. John Gamble, for instance, underscores an allegiance to brief and ephemeral forms when he says he wrote his volume "by hasty sketch, by short tale, and brief dialogue, rather than by formal dissertation."[76] Some of this, of course, is a tactic of disclaimer, an attempt to forestall the criticism of rapidly produced volumes. But it also foregrounds the way in which the informality of travel writing releases less the sobriety of cognitive or ethical discourse (the empirical or moral voice of truth) than the confusion of mixed modes noisily jostling together (a play of texts). Constituted by what Bakhtin calls "border violations,"[77] travel writing effects continual discursive crossings, mingling high-minded civic discourse with low comedy; juxtaposing information, gossip, and history; moving abruptly from modern political theory to picturesque landscapes to complaints about dirty inns.

Such texts block the emergence of a totality – a whole or general view – and herein lies the problem for the civic Irish tour. British public discourse urgently desired such a view of the "sister-island," impelled by a sense that Ireland had too long continued, as the *Monthly Review* notes, "a reproach to the empire of which it forms so considerable a part."[78] But its search for what John Wilson Croker, writing in the *Quarterly* in 1815, called "a general and enlarged view" was continually frustrated.[79] The Irish themselves, Croker argues in his review, have been unable to supply the deficiency of mistaken or blurred English perception, and he cites in evidence the text under specific review: a statistical account of Irish parishes by William Shaw Mason, a statistician and topographer working under Robert Peel, then Chief Secretary of Ireland. Throughout, Croker's review stresses that Mason's collection of data (valuable enough) is not properly ordered: he has not edited and reconciled reports; the statistical units are not comparable, thereby obviating the possibility of producing "general results"; the parishes are not arranged in any useful order; and so on. What is lacking in Shaw's text for Croker is not only proper method but a macro model to allow for the coordination of the data across sets. But if statistical accounts and surveys made difficult the construction of coherent "views" – the *Monthly Review* lamented that Thomas Newenham's *View of the Natural, Political, and Commercial Circumstances of Ireland* was simply "a mass of facts"[80] – the jumbled genre of travel writing seemed to obstruct them altogether. In an extended review of Wakefield's agricultural *Account of Ireland*, for example, the *Monthly* commends his enlightened approach to Ireland but reproaches him at length for his "desultory" composition, noting in particular the difficulty the volume presents in relating one thing to another. "Before one part of the picture is finished," the reviewer complains, "another is thrust into view without any reference to the degree of their mutual relation." And he sums up the overall problem: "As the book stands at present, so many superfluities remain to be expunged, so many transfers to be made from one title to another, and so many subdivisions to be laid down, that nothing less than a transcript of the whole is requisite to bring it into proper arrangement."[81]

Comments like this suggest that, rather than providing transparency and enacting totalization (as often charged), tour-texts tended to leave contemporary readers feeling far short of the "general view" or "comprehensive account" that would help orient not just the generic civic reader posited by the Irish tour but, more specifically, policy makers and enlightened landlords like the Edgeworths.

Moreover, the very gestures of analytic order made by the tour tended to reinforce rather than dispel the sense of disunity and fragmentation, generating less the coherence of a "survey" than the heterogeneity of a miscellaneous "collection." Travel writing in the period generally deployed a double-structured discourse, distributing analytic and narrative modes of representation unevenly as it worked out the problem of the relation of generalization and specificity in cultural representation. Unlike the later form of ethnography, which would set up different textual spaces – even different texts – for the two forms of representation, travel writing tended to operate in a rather untidier fashion, even when it enacted a similar split between the journey-narrative and analysis.[82] Arthur Young set the example for the modern Irish tour when he separated his survey into two parts: the "Minutes of the Tour," which detailed the "particulars" of agricultural practice in different regions of Ireland, and a section on "general facts" he derived from those particulars. Suggestively, however, the entire structure threatens to collapse in the final pages, when Young is forced to open up a text he had closed with an optimistic chapter on the "General State of Ireland" by adding another chapter to take into account a recent, negative turn in Irish affairs that undermined his earlier confident predictions.[83]

Early nineteenth-century tours prove even more textually unstable, adding appendix after appendix (generally for no apparent reason and often juxtaposing incompatible texts) and proliferating the divisions established by Young. Some travelers effect only a modest expansion, as in Thomas Reid's three-part *Travels in Ireland in the Year 1822* (History of Ireland, Tour of Ireland, and Reflections on the Foregoing Matters), but others subdivide more furiously. James Glassford's *Notes of Three Tours in Ireland*, for instance, divides each tour into two parts (Journal, General Remarks) and then concludes the whole with more General Remarks. Still others block entrance, as in Sir Richard Colt Hoare's *Journal of a Tour in Ireland. A.D. 1806*, which postpones the journal advertised in the title by first inserting a bibliographic survey (with notes), then adding a political history of Ireland, followed by a lengthy extraction from Beaufort's *Memoirs* under the title of "Civil and Ecclesiastical Division of Ireland."

Such texts can be entered or exited at almost any point. Furthermore, as it fluctuates between the generalizing mode of the treatise and the particularizing mode of informal genres (e.g., letters, journals, diaries, and anecdotes), the Irish tour keeps in play alternating forms of textual authority. If it is the case that the unofficial and empirical forms linked to the journey-narrative authorize theory and generalization, it is equally the case that these unofficial and empirical forms place theory and generalization in question. In the flat textual space that characterizes travel writing neither assumes clear priority; both exist on the same plane. In this sense a reading can always be reversed, and structural categories like "national character" or "the lower Irish" continually disarticulated and rearticulated.

What the tour encourages, in short, is what we might call reversible reading. Spreading in different directions, making connections both on and just beneath the surface, its crowded and careless texts defeat the desire to draw out a *line* of reading. Their extensive importation of texts and heterogeneity of modes, combined with the split form typical of the genre, foster a reading practice that dissolves or cuts across standard linear and hierarchical practices of reading. A magpie genre, the Irish tour generates a loose dissonance (rather than anything as coherent as contradiction) through an endless rummaging among texts which releases lines of continually crossing implication. Carr's *Stranger in Ireland* is once again symptomatic. Fond of jokes and broad humour generally, Carr cannot resist including sardonic and even subversive anecdotes, all the while assuring the reader of his orthodox English liberal allegiance to good sense and enlightened policies. In relation to the Union, for example, he declares early in the text that political reform is necessary to produce the "cordial cement" it requires, but he precedes this statement with a pointed jest: "But uniting Ireland to us in her advantages, and leaving her the gloomy dignity of unenvied independence in her wants and inconveniences, approaches a little too closely to the selfishness displayed in the fable of the two Travellers, in which the friendly pronoun *we* with respect to the treasure found was only recognized by the finder, when the hue and cry of the country were raised for the loss of the treasure" (74). The moment exists, one suspects, for the joke, but it nonetheless foregrounds asymmetry and offers a biting reading of the "we" of Union implicating both writer and reader. Repeating a tale belonging to the uncontextualized, migratory genre of the joke, Carr harnesses it to make a sharp comment in a very particular context; he then dissolves the sting by immediately offering his recommendation for "cordial cement" to complete the Union. The point, however, is that in a volume in which thoughts are not marshaled (to recall Carr's words) "according to rank and precedence" neither textual moment has clear precedence.

This sense of oscillating implication becomes even more apparent when the question of Union returns later in the volume, and Carr reproduces texts attached to the debate and to a prominent Anglo-Irish patriot active in both that debate and its aftermath. Two moments are conspicuous. About halfway through the text Carr asserts his ardent hope that the Union will benefit Ireland. There can then be no harm, he reasons, in printing examples of literary wit from the satirical periodical *The Anti-Union* (published at the height of the debate from December 1798 to March 1799). Among the reprinted texts he offers is a poem by a Mr. Lysaght, which argues the standard anti-Union line that Dublin will disappear as a town, leaving turnips and cabbages to grow where there used to be streets. Its chorus runs as follows: "*Chorus.* – Give Pitt and Dundas, and Jenkin a glass, / They'll ride on John bull and make Paddy an ass" (229). On the one hand, Carr's printing of anti-Union texts like Lysaght's confirms his confidence in the British incorporation of Ireland: such texts are irrelevant and may now be safely quoted. On the other hand, the inserted text reiterates the cynical note introduced by the joke about the "we" of Union earlier in the work: such texts remain relevant and need to be quoted. Neither reading can really be ruled out; nor can they be placed in firm relation to one another. A similar indeterminacy of implication marks the second moment. Late in his journey, Carr visits the admired politician Henry Grattan ("that great man"), and concludes the report of his visit with several extracts from Grattan's speeches. "I offer them *solely* as specimens of elevated oratory," Carr insists, "and not for the purpose of introducing political sentiments" (451). The emphatic "*solely*" works, of course, to raise the possibility of the very political reading it denies, and the extracts themselves prove to be arranged under titles like "Wretched Peasantry," "Toleration," "Illiberality," "Democracy," and "Self-Legislation." Does such a moment depoliticize a political genre? Or repoliticize the category of the literary?

In an important sense it does neither, for Carr is simply filling up his volume, making more text. And it is precisely this lack of directed attention that allows for lines of dissonance to emerge in so highly conventionalized a metropolitan text, enabling what I have been calling reversible reading. That Carr's text continues to operate in this way even in our own time is strikingly confirmed by two of his recent readers. Both Katie Trumpener and Glenn Hooper agree that Carr's tour enacts a colonial-imperialist reading of Ireland, but they differ markedly in how they *see* his text. For Hooper it is only "seemingly fragmentary and conflictual," its shifting positions in fact part of a coherent strategy for achieving the legitimation of colonial rule.[84] For Trumpener, on the other hand, Carr's text is all too incoherent, denying Ireland national wholeness and perpetuating stereotypes of incomprehensibility that reinforce an imperialist unconscious.[85] Both readings make a good deal of sense, and that is part of my point: they make sense where Carr really does not. If in that failure to make sense there lie some disquieting political possibilities, as Trumpener and others have argued, therein too lies a salutary power of dissolution that dislodges the order of representation, making text openly a pre-text (rather than an authoritative "work") and so opening out forms of representation to readings that reverse and traverse, as well as develop in orderly fashion.[86]

But the traveler-figure itself tends to remain outside that kind of reading, to move about untouched by the implications released by its own narrative. For all the discomfort evidenced by English travelers in Ireland, most travelers, as Harrington notes, did not basically examine their own assumptions.[87] The tour is governed by a chronotope of the random passage (i.e., most travelers' journeys simply get going and stop going), and this underscores the point of a certain inconsequence. Travelers may cross the terrain, but they do not cross into it. To put it in terms of narrative pragmatics, authorial enunciation may be discomfited but it is not really altered, and one way of understanding the new narrative form that emerged in directly rivalry to the post-Union Irish tour, taking the tour as at once model and satiric target, is that it sought to dislodge that enunciation. As the next chapter will argue, the Anglo-Irish national tale shifted and regendered the site of enunciation, rewriting the tour by moving the traveler-figure inside the narrative and making his (more rarely her) journey enormously consequential. It thus attempted to bring home the case of Ireland to English readers by moving them into its space in a new way.

CHAPTER 2

Public address: the national tale and the pragmatics of sympathy

It is pleasant, after ages of bad romance in politics, to find thus, at last, good politics in romance.

Thomas Moore "Irish Novels," *Edinburgh Review* (1826)

The politics Thomas Moore specifically had in mind when he made this remark was the support for Catholic Emancipation in the novels under review, and his comment underlines the way in which Irish fiction in the early decades of the nineteenth century was immediately understood by contemporary readers within the matrix of post-Union civic discourse.[1] It is not incidental that the paradigmatic *The Wild Irish Girl: A National Tale* appeared in 1806, the year following the renewal of Catholic agitation, nor that its publisher, Richard Phillips (earlier imprisoned for selling Tom Paine's *Rights of Man*), advertised the novel among a list of USEFUL AND VALUABLE BOOKS, all non-fiction and mostly travels, appended to John Carr's *The Stranger in Ireland*. Later readers, however, have been rather less sure than was Moore that the line of fiction inaugurated by Sydney Owenson (Lady Morgan) and her compatriot Maria Edgeworth does in fact represent "good politics in romance." Famously dismissed by Daniel Corkery in the 1930s as mere "traveller's tales" exhibiting Ireland to "alien eyes,"[2] early nineteenth-century Irish fictions continue to be regarded with a certain distrust in both Irish and British Romantic studies (Edgeworth is perhaps a partial exception). What has made these novels suspect by and large is their address, both in the sense of the location from which they speak (an Anglo-Irish writing usually published in London) and the location to which they speak (a loosely English reader). The narrative set to readers-at-a-distance in particular remains a sticky point. For Terry Eagleton this is a fictional mode that "constantly overhears itself in the ears of its British interlocutors," thereby enacting a debilitating self-censoring albeit one charged with some of the powerful energy, as well as blindness, Eagleton typically assigns to contradiction.[3]

Joep Leerssen puts the problem more bluntly: what undermines the national tale is its set toward "a readership of foreigners."[4] The difficulty, as he sees it, is that in addressing an English readership, the Irish novel distances itself from identification with an Irish subjectivity: "The destinatory vector towards an English audience is so strong that the author no longer identifies with the country which is represented, but becomes an intermediary, an exteriorized, detached observer."[5] On this reading, an authentic national writing is one that "identifies with" its country in a convergence of authorial and national consciousness which confirms the substantiality of both, and accords to language a transparency whereby it fuses with what it represents. Conversely, to produce words that are "intermediary" is to deplete both personal and national subjectivity, and to move language out of the meaningful realm of representation into that of mere signification where words are *only* words. Even for an acute reader of Anglo-Irish fiction like Leerssen, then, novelistic representation remains tied to a mimetic model that pretty much rules out the possibility of taking seriously any fiction that makes more active the pragmatic and performative notion of representation discussed in the Introduction: representation as a presentation of something to someone.[6]

The difficulty is compounded by the fact that the national tale is constituted as a genre less by a belonging (to one culture or another) than by a migratory impulse through which contending cultures may come into contact. It operates, that is, in much the same literary space as does translation, and translation inevitably takes on a charged status under colonial conditions. In Ireland, as Maria Tymoczko has shown, the question of translation was harnessed to a debate about the nation at least as far back as the late eighteenth-century controversy over Ossian. Technical and methodological disputes about the virtues of "acceptable" translation (oriented to the target language) as opposed to "accurate" translation (oriented to the source language) rapidly assumed a sharp, political edge.[7] For nationalists, source-based translation has typically represented the only faithful form of translation, oriented as it is to the Irish language and addressed to an essentially Irish audience. Theirs tends to be a strictly internal model of the nation, positing fidelity to origin as crucial in the making of an ideally self-sufficient national identity. By contrast, the model of the nation underlying a target-based translation offers a relational rather than substantive notion of national identity; in the case of Ireland, for instance, it meant arguing for a sense of the nation in relation to the dominant culture/language of England or, in more radical versions, to that of France. In this model, national identity is ungrounded and fluid, made out of disparate materials thrown up by the "middleness" of historical time rather than being understood as the necessary expression of an origin.

The instability of this second model of the nation means that (along with target-based genres like the national tale) it comes under severe pressure in sites of asymmetric power relations and at historical junctures when notions of national identity become unmoored from conceptions that have long pertained. But, in a more fundamental sense, it is the notion of translation itself, rather than the particular orientation of the translation, that presents the real source of unease. Translation implies the permeability of boundaries, and the intercultural figure of the translator (who lives in at least two languages) unsettles the notion of home space.[8] This may be why, in an odd footnote to his essay "On Patriotism," William Hazlitt, cryptically remarks: "He who speaks two languages has no country."[9] For different reasons, both a strongly monolingual culture like Hazlitt's England and one in which at least two languages stand in uneven, often violent relation like that of nineteenth-century Ireland regard as dubious those who do not live fully in one language. "Like the despised cosmopolitan of anti-semitic rhetoric," Michael Cronin has observed, "translators may indeed find themselves objects of suspicion because they are not wholly within one culture but occupy a space between cultures."[10]

In this space-between, the national tale set out (like the Irish tour) to complete the Union, specifically in arguing for Catholic Emancipation and more generally in attempting to reconcile Irish claims and English rule through a romance plot that typically concludes with the cross-cultural marriage of an English or Anglo-Irish landlord hero (generally an erstwhile absentee) and a displaced native Irish heroine. Invoking Morgan's *The Wild Irish Girl*, Robert Tracy has dubbed this "the Glorvina solution" whereby historical and legal right to the land are reconciled.[11] Drawing attention to the complicated work of legitimation performed by the marriage trope in the national tale, Tracy's influential article laid down the lines for reading it as imperial romance, and most readers have followed him in concentrating on the political allegory of union enacted by the romance plot.[12] But this is imperial romance with a distinctly abrasive edge, for the romance plot of reconciliation operates within a larger travel plot whose energies vis-à-vis English discourse and English readers are rather less accommodating. As Irish tours, national tales seek to displace the civic English genre they invoke (precisely by repeating it), so that the interlocutory relation to the implied reader is a peculiar mixture of the combative and the conciliatory. What matters is that the genre understands its address in interventionist terms recalling Bakhtin's definition of the dialogic utterance: "The speaker breaks through the alien conceptual horizon of the listener, constructs his own utterance in alien territory, against his, the listener's, apperceptive background."[13] Bakhtin's formulation captures the way in which the national tale, as a genre from the sidelines, moves on to the "alien territory" of a dominant discourse so as to wrest a place for its own utterance "against" the apperceptive background of that discourse.

It is not just that national tales take on specific travel-texts, although both Morgan and Edgeworth adopt this micro-tactic, but that they operate at a macro level to disturb the tour's center of gravity by disorienting the traveler-figure who anchors the travel narrative. The displacement they effect is nicely captured by Niilo Idman's pointed summary of the standard plot of national tales:

> A person of eminence arrives in Ireland; he (or she) possesses every qualification for a rich and interesting life, yet nothing noteworthy has ever happened to him, and he is full of spleen until, once there, he is dragged into a whirl of undreamt-of-adventures; his former habits, prejudices and ways of thinking suddenly give way to an all-absorbing passion, which irresistibly hurries him towards bliss or destruction, as the case may be.[14]

Idman's specific subject is Charles Robert Maturin, whose dark imagination sustains the language of rupture and whirl rather more persuasively than do Morgan's or *a fortiori* Edgeworth's fictions. But he derives his paradigm from *The Wild Irish Girl*, which inaugurated the pattern of transporting "a person of eminence" out of familiar categories and subjecting this figure to a *bouleversement* whose outcome was uncertain. Importantly, Idman sees this plot as releasing an aggressive energy located in the peripheries ("the revenge of a subdued and oppressed country upon her masters"[15]), so understanding it not as a move into but a turn on a master narrative.[16] It is by no means beside the point that the site of Idman's own enunciation was a small country, Finland, which had been absorbed into a very large one, Russia, as a quasi-independent province when Idman began his research in 1914 (by the time his book came out in 1923 Finland was an independent nation).

Idman's account draws attention to the fact that, as a romantic genre, the national tale is a genre of "minor" nations, that is, of small European nations that stand in a certain relation of hostility to a larger and oppressive nation with whose fortunes their own are intertwined. The idea of Irish writing in English as "minor" has become something of a commonplace following David Lloyd's applicaton of Deleuze and Guattari's influential notion of "minor writing" to Irish literature in *Nationalism and Minor Literature.* But my interest lies more in the obvious point that the national tale is a form of fiction invented in a small nation, and this sense of "minor" is caught more fully in the German phrase used by Kafka, "*kleine Literaturen.*"[17] The "kleine" in this instance also includes the sense of "trampled-down nations," as Thomas Moore called them,[18] so that the national tale is not simply a fiction that takes national matters or manners for its subject – *War and Peace* is not a national tale nor is *Persuasion*, although both are centrally concerned with the nation – but a fiction that locates itself in a contentious zone of discourse in order to articulate the grievances of a small people.[19] This helps to explain why readers like Idman and Tracy take *The Wild Irish Girl* as paradigmatic rather than turning to the earlier and better known *Castle Rackrent*, the conventional starting point of Irish fiction as a distinct mode of novel writing in English but not, in terms of my argument, of the national tale.[20] Morgan herself, looking back at the publication of her celebrated novel in the "Prefatory Address" to the 1846 edition of *The Wild Irish Girl*, offers perhaps the best definition of the novelistic project that made her name: "No work . . . of fictitious narrative, founded on national grievances, and borne out by historic fact, had yet appealed to the sympathies of the general reader, or found its way to the desultory studies of domestic life."[21] In a suggestive move, she adds a generous note to Edgeworth at this point but maintains their generic difference: "Miss Edgeworth's useful, admirable, and most humorous 'Castle Rack Rent,' had long preceded, as it surpassed 'The Wild Irish Girl,' but did not come under the same category."[22] Morgan does not specify why *Castle Rackrent* does not fall into "the same category," but her description of Edgeworth's novel suggests she may well have viewed her rival's odd and ironic tale as falling outside the three factors she stresses in her reference to *The Wild Irish Girl*: the foundation in "national grievances," the reference to "historic fact," and the appeal to "the sympathies of the general reader."[23]

The matter of grievance is crucial. To present Ireland as an anomaly, as we saw with the Irish tour in the last chapter, is to present it as a case for deliberation, and thus to move into the foreground the viewing/reading subject as the one who determines and judges. To present it as a grievance, however, is to write Ireland less as a problem to be resolved than as a claim that demands to be heard. It is thus to alter the narrative pragmatics of the case by directing attention to the one who presents the case rather than to the one who determines it, a point underscored by the derivation of "claim" from the Latin *clāmāre*: to call, cry out, proclaim, declare around, call upon. To recall Chandler's discussion in *England in 1819*, we could say that the scene of the representation remains the case (Ireland as a situation to be determined), but the focus has shifted to the claimant *making* a case for "the case." "Born and dwelling in Ireland, amidst my countrymen and their sufferings," wrote Morgan, defending herself against charges of being political, "I saw and I described, I felt and I pleaded; and if a political bias was ultimately taken, it originated in the natural condition of things."[24] Her tales constitute an equivocal "pleading," a term that conflates public and private scenes of address, overlaying the civic scene of a legal pleading and the domestic scene of a woman's plea, so as to infuse the public scene with personal affect while at the same time confirming the feminine propriety of her writing. The primary scene, however, is the agonistic scene of public speaking, and in placing her novels on this discursive stage, Morgan asserts not so much the truth of her representation as the truthfulness of her act of representing: a sincerity of performance.

Thus rooted in grievance, the national tale inaugurated by *The Wild Irish Girl* moved Ireland into a new kind of publicity, mobilizing the old romance trope of encounter on behalf of very contemporary and civic concerns. Although the Enlightenment genres of the picturesque and the survey remain importantly in play in the early national tale, it seeks to present Ireland less as a "picture" gratifying curiosity or as a territory to be inspected than as a participant in an event through which metropolitan perceptions themselves undergo a certain estrangement. Unlike the Irish tour, in which someone from "here" traveled "over there" and reported back, the national tale dislodged English readers from home space without securing the journey by a reassuringly English enunciation. Nor did it move the Irish into England, as had been the literary practice prior to the interventions of Edgeworth and Morgan. The significance of this latter point is underlined by T. H. Lister, writing in the *Edinburgh Review* in 1831, when he notes that until the turn of the century, the Irish were generally known to English readers only as "solitary foreigners, brought over to amuse us with their peculiarities." Since they were never represented "on Irish ground," he explains, "we never viewed them as natives of a kindred soil, surrounded by the atmosphere of home, and all those powerful accessaries [*sic*] which made *them* natural, and *us* strange and foreign."[25] Lister's memorable phrasing ("*them* natural, and *us* comparatively strange and foreign") draws attention to the reversal of trajectory in the national tale. Displacing its English readers in a way the Irish tour never did, the novelistic genre compelled them to consider Ireland as a habitat (a native and independent place) and not simply as the primitive, ridiculous, or dangerous colony of English imaginings. As a corollary, they themselves became "strange and foreign," thereby occupying a liminal position on which (as the next section of the chapter will argue) depends the notion of cultural sympathy activated by these fictions.

A brief sequence early in *The Wild Irish Girl* helps to throw into relief the debate with travel writing that conditions this rewriting of cultural encounter.[26] Setting out for the west of Ireland from Dublin, the aristocratic and bored English hero, Horatio M – (banished to Ireland by his father in punishment for a life of dissipation in London) ends up abandoning vehicular transportation to walk to his destination. Fearing he is lost, he comes across the standard Irish cabin of travel writing discussed in the last chapter, and seeks help but finds only a small boy and a large pig, both of whom run away, leaving him "alone in the centre of this miserable asylum of human wretchedness" (20). Contrasting this mean interior with that of an English peasant's dwelling, Horatio turns from it in a mixture of "compassion and disgust." At this point, Morgan inserts one of the many footnotes that constitute the novel's substantial (and literal) subtext, offering first a generic description of Irish cabins then a personal anecdote to contest her hero's disparaging account. What matters is the dynamic of contestation rather than the content of the rival representations, both of which in fact work within standard inflections of the cabin. Where Horatio offers a stereotypical colonial reading deriving from the anthropological categories of Enlightenment history (the barbaric Irish), the authorial reading draws on its sentimental tropes to proffer a pastoral reading of the cabin as a site of hospitality and courtly behavior. On one significant issue, however, the intersection of the two texts takes on a sharper resonance, underscoring the combative ground of authorial enunciation. This moment comes not, as might be expected, in the personal anecdote recounted by Morgan (a banal fantasy of peasant deference, wisely dropped by the author in the revised edition) but in a small and telling detail in the general description of Irish cabins. The cabin, Morgan pointedly states, "answers for every purpose of domesticity, though almost destitute of every domestic implement" (20). By so placing it within "domesticity," she not only counters the tour's general dismissal of Irish cabins as properly domestic space but implies that the English genre evidences a limited and technological definition of the domestic by reducing the notion of home to the possession of "every domestic implement."

The politics of genre (and gender) assumes an even more aggressive edge in the next moment of the sequence when, almost suffocated by smoke, Horatio hurries from the cabin to find himself attracted to a ruined barn by the sound of "a full chorus of females." There he finds a spinning circle of young women led by an old woman, and he listens to their song until it abruptly stops when the women perceive his presence. He reports that "the old woman addressed me *sans ceremonie*, and in a language I now heard for the first time" (21). Horatio responds in English, and his words are greeted by repressed laughter on the part of the younger women and by what seems a gesture of contempt on the part of the old woman. Never, he tells his London correspondent, did he feel himself "less invested with the dignity of [a man], than while I stood twirling my stick, and 'biding the encounter of the eyes' and smiles of the 'spinners in the sun'" (21).[27] Having gone for a look, Horatio is now himself subjected to an emasculating look, suddenly made aware of the existence of another world in which his usual (English, masculine) identity no longer quite sustains itself. Reinforcing this sense of dislocation, another long authorial footnote accompanies the episode, this time giving ancient provenance to the "*conventions* of female industry" characteristic of the west and north of Ireland and citing Charles Vallancy's antiquarian journal *Collectanea de Rebus Hibernica.* With some relief, Horatio welcomes the arrival of a young male who speaks English and offers to be his guide.

The travel journey in national tales thus begins to rebound on an ironized traveler figure, marking this figure rather than the Irish in terms of lack.[28] The scene of the cabin becomes a particular locus of such overturning and irony, for it allows at once a dialogic rejoinder to travel-texts and (inside the representation) an encounter with the Irish at the level of the lived body. Such encounters tend to press home in a visceral way the gaps and breaches in the cultural knowledge of those who govern the territory, as in a striking scene in Morgan's *Florence Macarthy*. In this scene an obtuse character named Lady Dunore, who fancies herself enlightened, visits the cabin of a forty-shilling freeholder (holders of the electoral franchise in pre-Emancipation Ireland) in the course of canvassing for votes for her son. The ramshackle cabin has the usual quota of children and pigs and is topped by a flourishing roof of potato stalks and grass sods. Utterly confounded, Lady Dunore turns to her companion: "What is this?" she asks. When informed it is a freehold, she repeats the word incredulously, holding a scented handkerchief to her nose: "I could not for a moment suppose that *this* wretched place, these wretched persons – in short, if I stay a moment here, I shall catch a typhus fever, or be suffocated by the stench."[29] Not only does the cabin defy English syntax – Lady Dunore cannot complete her sentence – but it also threatens contamination. Visitors flee or, like Edgeworth's Lord Glenthorn in *Ennui*, attempt to re-form the space only to find themselves stymied. When Glenthorn rides up to the surreal cabin of his old Irish foster nurse, Ellinor, he immediately finds his own sense blocked by an overwhelming heterogeneity of sheer sound: "the dog barked, the geese cackled, the turkeys gobbled, and the beggars begged, with one accord, so loudly, that there was no chance of my being heard!"[30] When he finally makes himself heard, he can make nothing of the local idiom, and the whole experience decides him on building Ellinor a house "in the most elegant style of English cottages" (189). But this too, when completed, resists his will and reason, uncannily turning itself into the Irish cabin he had attempted to erase. In frustration, he summons the stock anglocentric rhetoric Edgeworth makes a particular target in this novel: "I reproached Ellinor with being a savage, an Irishwoman, and an ungrateful fool!" (200).

Glenthorn's insistent "I" recalls that travel tales are always first-person tales ("I was there") and hence fall into the category of witness narratives, whose authority at once depends on and is rendered suspect by the personal enunciation. As they place pressure on first-person narration in their novels, both Edgeworth and Morgan retain the empirical bias that defines knowledge as a function of experience but at the same time foreground its framing and filtering by the often opaque workings of individual consciousness. For their first-person narrators, Ireland serves, at least initially, as a site that invites but defeats ideal self-projections, a function of their own tenuous subjectivity. So Glenthorn arrives at his Irish castle to receive thrilling confirmation "of my own consequence beyond any thing which I had ever felt in England" (178). Inspired by this sensation to try out the role of benevolent ruler, he lives out an incoherent fantasy mingling feudal and modern motifs, only to find himself (as we saw in the instance of Ellinor's cabin) somehow always beside the point. In the end, of course, Glenthorn discovers he is not who he thought he was, so that in a very real sense, he has always been beside the point in relation to himself as well. Only by assuming yet another family name and reinventing himself as a member of the gentry-professional classes (to whose cultural significance in the period Gary Kelly has drawn marked attention[31]) can the erstwhile Glenthorn find a meaningful place in the land and take responsible possession of his former estate.

As in *The Wild Irish Girl*, Irish feminine energies are crucial to the transformation and redemption of the English lord, but Edgeworth (unlike Morgan) is careful to defuse these energies of erotic charge.[32] Where the female figures in *Ennui* bring Glenthorn to a *concept* of civic and masculine duty, Morgan's Glorvina initiates Horatio (who, like Glenthorn, suffers from a "wretched state of non-existence," [34]) into a new *world* that revitalizes his consciousness. Glorvina thus operates in more controversial terms from the start because she encourages the conflation of nature and culture/nature and history characteristic of romantic nationalism, as Edgeworth's heroines rarely do.[33] Identified with a unifying trope of place and the nostalgic chronotope of the enclave, Glorvina adopts archaic customs and dress, and dances and sings her way into the hero's heart, at once erotic goddess of nature and ardent nationalist heroine. But even as she helps sustain Horatio's reading of the community of Inismore as a pastoral wherein atemporal figures perpetually enact "primeval virtues," Glorvina makes apparent the way in which this reading is in large part a function of his own modern desire. Seeking a "natural Irishwoman," he is seeking a pre-modern and childlike figure – innocent, spontaneous, vital, and uncultivated – who will anchor his own jaded, modern and reflective self. So he strives mightily to maintain his model of Glorvina who, for her part, does much to encourage his effort. But more disconcerting powers surface as well, for Glorvina too participates in the reversals to which Horatio has been subjected since arrival in Ireland. The process begins almost immediately in their encounter. Anxious to remain in Inismore but aware that Glorvina's father despises his own family as violent usurpers of the native estate, Horatio sheds his guilty name. Knowing he can gain entry into this place only on condition of a feigned identity, he announces himself as Henry Mortimer, itinerant artist. Strangely enough, the identity prudently assumed proves oddly compelling, bringing about an unsettling frame of mind: "By Heavens!," Horatio exclaims when he speaks to Glorvina for the first time, "I cannot divest myself of a feeling of inferiority in her presence, as though I were actually that poor, wandering, unconnected being I have feigned myself" (66).

On one level, this blurring of the lines of identity simply intensifies the erotic charge of the exotic, and Horatio lingers over the titillating contrasts Glorvina presents: her unexpected "elegance of manner," her smiles and blushes, her "wildly simple" looks, and the way in which she "speaks in the language of a court, [but] she looks like the artless inhabitant of a cottage" (66). But when he attempts to incorporate her into his fantasy through his own elaborate compliments, he meets a certain resistance: "I thought she looked wonderfully inclined to laugh in my face" (67). In a moment reminiscent of the humiliation suffered in the earlier scene with the female spinners, Horatio feels himself "looking like a fool" (67). What disconcerts in particular is that Glorvina's incipient laughter betokens a more knowing and adult consciousness than he is willing to grant the "wild Irish girl," and throughout the narrative she tends to keep him off-balance. Even as she explicitly performs as Gaelic heroine, Glorvina refuses the purity of belonging that informs the model of nostalgic nationalism: she reads English newspapers, quotes in Italian, declares "Milesian pride" fatal to the community, and claims that Catholic Emancipation will reduce "superstition." It is the outsider in *The Wild Irish Girl*, Luke Gibbons shrewdly notes, and not the insider who is heavily invested in notions of essence and the natural. In contrast to those who stress the Romantic essentialism of Morgan's novel, Gibbons sees it as exemplary of the way in which a particular strand of Irish Romanticism contains within itself "its own destabilizing moment," foregrounding its own artifice to deter attempts to mistake it for the real.[34] This is a point worth emphasizing. *The Wild Irish Girl* may demand an intimate and quasi-bodily reading, as we will see, but this is not because it wants to intensify a mimetic illusion. Rather, it exploits the powers of romance to provoke a new English orientation toward the matter of Ireland: it is *position* that is at issue. In the act of advocacy that constitutes *The Wild Irish Girl*, Glorvina herself is best understood as a provocative figure, a self-conscious stylization shaped by an acute sense of historical crisis.

Moreover, as Gibbons also notes, the journey into the wild landscapes of Ireland is not (like the journey into the American wilderness) a flight from society. Rather, the plot of the Irish journey typically pivots on an outsider who tries to gain access to a tightly-knit community and who has to learn that authenticity is not a matter of direct access to an essential nature but the substitution of one code for another.[35] The outsider, in other words, has to move – or be moved – into the zone of cultural sympathy, and to learn the category of synchronous as opposed to hierarchical difference. This travel plot defines the outsider as the one whose perceptions and conduct require alteration, and it is by placing the outsider in this position that Morgan and Edgeworth rewrote the Irish tour. Presenting it as a tour conducted from rather than to the peripheries, the national tale undercut the detached enunciation of the tourist through the romance figure of encounter, which offers precisely neither fusion nor survey but the uncertainty of a meeting.

DISLOCATIONS OF SYMPATHY

When the *Dublin Review* considered the category of "national novels" in 1838, it stressed the role of such novels as "vehicles for exciting interest and sympathy in the minds of those to whom the nation in question would otherwise have been a name and nothing more."[36] It thus defined the genre in terms of the gesture of making-familiar: the infusing of a mere name with interest and sympathy. In order to be moved into familiarity with the dimly known place, however, the targeted readers had, in a sense, to surrender their own national name: to become strangers. The pragmatics of sympathy in the national tale depend on the way in which the novels ask readers to operate neither as tourists (passing through for "a look") nor as foreigners (bringing along familiar norms), but precisely as strangers moving into a new zone. "A stranger," William Hazlitt reminds us, "takes his hue and character from the time and place."[37] To be a stranger is to suspend one's own identity – to become an "unknown" – and to enter what we might call the rim of another's space. Strangers do not belong within this space but nor do they invade it, as foreigners do. A stranger may certainly decide to become a foreigner – the two roles do not rule one another out – but the key point is that the stranger denotes a position in cultural or social encounter when the possibility of a shift exists. That possibility exists because, as Georg Simmel pointed out in his pioneering analysis, a stranger is a category *internal* to a group, representing a special synthesis of nearness and distance. The inhabitants of Sirius, Simmel explains, are not strangers to earthlings, since they "do not exist for us at all; they are beyond far and near."[38] By contrast, strangers operate within the horizon of the group – the trader is the classic instance – so that the category implies a relation, a specific form of interaction with the group.[39]

On Irish terrain, however, the word "stranger" had at least a double valence. "Stay, Sir, you are I apprehend a stranger in this country?" asks a judge in Morgan's *Florence Macarthy* when the unknown hero of the novel finds himself arrested on false charges:

"I am, my lord, an utter stranger."
"You have then, Sir, a prescriptive right to courtesy and protection, in a land where the name of stranger is still held sacred." (III: 44)

But "the name of stranger" was importantly a contradictory name, its positive resonance as a generic category (the "sacred" name) clashing with the strongly negative sense of "the stranger" as a particular reference to the English colonizer. Thus Daniel Dewar, an early nineteenth-century Gaelic-speaking Scottish visitor, comments more than once on the strength of Irish prejudice "against the sons of the stranger who have settled in his country." He makes special note of the fact that "no one can enter the cabin of an Irishman, and converse with him familiarly in his own language, without perceiving his strong dislike to the person and religion of the *Gall* [i.e., stranger]. He remembers that his country has been invaded." By contrast, Dewar adds, Scots are "never distinguished by this appellation. The Irish call them Albanaich."[40] Hospitality, as summed up by a character in Thomas Moore's *Memoirs of Captain Rock*, is only for strangers who "come to pass through our neighbourhood, not to settle in it."[41]

The English or Anglo-Irish landlord ("the stranger") was thus refused the particular form of entry granted to generic "strangers." To connect with the lived space of Ireland, then, landholders like Lord M – and his son Horatio in *The Wild Irish Girl* or Lord Colambre in Edgeworth's *The Absentee* have to move out of the category of "the stranger," a category of known identity, into that of "stranger," where identity is precisely not known, taking on unfamiliar names and identities. Lord M – underscores the point in *The Wild Irish Girl* when he explains why he assumed the rather bizarre role of anonymous rebel fugitive to gain access to the Prince of Insimore: "he who as an hereditary enemy was forbid your house, as an unknown and unfortunate stranger . . . was received to your protection"(233).[42] For his part Lord Colambre is fuelled not so much by guilt as by more rational interests, taking on an incognito so that "he might see and hear more than he could as heir apparent."[43] To encourage particulars about the estate agent in the area, he tells the landlord at an inn that he is "an Englishman, and a stranger" (131). As Colambre and Lord M – both know, a stranger denotes the point of hesitation in cultural encounter: neither side has yet made up its mind. Strangers operate in the buffer zone of language and decorum James Clifford has termed "stranger talk," a kind of talk that opens lines of communication between native and visitor but refuses intimacy, maintaining a distance that allows for a neutral space of contact.[44] In so eruptive a space as Ireland neutrality was admittedly difficult and precarious, where not absolutely impossible; nonetheless, the buffer role of the stranger allowed for the probing of questions of relation and identity within a highly stylized interchange that might or might not turn into actual engagement, either positive or negative. The key point for the national tale is that a stranger may find or make space where a known figure (like an English landlord) cannot. If, as several travelers reported, strangers sometimes fell under suspicion as they traversed the land, the national tale was more interested in how the zone of the stranger could suspend the weight of knowing linked to historical time in charged Irish space, and act as a lever that might push the present toward a future not strictly determined.

In both literary and political terms, sympathy was understood to be the crucial lever, and the distinctive contribution of the national tale to public discourse on the question of Ireland was to mobilize the powers of sympathy in a particularly acute way. Mobility was very much the point, for what impels narrative in the national tale is an understanding of sympathy as a dynamic of dislocation. "The ear is receptive to conflicts only if the body loses its footing," Julia Kristeva notes, pointing to a similar sense of the dynamic in a more contemporary context. "A certain imbalance is necessary . . . for a conflict to be heard."[45] Over and over again protagonists in national tales are moved into receptivity to the "conflict" of a submerged history and culture within their own realm through an actual loss of balance, a literal faltering. Even more particularly, the initial loss of balance tends to be brought about by the sound of an alien voice. Horatio in *The Wild Irish Girl*, Glenthorn in *Ennui*, Armida in Charles Robert Maturin's *The Milesian Chief* – all undergo a stumbling of the body on hearing an unknown voice in a narrative moment that is less mimetic than kinetic.

Horatio's entry to Inismore in Morgan's novel establishes the paradigm. On a spring evening he rides across a perilous bridge onto the isthmus where dwells the remnant of the Inismore clan, curious to see how these people live. Himself unseen, Horatio watches ("spellbound") the celebration of a mass commemorating the violent dispossession of the Inismores by his own ancestor during the Cromwellian wars, and his initial discomfort at the coincidence of dates soon gives way to the familiar aesthetic posture of the tourist. "What a captivating, what a *picturesque*, faith," he exclaims, identifying the nature of his scopic pleasure and then reinforcing it by drifting into narcissistic fantasy: "I . . . almost wished I had been born the Lord of these beautiful ruins, the Prince of this isolated little territory, the adored Chieftain of these affectionate and natural people" (48, 50). He turns to leave, but just as he does so, he hears "the low wild tremulous voice" of a woman playing a harp (50). This moment alters his entire history, jolting him out of the controling spectatorship of the detached gaze into the proximity and implication of response.[46] Like Wordsworth's speaker coming upon the solitary Highland reaper, Horatio is stopped by an unknown sound; unlike the Wordsworthian speaker, however, he does not stay to wonder what it means. Instead, forgetting caution, he moves toward it and loses his bearings. Following the "witching strain," Horatio climbs a ruined wall, and as he clings to the parapet "to prolong this rich feast of the senses and the soul," the loose stones give way. He falls, losing consciousness. Upon awakening, he finds himself inside the castle and experiences an "irresistible desire" to prolong his status as guest and patient at Inismore (50–52).

I have read this scene as an instance of what Certeau, in his account of the eroticism of ethnological encounter, calls "ravishment."[47] Ravishment is a moment of excess implicating the body and suspending (for the moment) linear and cognitive structures of temporality, language, and thought. For Morgan's Horatio, the voice of the unknown woman in a strange setting produces a response that bypasses the circuits of rationality. Where the earlier scene of the eye was governed by terms like "interest" and "curiosity," the scene on the parapet features "nerves" that thrill at what the ear hears: "I listened. I trembled" (50). The importance of such moments of ravishment, Certeau emphasizes, is that they *do* something rather than mean something, and what they do is prompt what he calls the "gesture of coming nearer." This gesture, reducing but not eliminating distance, represents the desire behind the narrative address of the national tale: its wish to turn the foreigner into the stranger-who-comes-nearer.

One way of understanding how the national tale (especially in its Morganesque inflection) sets out to accomplish this desire is to say that it infuses a Humean moment of "communication" into the rational Smithian model of sympathy as "concord" articulated in *The Theory of Moral Sentiments*.[48] Smith's inquiry into sympathy is part of an inquiry into the judgment of conduct, and his scene of sympathy functions as a highly structured thought experiment, which presents the interaction between agent and spectator in sympathetic exchange very much as the regulation of unquiet things. Elimination of discord and the establishment of social harmony are the goals that frame his analysis, so that (like most commentators on Ireland) Smith makes untranquil minds and bodies his target, and stresses tranquility as the desired state of both individual and social being. What encourages the achievement or maintenance of tranquility in his view is the sociability that makes us seek "fellow-feeling." In Smith's model, the agent (the one who is agitated by pain or pleasure) keeps emotions within bounds so as to ensure the sympathy of the spectator (the one who may become agitated by a kindred emotion). The person principally concerned, he explains, knows that sympathy is a second-order emotion, hence never as strong as the original emotion; but at the same time this person longs for the relief afforded by sympathy, by "the entire concord of the affections of the spectators with his own." Such sympathy, however, is possible only if the agent is able to "flatten . . . the sharpness of [his emotion's] natural tone, in order to reduce it to harmony and concord with the emotions of those who are about him." The spectator, in turn, generates emotion in response to the perceived situation of the agent, so that the one reduces while the other adds to the stock of sentiments in order to secure fellow-feeling. In the end, Smith argues, the two sentiments, while always different, may enter into "such a correspondence with one another, as is sufficient for the harmony of society." "Though they will never be unisons," he comments, "they may be concords, and this is all that is wanted or required."[49]

The appeal of such a scenario to a post-Union discourse on Ireland seeking concord is not far to seek: it casts the Irish as agents needing to cultivate the virtues of self-command (much advertised by Smith and the Scottish school), the English as spectators needing to develop the virtues of amiability and to nourish their sensibility. But for the national tale, focused as it is on the English spectator/addressee, the Smithian model possesses a fundamental limitation in identifying sympathy with a transposition that may add to but does not alter the materials of consciousness. Smith's famous account of sympathy as the changing of places in fancy with the sufferer directs its attention not so much to impulses received as to mental projections sent out by the spectator. In his oft-repeated phrase, we "bring the case home to ourselves," and this means that when we put ourselves in the place of the other, we do so *as* ourselves: "I judge of your sight by my sight, of your ear by my ear, of your reason by my reason, of your resentment by my resentment, of your love by my love" (19). This is exactly the problem. To recall the cabin scenes from Edgeworth and Morgan discussed earlier, in these scenes Glenthorn and Lady Dunore function as Smithian spectators who react to the scene in front of their eyes as if they themselves were in it. They become satiric targets because they do so. When faced with alien scenes, a sympathy based on simple transposition (a copying of the impressions of one's own senses, as Smith puts it) finds itself blocked, so that national tales – even those of the more rational and Smithian Edgeworth – find themselves experimenting with more dynamic models of encounter reminiscent of Hume's early account of sympathy in *A Treatise of Human Nature* as "communication."

Although operating within very much the same epistemological and psychological assumptions as his friend Smith, Hume's analysis of sympathy ends up yielding a different accentuation, for he directs his interest to the way the sentiments of others communicate themselves to us. In his model, the similarity of all minds means not so much that an individual subject can readily project itself into the situation of another as that all subjects move in a field of mutual vibration: "As in strings equally wound up, the motion of one communicates itself to the rest; so all the affections readily pass from one person to another, and beget correspondent movements in every human creature."[50] Hume's scene is a horizontal and fluid scene of "correspondent movements" – an acoustical rather than oracular scene – and it posits a porousness of consciousness minimized in Smith. Emphasis in Hume shifts to the dislodging of the subject through a rubbing up against other persons. No sooner does any person approach me, he writes, "than he diffuses on me all his opinions." He elaborates the point in a statement peculiarly resonant for the national tale: "And tho', on many occasions, my sympathy with him goes not so far as entirely to change my sentiments, and way of thinking; yet it seldom is so weak as not to disturb the easy course of my thought."[51] In this model, encounter produces a certain disturbance; significantly, what is disturbed is "the easy course of my thought." Sentiments are by no means entirely changed – one's subjectivity does not dissolve – but their unthinking flow is checked, brought up short.

A Humean notion of sympathy as an often disconcerting encounter shapes the national tale, and helps account for its interest in scenes that register the quite literal impact on protagonists of alien energies and, more particularly, of alien sounds. The Irish arrival scene in Maturin's *The Milesian Chief* provides a dramatic instance. Based on Morgan's plot of love between a dispossessed native and a dispossessing stranger but reversing the genders, *The Milesian Chief* rewrites Morgan's romance trope of the newcomer's fall from the parapet in darkly gothic tones as a potentially deadly plunge.[52] The Italian-English heroine, Armida, comes to the far west of Ireland with her father to take up residence in his Irish estate, formerly in the possession of the O'Morvens. As the carriage bearing them enters the castle of the O'Morvens, situated on a steep cliff, there rises a sound of anguish from the remnant of the displaced clan watching from the rocks below: "a cry, the most bitter that ever pierced the human ear, burst from the crowd below."[53] At this sound the horses bolt, and Armida's carriage hangs precariously over the edge. A figure suddenly appears; Armida assumes its murderous intent, and she loses consciousness. On awakening, she sees "the mangled horses wallowing amid the fragments of the carriage from which she had been snatched but a few moments before it was dragged down the precipice" (I: 59). More radically than in the case of Morgan's Horatio, this moment will prove to be a crossing, altering the entire trajectory of Armida's life and being.

The central role of sound in this scene, its capacity to generate deadly sympathetic vibration, underlines the degree to which national tales pay as much attention to the ear as to the eye. Unlike eyes, ears have been generally overlooked in recent critical writing, but the whole matter of Ireland in the Romantic period was as much a matter of ears as eyes.[54] In British discourse the Irish were regularly represented as "clamouring" for attention, and the clamor ranged from speeches by supporters of emancipation like Grattan, to the fashion for harp playing that Morgan herself helped engender, to the hugely popular series of *Irish Melodies* by Thomas Moore, which made their way into fashionable and middle-class drawing rooms all over the United Kingdom. For Morgan, her friend Moore's melodies performed the same kind of cultural work as her national tale, and she celebrated their capacity to draw attention to "the wrongs of Ireland, in her own touching melodies, – thus awakening sympathies which reason could not rouse, and making the ear a passage to the heart and understanding."[55] In their attempt to gain a fuller hearing for Irish claims and culture, her own novels are filled not only with scenes of song but with translations of Irish songs, explanations of bardic tradition, cultural comparisons of musical instruments, and so on. Glorvina herself is a musical figure whose name, a prominent footnote informs the reader, means "sweet voice."

For all her picturesque posturing, sound is this heroine's primary medium, and her voice unsettles the English hero as her visuals rarely do. It does so via two different modalities: first, as the musical power that attracts him in the first place and, second, as the linguistic facility that allows her to quote in several languages and to teach him to speak Irish. As Irish music, the voice of Glorvina moves Horatio beyond sense altogether, as when he finds himself haunted by a song she used to sing: "it breathes around me" (223). As Irish language, it makes palpable to him the presence of another sense, one that does not readily translate into his own language. Glorvina herself makes this explicit when she tells him that "no adequate version of an Irish poem can be given; for the peculiar construction of the Irish language, the felicity of its epithets, and force of its expression, bid defiance to all translation" (89). In both cases, her voice stands in critical relation to his own familiar sense, and its prominence in the novel throws into relief the way in which ears (in contrast to eyes) herald less the capacity of projection (of "framing") than the less controlled faculty of receptivity whereby something from outside comes inside.

Hearing underlines the middleness of historical being, as well as its sociality, for a listener typically stands in the middle of a scene rather than outside it or on the edge. To be sure one of the most famous and often criticized romantic scenes of hearing, Wordsworth's "The Solitary Reaper," features a listener who stands precisely on the edge of the scene. But it is notable that the poem initially establishes the reaper as a sight: "Behold her, single in the field." Even so, the activating impulse lies with the one who sounds, and the speaker's internalization of her *sound* ("The music in my heart I bore") is not, as often charged, an internalization of her *song*, for that remains opaque to him and in her keeping when he leaves the scene, no wiser than when he came upon it.[56] This reading aligns the poem with the bafflement of the traveler-figure in national tales, and it gains support from the second Highland girl poem in Wordsworth's 1807 volume. In sharp distinction to "The Solitary Reaper," the speaker in "To A Highland Girl" seeks to engage with the figure who has prompted his lyric, to make a "claim" upon her: "and I would have / Some claim upon thee, if I could." As the conditional phrasing suggests, the poet well knows the futility of such desire, and the poem repeatedly deploys the motif of incommensurability: "Thee, neither know I, nor thy peers"; "thoughts that lie beyond the reach / Of thy few words of English speech." Standard narratives of relation also fail, as he tries out a series of possible roles: pastoral lover, elder brother, father. Finally, as in "The Solitary Reaper," he takes away a memory as "recompense," but the key point is that the memory in both instances revolves centrally around a femininity that enables yet confounds his poetic powers.

These Wordsworthian lyrics, like the national tale, hinge on the doubleness of a meeting, and the importance of sound in romantic Irish novels lies in the way that its own doubleness at once provokes and impedes cultural crossings. As an emanation of the body (what the eighteenth century liked to call "the language of nature"), sound signals precultural energies through which disparate bodies may be pulled into proximity. As an emanation of culture, however, sound denotes the estrangement of disparate languages that do not understand one another. A small moment early in *Ennui* is emblematic. In another of the stumbles that set in motion the plot of encounter, Glenthorn falls to the ground when his horse is spooked by the voice of an old Irish woman. Lying there, he hears an anxious low voice near him: "I did not understand one word she uttered, as she spoke in her native language, but her lamentations went to my heart, for they came from hers" (156). Even as the voice pulls him into intimacy (my heart to hers), it is also the bearer of estrangement ("I did not understand one word"), and its sound underscores that they inhabit a world at once common and sharply differentiated. Such moments remind us that for eighteenth-century theories of language in the line of Rousseau – and Rousseau features prominently in Irish national tales – the auditory sense was perceived as *the* mediating sense, confirming the innate sociality of human beings and the priority of feeling over necessity (and reasoning) in the making of human community. "One does not begin by reasoning but by feeling," Rousseau characteristically asserts in his early "Essay on the Origin of Languages."[57] Speech, he maintains in this essay, began in an overflow of emotion and desire for another; to communicate physical needs, the visual signs of a purely gestural language were sufficient: "while visible signs can render a more exact imitation, sounds more effectively arouse interest."[58]

Downplaying mimetic forms and motives, Rousseau ends up devoting much of his essay on language to music, but the important point for genres like the national tale is his understanding of language as a non-mimetic surplus-effect generated by the desire to reach someone. "One can take nourishment without speaking," he writes. "One stalks in silence the prey on which one would feast. But for moving a young heart, or repelling an unjust aggressor, nature dictates accents, cries, lamentations" (12). In the surplus of this natural speech – pre-articulate and pre-rational – Rousseau locates the first social institution, and his valuation of sound persisted in European thought throughout the century even when his specific theory of the origins of language was disputed. Gottfried Herder, for instance, while dissenting from Rousseau in crucial ways, opened his own "Essay on the Origin of Language" with a memorable definition of sound as "a going out toward other creatures." Herder defines sound as an instinctive seeking for what he calls "an echo from one that feels alike, even if none is there" (87). For him this sound is not yet human language, which he identifies with naming, but in this outcry for recognition in and from the other he roots the "old wild languages" located in the body and the passions of the soul. Connections and communities (if not communications and nations), such arguments suggest, depend more profoundly on the somatic rather mentalist level of language.

But if voice is that which bridges cultural difference as sound (a cry, a song), it is also that which, in its manifestation as speaking, concretely marks such difference. "Sound is not in the organism and not in nature," Bakhtin and Medvedev testily assert, "but is between people, between socially organized people."[59] Their concern is with what they call "socially meaningful sound," and in the organization of this sound a "social audience" is constitutive, so that to register sound as not meaningful is at the same time to register oneself as not part of the constitutive audience. To be amid the sounds of an unknown language is to become aware of oneself as alien, a point nicely illustrated by Hazlitt when he contrasts domestic as opposed to foreign travel. When travelling the familiar terrain of England, he observes in "On Going on a Journey," he prefers to travel alone, enjoying the suspension from his everyday identity made possible when dealing only with strangers: "In his ignorance of me and my affairs, I in a manner forget myself."[60] But in foreign lands Hazlitt finds such loss of identity less liberating, and wants a companion. When travelling abroad, "one seems a species by one's-self," and to counter this sense of alienation, Hazlitt seeks the reassurance of a fellow English speaker: "I should want at intervals to hear the sound of my own language."[61]

If Ireland is not precisely a foreign land, it resounds with foreign words – travel-texts typically made a special note of the sound of Irish – and in *The Wild Irish Girl* Horatio soon learns that the sound of a foreign language marks the boundaries of one's own world, as well as establishing a palpable sense of other worlds. Throughout the novel, he repeatedly finds himself excluded from Irish scenes, as when a crowd is somehow placated or mourners make incomprehensible appeals to the local priest. Even when English is spoken, as in the case of the Prince of Inismore, the language does not sound quite the same: the Prince, we are told, does not so much speak English as translate the Irish. Dependent on translators and guides, Horatio cannot make his own way around the place, and he experiences a vulnerability and limitation new to him. The sound of the Irish harp may generate a sense of erotic communion, but Irish speech makes apparent a sense of community deriving from a language, custom, and history from which he is excluded. Moreover, Morgan's own text is crowded with words in many languages, including Irish words, so ensuring that the English reader will experience a decentering as well. When foreign words appear on the page, readers can no longer read past them to their meaning; generally, in fact, they "sound" them out in silent reading. A certain stickiness in the text is thus central to its project of moving the reader into a new kind of cultural awareness. As Johannes Fabian puts it in *Time and the Other*, awareness is "fundamentally based on hearing meaningful sounds by self *and* other," so that for him (as for his eighteenth-century predecessors) hearing stands as the "noblest sense," the starting point of a materialist anthropology.[62] Attempting to turn Ireland from meaningless "clamour" to meaningful sound for English readers, the early nineteenth-century national tale embodied a similar understanding albeit from a very different position, as it activated the romance plot of encounter to clear a space in the literary field wherein Ireland could move from cognitive object of knowledge to ethical subject of acknowledgment.[63]

PUBLIC PERFORMANCE

To gain a hearing for the matter of Ireland was also to place the woman writer within civic discourse, for the enunciation of the national tale was inflected not only by nationality but by gender. The flamboyant Morgan aggressively highlighted both inflections, while her more reserved compatriot Edgeworth tended to downplay both her nationality and her gender, eschewing overt identification of her sex in the narration and presenting her Irish tales as part of fashionable metropolitan genres rather than labelling them "A National Tale." This does not mean, as Mitzi Myers has been pointing out, that Edgeworth's novels were not interventions in public discourse but that Edgeworth constructed herself as author in terms of a genteel feminine reserve that either eluded or did not interest the more lowly born Morgan, whose family ties to "the *strollers' barn*" hostile reviewers liked to point out.[64] Where Morgan presented herself as a Wild Irish Girl and actively courted publicity, Edgeworth was habitually distrustful of what in *Ormond* she calls the "desire to *produce an effect*, to have a scene."[65] In an often quoted remark later in her life, she refused a request for prefaces to an edition of her work by saying: "As a woman, my life, wholly domestic, cannot afford anything interesting to the public."[66] By contrast, Morgan produced a steady stream of prefaces, pamphlets, travels, memoirs, and anecdotal essays, none of which is particularly intimate (Morgan had her own form of personal reserve) but all of which are bent on deliberately and provocatively placing her in public discourse as a female and Irish author. From the start her work met with critical disdain, as well as with a certain amount of approval, and Morgan herself intensified the debate by prefacing her travel book on France in 1817 with an extended attack on the *Quarterly Review*'s early and derisive review of her fiction in 1809.[67] Those provoked by Morgan responded in kind, and she was fiercely attacked not only in the *Quarterly* but in various other reviews like the *Antijacobin* and the post-Colburn *Literary Gazette.* "I think it a pity so much good invective should have laid out upon her when there is such a fine field of us Jacobin gentlemen for you to work upon," Byron joked to John Murray after Murray's *Quarterly* published its own stinging response to Morgan's *France.*[68] His remark usefully reminds us that the now mostly forgotten but once lively controversy over Morgan constitutes a significant minor moment in the well-known battle between Bards and Reviewers in the Romantic period.[69] It is not only that the controversy was the direct stimulus for Colburn's founding of the influential *Athanaeum* in 1828 but that it represents a determined and unusual female intervention in the generally male struggle over literary authority in the period.[70]

In taking on the critical reviews, Morgan argued for female authorship as a properly public activity answering to a "general public" outside the controls instituted by the literary field. She may have placed her national tales under the sign of conciliation and repeatedly imaged herself as a young, small, and unprotected woman – a minor – when she entered the literary field, but she nonetheless wrote herself as national author under the sign of an adult politics and polemics, and she approached the institutions of British public discourse with a marked irreverence. Viciously attacked in the *Quarterly Review*, she answered in her novel *Florence Macarthy* with a wickedly satiric portrait of her reviewer, John Wilson Croker (Lord of the Admiralty), casting him as a member of the sleazy Crawley clan, a clan Thackeray was to remember when he came to write *Vanity Fair* (as he remembered too the name of Glorvina).[71] Reviewing the novel, the *Edinburgh Monthly Review* complained that critical attack had simply increased Morgan's bouyancy, encouraging her "to caper away in the highest regions of impertinence."[72] When condescendingly reviewed by Hazlitt in the *Edinburgh Review* in a notice of her biography of Salvator Rosa, Morgan dashed off an informal essay in which she dismissed the article as the made-to-order product of a "little unknown" hired by the "great well-known of a great review"; on another occasion, she produced a spirited pamphlet replying to the reviewers of her book on Italy wherein she took great delight in hurling satiric epithets at the periodicals concerned (e.g., "that heavy nondescript, the Literary Gazette").[73] The same pamphlet, incidentally, directly invokes the battle of Bards and Reviewers, bringing up the usual charges about *Blackwood's* and the death of Keats, along with the recent duel that had taken the life of John Scott, gifted editor of the *London Magazine*, in a quarrel involving the same magazine ("the blood-stained pages of Blackwood's publication," [19]).

As with the national tale, what is telling is less the content than the address and tone of these texts. "Lady Morgan was essentially an aggressive writer," observed Julia Kavanagh of her countrywoman, acutely noting that although Morgan's views were often moderate enough, their enunciation was always provocative: "There are few of her works which are not written in a tone of defiance."[74] The defiance was directed in particular at the claim of what Morgan scornfully termed "professional criticism" to represent public opinion. The centrality of public opinion was fundamental to Morgan's liberal understanding of the modern nation – "The appeal of public opinion belongs to the age in which we live," declared the Advertisement to *Florence Macarthy* – but she placed this "public opinion" outside both the rationally derived consensus of literate persons we know as the eighteenth-century public sphere and the newly professionalized critical discourse of the reviews that was one of its nineteenth-century avatars. For the notion of the public sphere, Morgan had a nostalgic affection, linking it to the idealized moment of Grattan's Protestant Nation when in her eyes Ireland had a real press and an informed reading public of "genuine and educated Irish gentry" to serve as a vehicle of "public feeling."[75] Vestiges of this moment lingered, as in Morgan's own Dublin salon, but the mantle of the public had passed to a "general reader" and "general public" now linked to an amorphous literary market rather than to the more firmly located public sphere.

For Morgan this public acted as a bulwark of "opinion" and openness against both the powers of force and the more sinister powers of government secrecy and control. To this public she dedicated her *Memoirs*. Opposed to it stood the professional criticism that was her target, a discourse she charged with being in secret and cowardly complicity with government power and party aims: "the anonymous slander with which party spirit arms its strictures, under the veil of literary justice."[76] Deploying a political whig scenario for her literary point, she accused the *Quarterly* reviewers of being simply "subaltern scribes" for the government, "nameless assailants" shooting arrows at her from behind "masked batteries."[77] For her part, she presented herself as disdaining any such masking, a woman author who openly took her ground. "Mine, I trust will be true lady's archery, fair, though irregular; my aim taken in the garish eye of day – my name announced."[78] Enhancing her own femininity, she shrewdly diminishes the virility of her adversaries.

If the boldness of Morgan's assault on the critics was unusual for a woman writer in the period – and unusually inflected for nationality – the quarrel itself was not. As Frank Donoghue has pointed out, by the late eighteenth century writers and reviewers were engaged in a struggle over the power of literary legitimation and definition, impelled in large part by concern with the "phantom of the English reading public." This "phantom," product of the market and largely outside institutional purview, haunted the literary field because it at once sustained its viability and threatened its authority. Within the field itself authors and reviewers vied for control over literary naming, each authorizing itself, Donoghue notes, through "a partisan representation of the 'public in general.'"[79] The Morgan affair is thus a classic instance of this intramural struggle within print culture. Morgan consistently sanctioned her authorship by elevating the "public of an enlightened age," claiming for it (rather than critical discourse) the power to grant authorial status. When denied that status by reviews like the *Quarterly*, she invoked the superior power of the public to overturn critical decision: "Placed by that public in a definite rank among authors."[80] Not surprisingly, the *Quarterly* itself was not much impressed by her claim: "Lady Morgan . . . appeals from our judgment to that of (what she calls) the public."[81] Such appeals and disclaimers can never be resolved because "the public" functions as a strategically empty third term, ready to be harnessed by either side and in different ways. On the one hand, the turn to this third term sustains the rivalry that structures the literary field; on the other, it also contains the potential to dissolve it, or, more precisely to differentiate a field that each side implicitly seeks to keep a whole ("the public" rather than various "publics").[82] The author-public alliance, that is, points to a potentially mass audience or mass culture bypassing the judgment of critics; that of critic-public to an elite or high culture audience bypassing the desires of authors.

The vehemence of the attacks on Morgan – vehement even according to the standards of the day – stems from the way in which her volatile mix of low forms and high ambition, of Irish nationality and female sex, romance and politics, cut across the divisions that kept the triangular relationship of author-reviewer-public in regular, as opposed to dissonant, play. Hence it seems to me the insistence on Morgan's writing as but a cheap imitation of authorship, a tawdry simulacrum made of "tarnished tinsel and cast-off frippery."[83] For the *Literary Gazette*, for instance, her whole career amounted to an absurd copy of that of Mme de Stael, and the review presents the Irish writer as Stael's "little grotesque mimic," who has spent twenty years "following at an humble distance that dashing hater of monarchs and *lover* of *men*."[84] In only "seeming," she becomes unseemly and potentially dangerous, so that the vocabulary of second-hand authorship combines with that of infection, as in the *British Review*'s declaration that "we, as guardians of the intellectual health of our readers, must not suffer our watchfulness to be beguiled by the meanness of the vehicle. The plague has sometimes been conveyed in a bundle of old clothes."[85] Charged with a range of political and social vices (e.g., jacobinism, blasphemy, and licentiousness), as well as a host of literary sins (e.g., inflated prose, bad grammar, slovenly style), the figure of Morgan's authorship – aggravating, indecorous, sprawling – tended to double that of the Irish nation itself, a point neatly underlined by *Blackwood's* in 1828 when it conveyed her abrasiveness via the trope of the rude nation so often featured in the Irish tour: "the bog-trotting buskins of Lady Morgan; who, wild as her fictions are, is somewhat more at home in endeavouring to paint the rude manners in which she was bred, than those of the civilized countries into which she has intruded."[86]

Morgan clearly relished her celebrity and success – this in itself was not the least of her offences against decorum – but at the same time she became increasingly aware of some of the troubling ambiguities of the project she had initiated. As a narrative act rooted in pragmatic notions of performance and effect, the national tale founded by Morgan constantly risked producing simply a picturesque thrill for jaded urban palates or material for a fashion statement. If the figure of Glorvina dislodged some English preconceptions and shed a glamour for the Irish themselves over their degraded national identity, it was also readily recuperated into metropolitan categories. "I have finished the picture in that light tinting, so effective in these kind of characteristic drawings," writes Horatio of a drawing he has made of Glorvina singing Irish songs. "That beautifully pensive expression which touches the countenance of Glorvina, when breathing her native strains, I have most happily caught; and her costume, attitude, and harp, form as happy a combination of traits, as a single portrait can present" (98). Thus "happily caught" and turned into artifact, Glorvina and her Gaelic trappings threaten the transformation of history into decor and point to the "staging" of folklore that Susan Stewart finds typical of literary ballads of the period.[87] Morgan's novel may have helped to shape serious cultural-political formations in nineteenth-century Ireland (such as the Young Ireland movement of the 1840s), but, as she well knew, it also produced on the mainland what Ian Dennis has wittily termed a rage for the Wild Irish Look.[88]

Starting with her second national tale, *O'Donnel*, Morgan began to place both the question of publicity and her own fictional project under a certain scrutiny. *O'Donnel* makes theatricality and self-display central motifs, and both the embittered Irish Catholic hero and the odd Irish heroine of the novel repeatedly reflect on the question of performance for an English audience. The heroine in particular evidences a high degree of self-consciousness about her own performance. "What did you think of my face when I sang?" she asks at one point. "I always make a pretty face upon those occasions. You cannot think how it tells . . . I make the face, and they all cry 'how interesting she looks when she sings!' The truth is, the world loves a little acting."[89] As she also knows, "the world" admits her only on sufferance, and she is quite aware that she is not *bon ton*: "We Pamelas . . . are never supreme bon ton. No, we are at best but 'the fashion': we are for a time shown about, and followed and gazed at, and we exhibit and are exhibited" (198–99). In such statements we hear the resentment of young Sydney Owenson, taken up by the aristocratic English circle of the Abercorns and playing for their entertainment the role of Glorvina. In colonial Ireland, Seamus Deane remarks, "there was an irresistible temptation to impersonate the idea of oneself which was entertained by others," and he cites as a prime example Morgan's impersonation of herself as Glorvina.[90] At the same time, the clear-eyed recognition of role-playing evidenced by a figure like the heroine of *O'Donnel* points to a certain colonial self-possession, and the novel registers less the temptation of impersonation than its bitter anxieties. An extended reflection on the question of self-staging in a colonial context – the hero is referred to at one point as "a pet Irishman" (220) – *O'Donnel* testifies to a troubled sense that the distinction between role and being or between pragmatic demands and authentic action may entirely erode in such a context, become illusory, or serve only as a sustaining fiction.

For a national tale writer like Morgan the question of publicity was inevitably mired in ethical ambiguity, and her own authorial anxieties enter into the construction of the heroine of *Florence Macarthy* as a national novelist, acutely aware of producing Irish tales for an English market: "With Ireland in my heart, and epitomizing something of her humour and her sufferings in my own character and story, I *do* trade upon the material she furnishes me; and turning my patriotism into pounds, shilling and pence, endeavour, at the same moment, to serve her and support myself" (III: 264–65). Drawing on standard explanations in the period for women's writing, Florence invokes the alibi of both social service and personal economic survival.[91] But what rankles is precisely the overlap whereby national injuries become a commodity for personal gain. To mitigate the sting – to transform the private civil act of "trading" and "selling" into the properly civic act of public good – Florence Macarthy calls on the specifically female and traditional act of spinning. As she works at her spinning wheel, she finds in spinning confirmation of a genuinely national and gendered heritage ("our grandmothers of the highest rank in Ireland were all spinners,"[III: 264]), and she conflates spinning and writing in metaphoric interchange: "Meantime my wheel, like my brain, runs round. I spin my story and my flax together; draw out a chapter and an hank in the same moment; and frequently break off the *thread* of my reel and of my *narration* under the influence of the same association" (III: 265).

Such a moment transforms text into tradition, linking the literate, commercial heroine and the nation she writes with the rural and oral rhythms of preliterate community. In an important sense this exemplifies the kind of standard modern nation-building to which Ernest Gellner draws attention when he argues that the literate elites who typically forge the modern nation tend to validate it through appeal to a preliterate "folk."[92] But the fractured narrative and mobile heroines of Morgan's later national tales, the next chapter will argue, complicate this model by deploying archaic or regressive forms not so much to confirm national origin as to open up quasi-utopian spaces in which questions of nation, gender, and public action can be parsed in different ways. In particular, the femininity that broached the literary field via polemics and publicity now rewrites itself as a peculiarly theatrical reticence or reserve which allows for notions of female agency outside, though not directly opposed to, the domestic understanding that shaped most British fiction in the Romantic period.

CHAPTER 3

Female agents: rewriting the national heroine in Morgan's later fiction

> it is the peculiar advantage of woman's interference, that its sphere of action is all-pervading, and that its applicability commences there where all other agencies have no *prise* or lever to act upon.
>
> Lady Morgan *The Princess* (1835)

> a scene got up is always well worth a case stated.
>
> Lady Morgan *The O'Briens and the O'Flahertys* (1827)

"Politics can never be a woman's science," Morgan declared early in her career, "but patriotism must naturally be a woman's sentiment."[1] What made patriotism "naturally" a sentiment for Morgan, as for her compatriot Edmund Burke, was its roots in the intimate sphere of the local and domestic. Domestic affections expanded into "sentiments of national affection," establishing a national-cultural whole in which forms of public subjectivity were not only continuous with but grew out of the private sphere of the conjugal family. But even as Morgan continued to authorize her writing in terms of an acceptable "female patriotism" throughout her career (as in the preface to her last Irish tale *The O'Briens and the O'Flahertys*), her national tales increasingly began to interrogate the smooth flow from private to public implied by this model, troubling rather than consolidating the domestic articulation of women and nation rapidly, if not always straightforwardly, achieving prominence in post-Revolutionary Britain.[2] Where Edgeworth turned to a renovated domesticity founded on a notion of family that scrambled traditional models of birth and inheritance to confirm a virtuous femininity as the core of the new nation, as in *Ennui* and *The Absentee*, Morgan's later tales bypass the family and the rule of the couple as at once the affective and theoretical basis of national order. Instead, they posit a more precarious and amorphous principle of sociality forged in unofficial associations, at once local and cosmopolitan, and typically attached to an unconjugal and performative female figure with continental and Catholic ties.

In apparent paradox, Morgan's later tales rewrite the national heroine as precisely not "natural" but somehow all the more "national" as a consequence. The pastorally inflected Glorvina, devoted daughter and Gaelic nationalist, may have signaled a "pure national, natural character"(albeit not transparently, as the last chapter has shown), but her successors refuse any such identification and conflation. As Christian Isobel Johnstone complained in *Tait's Edinburgh Magazine*, they are all "dazzling actresses,"[3] and the ever acute Julia Kavanagh observed that "a spirit of mischief and intrigue, an aversion to the straight ways of life, mark them all save Glorvina."[4] These wayward figures, Kavanagh adds, "seem always to want some tie to break, some recognized standard of womanly decorum to violate."[5] Self-consciously theatricalized, Morgan's later heroines operate *aslant* the domestic, turning femininity into a "*prise* or lever," as she puts it in the epigraph to the chapter, one that unhinges if it does not overturn notions of agency, belonging, and history underwritten by emergent middle-class constructs of gender and the nation.

In an important way, Morgan's national tale resists the aesthetic of intimacy and interiority linked to the domestic genres, activating an aesthetic of estrangement whose implications for women's writing in the period have received rather less attention than they deserve. At the core of this aesthetic is a rethinking of questions of femininity and political agency that can best be understood as effecting a shift from questions of place to those of space. As Michel de Certeau puts it in his influential distinction, a place (*lieu*) is governed by the rule of the proper: each element is situated in its own distinct location, and all elements are distributed in relationships of coexistence, so that two things cannot occupy the same place. As a stable or, more accurately, stabilized "configuration of positions," a place is attached to notions of mapping and seeing, and thereby constituted as an object available to knowledge. By contrast, a space (*espace*) is not a structure but an itinerary, a function of "going" rather than seeing or knowing. The key point for my purposes is that a space, marked by ambiguity and polyvalence, comes into being when time is introduced into the field: velocity, temporal variables, vectors of direction.[6] Hence spaces not only imply agents but define them as subjects-in-time, that is, as moving figures rather than positions in a system. And it is precisely through modalities of temporality, this chapter will argue, that Morgan's later fiction opens up the figure of the heroine and the trope of the nation.

Starting with *O'Donnel* and culminating in the sprawling, web-like *The O'Briens and the O'Flahertys*, both Ireland and the performative heroine become detached from the unifying figure of place and reconstructed in the disjunctive temporal terms of mobility and metamorphosis. The drive to a Gaelic origin that characterized the narrative of *The Wild Irish Girl* dissipates, and the Irish nation now "appears" in different locations and among different groups, an internally stratified and dispersed category. The heroine herself undergoes a similar scattering, as Glorvina's *thereness* – her fullness of being, her rootedness, her iconic visibility – gives way to an oddly elusive and deterritorialized being who belongs nowhere, exactly, and who typically operates in the interstices of culture, keeping herself hidden and in reserve. While the erotic power of voice persists, the innocent blushes of the Rousseauean Glorvina are replaced by worldly verbal play and a peculiar delight in shape-shifting and disguise. As Morgan's biographer, Geraldine Jewsbury, notes of the eponymous heroine of *Florence Macarthy*: "Florence Macarthy appears always in disguise and masquerade – flits about like a will-of-the-wisp, mystifying everybody."[7] Of Spanish-Irish parentage, this heroine – like all of Morgan's later heroines – is a hybrid, and she plays at least three distinct roles in the narrative (including one in a disguise impenetrable to the reader). She has several names, the most prominent being Lady Clancare, a title that signals her link to metropolitan genres like the fashionable tale, the comedy of manners and the national tale (which she herself writes). She is also the Bhan Tierna, and in this role she is linked to the traditional and rural genres of Gaelic Ireland, familiar with Irish language and lore. As Florence Macarthy, meanwhile, she features in a romance with the dispossessed Anglo-Irish hero, but the name itself proves an equivocal sign, at once of uncertain gender (it is also the name of her father) and pointing to more than one female referent (it is also the name of a female cousin).

Such slippages and proliferations characterize the fully developed Morgan heroine, an oddly fluid and unlocated creature who derives not from the English conduct books, domestic tales and pastoral lyrics that have largely governed critical generalizations about women and the nation in the Romantic era but from a Continental line of fiction exemplified most prominently for Morgan's first readers by Mme de Stael's *Corinne* (1807).[8] Morgan herself expressed admiration for Stael on various public occasions, notably in her popular travel book *France* where she identified Stael as a writer "from whose works I had received infinite pleasure, and (as a woman, I may add) infinite pride" (231). References to *Corinne* pepper Morgan's correspondence, and include a memorable occasion in May 1808 when, as she reports to a correspondent, "We sat up till two this morning talking of Corinne."[9] Reviewers linked the Irish writer to Stael's novel throughout her career, starting with the publication of *Woman: or, Ida of Athens* in 1809, initially as a form of compliment but increasingly as a way to underscore Morgan's status as an inferior and imitative writer, as in Christian Isobel Johnstone's dismissal of the heroine of Morgan's last novel as "a kind of second-hand Corinne."[10]

Most readers of *Corinne*, then and now, have understood Stael's heroine as primarily a "performing heroine," to use Ellen Moers' handy phrase, but Morgan herself was fully alert to the fact that Corinne is in the first place a national heroine of a national tale.[11] Although *Corinne* is rarely discussed as a national tale, it is of paramount importance that it takes as its focus an unofficial nation: the not-yet-unified nation of Italy. From the outset it stresses that its heroine "performs" a nation that in a very real sense does not exist, and links Corinne's femininity to the conditional tense. As one character puts it, she is what Italy "would be," so that her performance does not so much represent a given entity as present a potential or virtual one.[12] The idea of a unified Italy in the period, Martin Thom reminds us, was a utopian notion largely constructed by those outside the country, *Corinne* itself being a prominent example. But as he also notes in passing, *Corinne* treats Italy less as a unified nation than as a collection of very different cities, so that it falls somewhere in between the receding classical republican model of the "city-state" and the emergent German Romantic model of the "tribe-nation," to both of which Stael owed ambiguous allegiance.[13]

The consequential point for the national tale is the indeterminateness of the nation, its unclear shape and boundaries. Attached to such a space (not yet a "place" in Certeau's terms), Corinne's femininity works less to consolidate native ground – to found an order – than to hold open the question of the future. Importantly, the condition of its doing so is that it must lie outside the reproductive domestic economy underwriting the model of nationhood coming to dominate much of the thinking in the period. If Stael's novel – much debated, imitated, satirized, and celebrated in British literary discourse – helped establish national history and culture as "a particularly feminine domain," as Gary Kelly has argued, it did so in terms that contested rather than confirmed the familiar domestic register.[14] Corinne herself is a profoundly undomestic figure – passion, not marriage, is her medium – and the significant and striking point is that Stael chose to invest this unaccommodated femininity with civic and national authority. Corinne's entire performance as patriot is predicated on a radical break with familial order and its rules of nomination.

Self-named, she constructs herself as national bard by repudiating not only her paternal land and name but also, more remarkably, her maternal roots. Corinne may return to her mother's land, but she does not do so as her mother's daughter. The narrative thus hollows out the act of return to Italy as a return to origins, reinforcing the way in which Italian space in the novel functions as a zone of potentiality.[15]

To move into such a zone does not mean a move out of the cultural imaginary and its strategic misrecognitions – indeed, the contrary is often the case – but the crucial point is that such zones drive a *wedge* between history and the nation or between nature and the nation, blocking the easy assimilation of terms whereby passage from one to the other is simply a matter of common sense. For obvious reasons, a construction of the nation as potentiality and as non-native space would appeal to a colonial writer like Morgan, but the main lesson of Stael's novel for her lay in the presentation of femininity as that which holds open the national future by keeping apart, rather than bridging, the mutually authenticating terms of nationalist closure, political and aesthetic. Even as femininity continues to be understood as a principle of national mediation in her later tales (although now more within Ireland than between Ireland and England as in the early *Wild Irish Girl*), Morgan's national heroine begins to manifest a more astringent ethic of estrangement through which the Irish novelist repositions the Staelian heroine to expose the ambiguities of agency in colonial spaces.

MOVING ON THE DIAGONAL

Halfway through *The O'Briens and the O'Flahertys*, the hero, Murrough O'Brien, goes directly from being sworn in as a member of the secret United Irishmen to a masquerade ball at one of the main sites of Ascendancy power in Dublin. What drives him to the ball is illicit sexual desire for Lady Knocklofty, wife of an Ascendancy grandee, and it is in this worldly and politically charged context of disguise and transgression that he encounters the figure who will prove to be the heroine of his story and of Morgan's novel. Upon his arrival at the ball, an unknown woman shrouded in the garments of a penitent engages O'Brien in sardonic and enigmatic conversation, provoking but eluding his scrutiny and identification. "You attract attention only to evade it," he accuses her, registering the deliberate theatricality of her elusiveness.[16] Throughout their exchange, he is uncertain whether "nature or art" dictates the gestures she directs toward him, and he remains disconcerted by "something ironical" in her tone (325). Moreover, he finds himself completely at sea as to who she might be, although for her part the mysterious mask seems to know all about him. Eventually, she allows him to recognize her as the same female figure who intervened in Rome during carnival some years ago when, as now, he was toying with the idea of adultery. This revelation, however, brings no clarification, for on that earlier occasion as well she had been in costume. One disguise thus simply gives way to another in the multiple and receding acts of masking that will continue for most of the narrative, as – in one form and another – this female figure darts in and out of the hero's (and the reader's) range, continually snatching O'Brien from danger but refusing to reveal her identity.

Clearly, this is a heroine-who-acts in more than one sense, and she exemplifies the way in which Morgan's later national heroine deliberately provokes the question of the relation between impersonation and agency when it comes to the "female patriotism" advocated by her author. Inhabiting the margins between classes, religions, nationalities, and genres, this patriotism seems to achieve agency (understood as the taking of initiative to set in motion some alteration of the given) only on condition of a certain hiddenness and disguise. It thus stands in highly equivocal relation to the liberal political logic governing the very project of the national tale. In rewriting the national heroine, Morgan not only detaches female visibility from the spontaneity of "natural" appearance (as in *The Wild Irish Girl* where Horatio was typically enchanted by glimpses of the unselfconscious Glorvina playing the harp, reading, dancing, and so on) but implicitly places in question notions of legibility and transparency sustaining the public sphere and its civic model of the nation. Even as the Morgan heroine continues to articulate a liberal politics, she operates well outside the openness and publicity valorized by its ideology, exploiting by contrast the powers of secrecy and reserve.

In Irish tales like *Florence Macarthy* and *The O'Briens and the O'Flahertys*, enlightened male patriotism typically finds itself stymied not just by the counter-revolutionary forces unleashed by the French Revolution but by an ambiguous female patriotism that "confounds" – to use one of Morgan's own favourite terms – its authority and confidence. Murrough O'Brien himself offers an exemplary instance, articulating a liberalism at once affirmed and baffled by the narrative in which he features. The son of a tormented and demented Gáelíc nationalist father who bears a bitter history, the young O'Brien has chosen a more moderate and modern model of national allegiance. As a student at Trinity College, Dublin in the period leading up to the United Irishmen's rebellion of 1798, he is an enthusiastic reader of the civic discourse of Locke and Rousseau, a writer of political pamphlets in the cause of Ireland, and a supporter of the liberal ambitions of Henry Grattan's "Protestant Nation." But the volatile politics of Ireland enmesh him in various confrontations with government authority. O'Brien is expelled from the university, and this leads to his initiation into the United Irishmen by the charismatic Lord Walter Fitzwalter (a fictional portrait of Lord Edward Fitzgerald), though he ends up at a distance from the failed rebellion that ensues. His father dies, the family mansion in Dublin literally collapses, and near the end of the novel he finds himself accused of murder. Rescued from prison and death in Ireland, he goes into exile in Paris, serving as an officer in Napoleon's army and holding on to those liberal principles defeated in Ireland and now threatened in Napoleonic France as well.

Murrough O'Brien is explicitly identified by Morgan with the favored liberal causes of the day: Greece, Poland, Ireland, and – most important – France, whose revolution established for Europe the modern sense of the nation as the sovereign "people" in whom rests all legitimacy. Exemplary theorist of the public sphere, he argues that a new political day has dawned because "learning and opinion" are no longer the monopoly of the few, so that the power of the nation-as-state is counteracted by the power of the nation-as-public. Literacy is the key: "the education which the public gives itself absorbs and neutralizes the instruction prepared for it by governments and hierarchies, whenever the results of both do not coincide" (367). At no moment, perhaps, is his status as precisely *public* hero more clear than when he balks at the idea of joining the United Irishmen because of the secrecy of the organization: "It was in no secret association . . . that the great principle of American Independence originated. It was the free and bold explosion of public opinion, which, in giving birth to the French Revolution, worked openly, and in the face of day. I distrust, I dislike secrecy" (298). In the end, however, he does join the United Irishmen, and he does so partly out of the recognition that (as a leader of the organization maintains) "wretched Ireland has no public opinion, no public to express an opinion" (298).

Grounded in texts and in the example of the French Revolution, enlightened patriotism works deductively from assumptions about liberty and universal rights as it seeks to realize a civic ideal of the nation, and Murrough O'Brien is inspired by its centripetal and rational model of the nation-as-project to enlist in the task of unifying the disparate nation and of harnessing into coherent action the disjunctive energies of the Irish crowd that haunts the novel. His model of the nation (like the public sphere itself) depends on the rational temporality of linear time: the time of modern history. From his liberal constitutional reading of the French Revolution, O'Brien has derived a historical *series* into which he and like-minded others seek to enter Ireland. But the drive for modern nationhood is blocked with the defeat of the United Irishmen's rising, and Murrough O'Brien himself must literally go underground and travel into the hinterland. Here he encounters another Irish nation, attached to temporalities outside the cursive flow of history and the rational structures of the law, as the novel increasingly begins to activate the disjunctive temporality Homi Bhabha has called the "double-time" of the nation.[17] Here too he finally encounters face to face the mysterious female protector who has repeatedly effected his rescue in the course of the novel.

She turns out to be his cousin, Beavoin O'Flaherty, an uncloistered nun who runs an abbey in the hinterland, and her actions and eventual romance with O'Brien replay earlier events in the long and complicated history of their two families. She thus evokes repetitive and recursive temporalities that counter the cumulative temporality of modernity affirmed by the enlightened hero, but the crucial point is that the hybrid Beavoin, who is half-Italian and half-Irish, does not herself exist in any one temporality. A modern cosmopolitan raised on the Continent, she is also an Irish native with roots in Gaelic female culture; a nun in an ancient patriarchal institution, she uses its resources to teach modern liberal ideas to local girls. Endowed with the almost magical powers of mobility that characterize Morgan's later national heroine, she moves about Europe and Ireland apparently at will: "from the choir of the Gesú Bambino, to the pavilions of the Borghese palace – from the saloons [*sic*] of the castle, to the fallen ruins of O'Brien's house – from the caves of Cong, to the smoky chambers of Bog Moy" (510). As she flits in and out of the hero's view, always veiled and under cover, the narrative makes increasingly apparent that it is she who controls the form and rhythm of their encounters. "You have too long assumed a power, only belonging to Providence itself," an exasperated O'Brien tells Beavoin when he finally confronts her, and he has in mind not just her power of protection but also her knowledge of "who and what I am" in contrast to his own utter ignorance of her identity. "I demand who and what you are" he insists, and she responds by finally revealing her history (518).

The figure of Beavoin O'Flaherty encapsulates the strangely atopic nature of Morgan's later national heroine, who is typically removed from immediate family ties and operates outside the locatedness and openness of being associated with the domestic heroine. Eschewing both the sincere speech of proper femininity and the rational discourse of enlightened masculinity, this heroine opts for an ethics of performativity. "Men . . . are always more readily convinced through their sensations than their reason," Beavoin tells Murrough in her scene of explanation, " – for arguments are words, but images are facts; and a scene got up, is always well worth a case stated" (526). Like her better known fictional cousin Flora MacIvor in *Waverley* (who produces herself as the Celtic Muse for the susceptible young English hero), Beavoin turns to her particular advantage the iconic power conventionally assigned to the female body-that-grounds, but at the same time she estranges this body from the natural order by identifying it as a cultural reservoir of effects. In so turning her body into image-matter, Morgan's national heroine not only "lays bare," as the Russian Formalists liked to say, the "devices" that pass for nature but asserts a certain control within the gendered code of signification and representation. To the extent that the female figure no longer simply inhabits this code but self-consciously acts within it, she unhinges the taken for granted tie between signifier and signifed, and so refuses the status of a naturalized first-order representation. Indeed, the Morgan heroine delights in obtruding precisely her second-order status, her role as the representation of a representation.

A striking example appears in the stagy introduction of the heroine of Morgan's last national tale, *The Princess; or the Beguine* (1835), a title that itself nicely raises the question of female roles. This heroine, whose original name we never learn, enters the novel under the rubric of the Princess of Shaffenhausen. She appears in the audience at a performance of Bellini's opera *Norma* in London wearing a costume identical to the one worn by a former Princess of Shaffenhausen in a portrait by Velasquez: "the picture was perfect."[18] The original painting exists abroad, but the current princess has made a copy and hung it in her London house, so that when she displays herself in the opera house, multiple and receding acts of reproduction converge on the scene. More emphatically even than Beavoin O'Flaherty, this heroine is characterized by role-playing: she is now an earthy, middle-aged Belgian nun, now a young Polish-Irish artist, now the widow of a minor European prince, now a muffled unknown, and so forth. As with Beavoin, who confesses that "caprice" came to govern the "fantastical" behaviour she initially adopted on grounds of necessity (523), the masquerade exceeds the notions of purpose and end that typically explain actions. Christian Isobel Johnstone noted with some exasperation in *Tait's* that the heroine of *The Princess* was "an ambiguous personage . . . without adequate motive or object in her endless shifts, subterfuges, and manoevres."[19]

Such "ambiguous personages" remove femininity out of categories of purity and wholeness, but in Morgan they do so *without* thereby losing authority as national heroines. Herein lies her primary contribution to the thinking about women and the nation in the first decades of the new United Kingdom. Unusually for British women's writing of this time, Morgan valorizes a femininity that not only knows itself to be compromised and estranged but makes such knowledge the condition of its national authority. This national heroine knows no category of the "pure" act, and this helps explain Morgan's rather peculiar tendency to shadow her female protagonist with a parodic double. In both *Florence Macarthy* and *O'Donnel*, for instance, the heroine's patriotic commitment is taken up and "parrotted" (as Morgan puts it) by a sharply satirized aristocratic woman, Lady Dunore in the former and Lady Singleton in the latter. Rather than securing the distinction between inferior/superior or mimic/authentic forms of femininity, as in most cases of doubled female figures in fiction of the period, however, Morgan's doubling tends to blur instead of clarify the difference between the fake and the true. Not only is the national heroine herself typically linked to motifs of citation and imitation but her vapid aristocratic copy parrots her so skilfully that her words threaten to be indistinguishable from those of the heroine herself. Thus Lady Dunore delivers an entirely convincing argument on the need for rural employment and manufacture in the final volume of *Florence Macarthy*, declaring that her Irish friend has "given me an entirely new view of things" in relation to the country (IV: 19–24).

Morgan's argument is not that one cannot distinguish between a Lady Dunore and a Florence Macarthy but that the colonial nation lies outside the coherence of unity, an unstable compound whose temporality (in contrast, for example, to that of the Burkean nation) is shaped by the fractious and shifting intersection of conflicting lines. On such terrain words and acts are inevitably embedded in an impure matrix. Compounding the sense of implication in such a matrix is the fact that the heroine's mobility – that which allows her to move between not always congruent social and national layers – enmeshes her own acts in crossed contexts and gives them mixed bearings. Thus, as we saw in the last chapter, Florence Macarthy feels uneasy about the way in which her national tales, directed at the English market and written under the name of Lady Clancare, "trade" in Ireland's wrongs for personal gain. Both her defence of her writing and her moral uneasiness make a good deal of sense but not in entirely compatible ways, so that such a moment points to a friction and lack of fit between positions simultaneously available within a culture. Morgan's national tale not only refuses to harmonize such a condition but makes it the key to the peculiar power wielded by its national heroine. As a figure who moves laterally rather than vertically, she blocks both the transcendental move "beyond" and the interior turn to a "deep" subjectivity.

Hybridity – indeed hyper-hybridity – is the signature of femininity in such a place, and Morgan's female protagonists are typically amalgams in more than the obvious national sense. They are all in the first place hyphenated nationals – this seems to be the basic condition for heroine-hood in the later Morgan – but they are also mixtures in terms of class (residual aristocrat/emergent bourgeois), secular status (half lay/half nun), and habitation (rural/urban; Ireland/Italy, etc.), to mention only the most prominent categories. This hyper-hybridity establishes the national heroine as precisely not a pure whole (an integral being) but as someone willing to live in and among parts. To live-in-the-partial in this sense is not so much to be *outside* a particular cultural discourse or category as not to be fully *within* any single discourse or category. Thus from the perspective of any particular formation within the culture, part of the heroine is always "elsewhere." From this dissonant capacity to be "elsewhere," at once in surplus and in reserve, the heroine derives the levers allowing her to find purchase and take initiative.[20]

Through this interstitial heroine, Morgan rewrites what Kristeva has called "women's time": that specially gendered archaic temporality of reproduction marked by repetition and immobility, which stands in problematic relationship to the linear time of history, that is, to time as project, as departure and arrival.[21] Women's time, as Kristeva notes, acutely poses the question of female agency and subjectivity in history, for it threatens the kind of inertness exemplified in iconic figures, immobilized in repetition and symbolization. But hybrid heroines like Beavoin O'Flaherty and Florence Macarthy harness women's time, make it tell in history by transforming it (to paraphrase Kristeva) into the time of the diagonal. In Kristeva's account socio-cultural groups defined by their role in the mode of reproduction (e.g., gender, age) stand in "diagonal" relation to the particular formation of which they form a part because, although they bear the specific traits of this formation, they also bear the more general traits of their place in the universal structure of reproduction. Hence, she states, the group "women in Europe" has its own particularity, but at the same time that which defines the members of the group as "women" connects them ("places them in diagonal relationship") to similar categories in China or North America. Morgan evidences a similarly "diagonal" cosmopolitanism in much of her writing, declaring, for example, that the "same womanly sympathies" that prompted her writing on Ireland "governed my writings and directed my views for other countries,"[22] and her final work is an ambitious and unfinished general history of women titled *Woman and Her Master* (1840). What interests Morgan, however, are less structural relations across systems, although these certainly attract her attention, than what she calls the scattered "track" of women in the historical life of nations.[23] Where Kristeva presents the diagonal as a spatial connector uncovering deep-rooted structural convergences, Morgan highlights it as a point of intersection, the meeting of two lines (or kinds) of time.

To move on the diagonal, as Morgan's heroines do, is neither to collapse into nor to remain outside but to connect with the line of history by meeting it aslant. Importantly, this movement plays in the full ambiguity of the term "agency" as meaning both initiative and instrumentality. Agency refers on the one hand to self-determined actions (becoming an agent); on the other, it denotes actions determined by others (being an agent for someone). Both meanings come into play, for example, when the narrator of *The Princess* notes that the struggle between conservative and progressive forces in post-Revolutionary Europe has produced "an under-current of female agency." The specific reference is to the way in which church and state have used women as agents to cement their power, but the usefulness of women as agents turns on their special power of action in spheres "where all other agencies have no *prise* or lever to act upon."[24] Oddly enough, the activities noted as illustrations of such "female agency" belong to traditionally male spheres – mathematics, politics, philosophy, and preaching – rather than to the unofficial realms of influence assigned to women and ostensibly at issue. *The Princess* as a whole, in fact, is virtually a textbook instance of what we now call "feminist recovery," a foregrounding of women's share in the establishment of Belgium as a modern nation: it inscribes female contributions to institutions of literacy such as the ducal library, draws attention to the obscured history of women artists in Belgium, and (in a long footnote in French) celebrates the "heroic" conduct of women during the Four Days of the 1830 revolution in Brussels that won Belgium independence from the Dutch.

Morgan's main purpose in raising the question of women as agents, however, is to argue for power on the part of secondary agents to counter the designated intentions of principals. The thematic of agency in her texts thus pivots on the potential for reversal within an exigency, a thematic worked out most fully in *The O'Briens and the O'Flahertys*, whose heroine has founded an order of nuns under the aegis of the Jesuit order, ostensibly to further its influence and interests. To the enlightened Murrough O'Brien such an act is reactionary and abhorrent, and he scorns Beavoin O'Flaherty for "upholding a system he detested," seeing her as at worst an "imposter" and at best a "dupe" (511). In explaining her activities to him, Beavoin declares that because "my agency is limited," she has had to avail herself of the means at hand, appropriating the power of the church but directing it to her own ends (523). "I wield the power and influence they have given me," she says of her Jesuit teachers, "for purposes directly opposed to their intentions" (521). Suggestively, Murrough O'Brien simply fled the Jesuits when he found himself unwittingly co-opted into their enterprises, and then searched for an alternative authority. Beavoin, by contrast, remained on the suspect terrain but exploited her distance from the formal center of rule. The heroine of *The Princess* will make a similar point in relation to the secular power of a Tory government that seeks to use her. Both thus define themselves in terms that recall Bourdieu's distinction between agents in and subjects of a system. "And I mean agents, not subjects," Bourdieu says, explaining his interest in reintroducing agents into social theory: "Action is not the mere carrying out of a rule, or obedience to a rule."[25]

In that break between rule and act, as writers on both sides of the Irish Sea well knew, lay the possibility of moral agency and resistance on the part of colonial subjects, including elite subjects. British discourse on Ireland had long featured double-speaking Irish peasants, tricky local agents, deceptive bogs, and so forth. To these Morgan added a wayward colonial femininity, all the more unsettling because it stood in skeptical and sardonic, rather than directly oppositional or transgressive, relation to the cultural order. So the *Edinburgh Monthly Review* declared itself filled with a "sentiment of disgust" when Florence Macarthy interrupts her proposal scene ("the most passionate, the most important moment of her life") "to place herself in an attitude."[26] Such a response draws attention to the fact that the Morgan heroine not only characteristically subordinates romance to political or patriotic ends but stages a courtship that deliberately avoids intimacy, the special province of the domestic heroine. Performative and unconjugal, this wayward femininity overlaps with the colonial nation in foregrounding dissonance and asymmetry rather than (as in the domestic model promulgated by Hannah More and her allies) consolidating an ideally symmetric national space of rational consonance. For a writer like Felicia Hemans the main point of womanhood may well have been to make "the humblest hearth / Lovely but to one on earth,"[27] but Morgan's female figures are more interested in public circulation. So at the end of *The O'Briens and the O'Flahertys*, Beavoin O'Flaherty (now married to her cousin) becomes the subject of public talk in Paris, where she runs a salon opposed to Napoleon: rumour has it she is about to be banished (à la Stael) from the city. At the moment of narrative closure, then, this heroine continues to circulate, refusing the intimacy of the hearth valorized by Hemans and central to the Burkean model of the imperial nation as a circle of loyalty and love. Morgan's colonial nation emerges by contrast as a confused intersection of different lines or, to adopt a more geological metaphor, as a heterogeneous complex of different strata, and it is as a figure peculiarly suited to negotiate the conflicting pressures of such asymmetric national space that the heroine achieves her narrative centrality.

Increasingly, she features in a narrative structure marked by the shifts, tangles, and discontinuities that prompted one reviewer to describe *The O'Briens and the O'Flahertys* as a "splendid phantasmagoria."[28] Responding rather less sympathetically to it as a "saturnalia of Irish life," another reviewer suggestively complained that "[w]e have a complete rifacciamento of languages in every third page – Latin, Irish, French, Italian, Spanish, &c. in abundance, as if the author could not express her meaning in English."[29] As early as *The Wild Irish Girl* Morgan had made the point that "English" would not in fact suffice, but she was now asserting it in a narrative that had dissolved the unifying power (no matter how problematic) of the Gaelic chronotope.[30] This late fiction uncovers an Ireland of different layers and different histories which stand in tense and shifting relation to one another.[31] Descendants of the "old English" (the Norman Catholic layer of Ireland's history), for example, mingle in the countryside with the Gaelic Catholics through intermarriage and shared suffering, but they nonetheless remain a distinct group; while in the urban space of Dublin different strands of Irishness now intersect and now diverge. Such entanglements yield a density of time, language, and history that Morgan increasingly signals through what might be called an "infolding" (rather than simple juxtaposition or parallelism) of genres and discourses. Later novels like *The O'Briens and the O'Flahertys* may present a smoother, more conventional narrative surface than *The Wild Irish Girl* with its sharply separated upper and lower texts, but they contain within themselves narrative cuts and folds, not to mention a plethora of genres (e.g., letters, annals, gothic, carnivalesque), that fracture any sense of the wholeness of national-historical time.[32]

Thus when Morgan adopts the gothic technique of embedded texts, she activates it to convey the way in which one kind of time contains, often unexpectedly, other kinds of time and present intervals are traversed by unharmonizable traces of the past. Her second national tale, *O'Donnel* (1814) initiates this practice, including an interpolated text of a historical figure, Red Hugh O'Donnell, rebel ancestor of the fictional titular hero. Placed in a highly resonant scene, this interpolation is triggered by a suggestive interplay between a contemporary, upper-class English tourist, Lady Singleton, and an Irish servant, M'Rory. Lady Singleton and her party have been touring Ireland in search of the picturesque and the sublime, and one dark night they find themselves stranded in a region where the militant White Boys are said to be operating. They take shelter in the cabin of the absent Roderick O'Donnel (impoverished and dispossessed descendant of the chiefs of Tyrconnel), where Lady Singleton glances with some apprehension at a large sword hanging over the chimney-piece. At this point, M'Rory (who has already demonstrated his ability to gull the tourists while pretending to be obliging), identifies the marks on the blade as blood, and boasts of "the great O'Donnel, my lady, who bate the English troops fairly out the province." Was this lately? asks the lady, and M'Rory asserts that indeed it was (86). The exchange that ensues plays off M'Rory's sense of "lately" (he is referring to the end of the sixteenth century) against Lady Singleton's more immediate sense, heightened by anxiety about the reports of very recent White Boy raids. A comic moment, its linguistic doubleness nevertheless generates a hermeneutic instability that opens up a gap, and in this gap appears the interpolated text titled "O'Donnel the Red; or The Chiefs of Tirconnel. A Fragment." This text, not in fact one fragment but a set of fragments, tells a story of injustice, rebellion, and murder in the final days of the Gaelic order.[33] Lady Singleton reads it aloud to pass the time while awaiting the appearance of their reluctant host, after which the regular chapters resume.

This dark, alternative history of Ireland, which (briefly) intrudes into the contemporary comedy of touristic manners, is precisely a kind of fragment within the dominant colonial national narrative.[34] As fragment, this history can be readily dismissed or, as Lady Singleton demonstrates, incorporated as simply a diversion. But its interpolation testifies to the simultaneous circulation within the nation of unassimilable kinds of memory and desire. In the hands of a M'Rory (who literally gives the text to Lady Singleton) the fragment serves to unsettle the colonial story, while in the fugitive bands of White Boys this text of the past finds a material echo and re-enactment. The gothic swerve of interpolation thus takes on a decided political edge, foregrounding a sense of national time not only as dense and layered but as an ongoing contestation between asymmetries of remembering and forgetting. The standard linear tropes of Enlightenment history and of colonial history (not necessarily convergent) serve to resolve such layers and asymmetries, and Morgan's narrative keeps these tropes in place, but it renders them precarious by crossing them with murkier and less stable temporalities.

The striking interpolation of the Annals of St. Grellan into *The O'Briens and the O'Flahertys* (vol. II, chap. 6) offers a telling instance. Murrough O'Brien finds the volume of annals in the deserted and decaying house of his bankrupt, Gaelic-obsessed father, and he sits down to read them. This annalistic history of Ireland, which begins before the proverbial flood, is focalized through the region in which the O'Briens and the O'Flahertys have long played out their rivalry ("greate strife and hurly-burly between the O'Flahertys and the O'Briens"). The annals assemble local, familial, and national histories; the entries, of varying lengths, deal with a miscellaneous range of topics: invasions, oysters, prophecies, transportations, frogs, lawsuits, abductions, and so on. Even more dramatically than the embedded fragments of Red Hugh O'Donnell, the Annals of St. Grellan draw attention to the unevenness of history and of writing. The text read by O'Brien is a copy of the original, smuggled out of Ireland to the Vatican when the Elizabethan governor, Sir George Carew, ordered the destruction of all Irish manuscripts in the area. The actual volume he reads, bound in rich Roman binding of white vellum, stands out as an incongruity in the crumbling Dublin mansion in which the reading occurs, but it proves to be very much connected to its site. The volume contains unfinished drawings of some of the family relics, drawings that are clearly still in process. These underscore the open-endedness of the annalistic genre, the ongoingness that distinguishes it from standard historiography. Unlike standard historiography, annals are an assemblage rather than a configuration of events, a compilation rather than a narration. The characteristic tense of the genre is the present ("The saintes multiple exceedingly"), and this leaves the annals always open to addition. Authorship is then necessarily multiple, as different scribes make their entries over different periods of time. In the case of the Annals of St Grellan, even the modern volume containing the annalistic text is very much a composite production: it is illuminated (it will turn out) by Beavoin O'Flaherty, translated by the Abbot Malachi O'Flaherty, and annotated by the elder O'Brien who (like Morgan herself in *The Wild Irish*

Girl) mingles quotations from authorities with comments of his own. One layer of the text gives way to another layer, while the annalistic entries themselves follow the discontinuous style of the genre.

Where the fragments on Red Hugh O'Donnell functioned as a cut in the narrative line, underlining history as rupture, the Annals are folded *into* the main narrative. Narrative attention keeps shifting from annalistic entries to the response of Murrough O'Brien, and this infolding exposes a certain fluidity of time and consciousness that threatens the clarity of the line of modern history and the coherence of modern subjectivity. O'Brien himself is a modern subject ("an epitome of the regenerated age to which he belonged"), but his immersion in the unstable matrix of Irish temporalities has made him a peculiarly conflicted subject. His mind may belong to the Enlightenment but, we are told, his "prejudices and sentiments" have been unconsciously formed by his father's obsession with the Gaelic past, while his "memory and imagination" have been profoundly shaped by the tales and sufferings of his Irish foster-mother, the uncanny Mor ny Brien (212). His reading of the annals enacts this splitting and confusion. On the one hand, he reads at the distance of precisely modern rationality, finding in the annals "sanguinary absurdities, and confused and barbarous details of the wars of his ancestors" (220-21). Condescending and fascinated by turns, O'Brien reads the past as an exotic text with which his own modern self has little to do. At the same time, however, he experiences moments of identification, of weird recognition, that betray his rational sense of time, place, and identity. Such moments move into the foreground a stranger temporality, one that places the present inside the past and the past inside the present.

Two such moments of temporal merging are of particular interest. In the first instance, O'Brien encounters in the annals the name "Beavoin O'Flaherty," a name he does not consciously know but one that seems "familiar to his memory" and somehow linked to his infancy on the isles of Arran with Mor ny Brien. He repeats the name aloud, and the sound resonates "as the echo of sounds known, and half forgotten" (222). It echoes not simply because (as he will later learn) O'Brien did in fact meet Beavoin in childhood but for less empirical reasons as well: an earlier Murrough O'Brien was involved in an ill-fated romance with an earlier Beavoin O'Flaherty, and their eighteenth-century namesakes will play out that romance to a rather happier end. O'Brien, of course, knows nothing of this, but the original story of Murrough and Beavoin does stir in him a sense of history as re-enactment, as when he notes how the lives of his grandmother and aunt have replayed parts of the old story. Time increasingly appears as a "repetitive loop."[35]

In the second instance, the memory of a certain death leads to another kind of blurring of temporal boundaries. Reading the final entry of the annals, O'Brien is brought to tears by the account of the brutal extermination during the reign of William of Orange of the outlaw Irish figures known as "rapparees." The report of their executions stirs his memory of the death of his foster-brother, Shane, who had gone "from a mock trial to instant execution" seven years previously (244). Ashamed of his "womanish sensibility," O'Brien stops reading only to catch sight of a drawing representing "the rapparee or wild Irishman," which he recognizes as a portrait of the very foster-brother he has been remembering. At this point – in a classic gothic moment – the dead Shane himself materializes "on the threshold of the door." Inevitably, the narrative goes on to naturalize the apparition, as it does the echo of Beavoin O'Flaherty's name, but such doubling places within modern Dublin an archaic power, a literal return from the dead. Folded into rational temporality, it suggests, are nonrational temporalities that cannot be disentangled from it. These give to national time a stereoscopic depth confounding modern analytic reductions; more particularly, they point to the unfinished character of history in that the persistence of the archaic undoes the primary separation (i.e., the line drawn between past and present) that founds a distinctively historical understanding.

Morgan's national heroine seems to me best understood as the characterological reflex of such a skeptical historical sense, herself a form of infolding. An emblematic scene near the end of *Florence Macarthy* helps to illustrate. Immediately after the marriage of the heroine to General Fitzwalter (Marquis of Dunore), soldiers appear to arrest Fitzwalter on a charge of murder. The crowd of local peasants escorting the bridal couple immediately forms a protective phalanx around them, flinging stones and turf at the military. Both General Fitzwalter and the officiating priest, O'Sullivan, try to calm the crowd but to no avail. As the soldiers prepare to fire, "the voice and interference of Lady Clancare produced an effect, as unexpected as singular." The key to her effect is a change in language and in genre: "She addressed them in Irish; but it was evident neither in command nor in supplication. Whatever she said produced bursts of laughter and applause; every eye, flashing humour and derision, were [*sic*] turned on the constables and their satellites." Their anger dissipated and exchanged for contempt, the crowd pulls back and proceeds "in regular order" (IV: 235–36). A certain nostalgic feudalism surfaces here, as so often in the closural moments of Irish national tales (including those of the resolutely modern Maria Edgeworth). At the same time, however, the scene pivots on the collapse of the masculine institutions on which feudalism depends. As the discourses of military, ecclesiastical, and aristocratic authority fail, a female voice intervenes, drawing on local tradition and on unofficial, notably comic, genres. This voice moves *around* official discourse, addressing the crowd "neither in command nor in supplication," and the intervention itself, significantly, lies outside representation. It remains a moment of narrative opacity, connecting with official discourse and moving into representation only in its effect.

In so rewriting the national heroine as a mobile figure who refuses to operate as a unified body and under a single name, Morgan links her energies to fissures within national time and place. A peculiar combination of conciliation and provocation, this stylized character recharges standard feminine traits (e.g., obliqueness, local attachment, unofficial status) by giving them a destabilizing and interventionary power on colonial ground. In all this, as Morgan's reviewers were quick to notice, there was a good deal of transparently embarrassing self-idealization and tawdry aristocratic fantasy.[36] But this does not diminish the innovative feminist force of this heroine in British fiction of the period nor Morgan's provocation in carving out a public role in the British literary field for a femininity at once outside strictly domestic and (ambiguously) inside Catholic space. Morgan herself, to be sure, regarded the Catholic religion with a good deal of suspicion despite her firm support for Catholic Emancipation as a civic cause. Indeed, *The Wild Irish Girl* had suggested that one of the benefits of emancipation would be a de-Catholicizing of Ireland. But the late novels evidence a curious attraction to Catholic spaces as paradoxical sites of the "undercurrent of female agency," and strangely recuperate them for Morgan's liberal-feminist project. Reinflecting in particular the gothic tropes of the nun's chamber and the confraternity, she reworks them into quasi-utopian but necessarily compromised spaces of female agency, advancing a pragmatic politics of the interim, which stands in critical relation to the foundational ambitions of the secular and civic liberalism to which her novels continue to adhere.

SEQUESTERED (CATHOLIC) SPACES

On a trip to Italy in 1820 to write a book of travels, Morgan visited Parma where she heard about and became intrigued by a local episode involving an early sixteenth-century Benedictine nun named Giovanna da Piacenza, the powerful abbess of the congregation of San Paolo in Parma; an unknown young artist, who was to become very well known as Correggio; and the repressive authority of the Catholic Church. A telling instance of both the tenuousness and tenacity of women in history, the incident so compelled Morgan that she not only wrote up an account titled "Corregio and Johanna of Placentia" in her *Book of the Boudoir* (II: 197–210) but also incorporated aspects of the Renaissance abbess into her own fictional Abbess of Moycullen, Beavoin O'Flaherty. Importantly, the episode involves two widely separated historical moments. Its first moment is the early sixteenth century when Giovanna da Piacenza, an uncloistered nun and prominent reformer of the period, commissioned frescoes for her private apartments from a young local painter, Antonio Allegri da Correggio. The frescoes produced by Correggio in response to her invitation are remarkable for their sensuous design and secular (classical) subjects, neither of which was regarded as seemly for a nun's chamber. When the abbess fell foul of the ecclesiastical authorities some years later, her chamber was sealed, and the frescoes disappeared from public view. The second scene of the tale takes place in the 1790s, when the persistence of a "vague tradition" in the area that Correggio had painted something in the sealed apartments led to their unsealing after almost two hundred and eighty years. The frescoes were examined by a panel of eminent artists, and in 1795 the panel declared them to be indeed the work of the famous painter. But whether he or his female patron chose the controversial subjects of these frescoes remained – and remains – a subject of debate.[37]

Morgan, however, is in no doubt: "she herself selected those subjects which he so beautifully executed" (II: 208). Nor does she read this as a story of hidden paintings; through a suggestive transfer of epithets, she turns it into the story of a hidden woman, "the long-concealed and celebrated abbess" (II: 201). The episode now belongs not so much to the history of European art as to the history of European women, and for Morgan the dissonant space forged by the Italian abbess inside the very structure of the church comes to stand as a resonant emblem of that "undercurrent of female agency" in history in which she was becoming more and more interested. Morgan presents Giovanna da Piacenza as preeminently a representative of what she calls "the rebellious mothers of the Christian church," and she reads the frescoes in her private apartments as allegories of such female rebellion (II: 205). Thus she glosses the representation of Jupiter's punishment of Juno, for example, as a comment on "the severity with which the rebellious mothers of the Christian church, the powerful abbesses of the fifteenth century, were occasionally treated by the Jupiter of the Vatican" (II: 205). More generally, she links the abbess's classical subjects to a progressive politics of resistance, a turn to ancient models of "liberty" and "independence" as a way of sustaining her own (modern) battle against the bishops and the pope (II: 208).

In the end, of course, the abbess was defeated by these institutional forces – or so it would seem. Her convent was cloistered, and she herself did not long survive what Morgan terms "her living entombment." Her inner sanctum, the site of her resistant subjectivity and agency, was shut up and "at last forgotten" (II: 209). But an unofficial memory, as we have seen, persisted in the form of a "vague tradition" in the area, and the pressure of this memory eventually prompted the custodians of a now secular and aestheticized national culture to uncover and reintegrate that which had been excluded by an earlier, ecclesiastical authority with similarly canonical ambitions. This reintegration, however, did not mean a symmetric reversal of the earlier banishment, for it brought back to view not so much Giovanna da Piacenza as the young Correggio. The story of a woman's patronage and of her resistance to orthodoxy became subordinated to a story of free-standing male genius. In response, Morgan enacts her own micro-tactics of compensation, transferring the epithet of oblivion from the paintings to the nun and transporting Giovanna da Piacenza's inner sanctum to the hinterland of Ireland in the description of the heroine's study in *The O'Briens and the O'Flahertys*.[38]

Significantly, however, the paintings that dominate this fictional study are not those of a scandalous masculine imagination. Morgan confines incongruous "heathen" frescoes such as those found in the sanctum of the abbess to a linking corridor, devoting the walls of her nun's private apartments to portraits of "the *mothers* of the church" and of "saintly women of all ages."[39] It is to these Beavoin turns for sanction of her own activities as patriot, abbess, and educator. Three are singled out for narrative attention: the sixteenth-century Spanish writer and mystic St. Teresa, who founded and reformed religious houses all over Europe; the fifteenth-century Italian saint Catherine of Siena, who mediated in the great papal schism and corresponded extensively with the powerful men of her time; and the eighteenth-century French patron and writer Alexandrine de Tencin, who broke her religious vows, took a series of lovers, and founded an important salon in Paris. Beavoin herself will become a more respectable Tencin, but the point is that all three women used their role in the religious sphere to intervene in the public world of action and discourse. Even as Morgan reiterates the standard gothic motifs of oppression and repression in her fiction, then, the Catholic convent exemplifies at the same time – and on the *basis* of its oppression and repression – the dynamic of a certain kind of public female power.

Morgan reconstitutes the nun's chamber as a counter-space of women's agency and persistence in history. She does so generally in the idealized aristocratic form exemplified by Beavoin O'Flaherty's apartments, but she turns as well to more lowly and comic forms, as in the story in the same novel of the remnant of the order of Mary, John, and Joseph of St. Grellan. The order, repeatedly exiled over three centuries, has as repeatedly returned, but by the mid-eighteenth century it has dwindled down to four old nuns. The government, however, once again decides to dispel the order, and the mayor searches the premises to find only ten empty beds. He assumes the aged nuns have fled, but it turns out that the four women "still held their ground *perdues* under the beds, where the mayor had forgotten to look for them" (37). So hidden and overlooked, the rustic sisters share important traits with the enigmatic upper-class abbess, but the key thing is that in neither case is the interior they inhabit preeminently a space of innerness or private subjectivity. These interiors thus stand in contrast to the private female closet influentially established by Samuel Richardson and developed in the late eighteenth-century domestic gothic by writers like Ann Radcliffe.[40] In their narratives the closet functions as the place wherein female subjectivity, pushed to a limit in its contention with the symbolic and institutional order, unlocks its own powerful interiority, an interiority that will anchor the very notion of femininity in middle-class English fiction for at least two centuries.[41] By contrast, in Morgan's national tale the inward turn whereby a Pamela or an Ellena gather together their psychic and moral resources tends to be replaced by outward-going enterprises of administration, education, and publication.

Female activity rather than feminine subjectivity becomes the hallmark of her nun's chamber, and in this reaccentuation of the gothic trope the real-life example of Morgan's much admired Mme de Genlis was paradigmatic. Celebrated as an educator but also (like Stael) regarded as a dubious figure because of her irregular sexual life, Genlis had retired to a Carmelite convent by the time Morgan met her on her first trip to Paris in 1816. Morgan's account of her visit to Genlis in her convent study, however, completely elides any sense of retreat or retirement, presenting the study instead as a space of energetic and worldly pursuits. Genlis is preparing a new novel for publication, abridging old French memoirs, and copying out a list of the plants mentioned in the Bible. Her piano, Morgan notes, is covered in new music, and her harp is tuned: "All was energy and occupation," Morgan records with approval.[42] And the aristocratic Genlis herself frames her enterprises as labour rather than art: "What I pride myself in," she tells her Irish visitor, "is knowing *twenty trades, by all of which I could earn my bread.*"[43] Harnessing for her own use both modern energies (commerce, print) and pre-modern forms (feudal rank, ecclesiastical institutions), Genlis mobilizes the confined space of the convent chamber so that it no longer works to separate but to connect woman and world.[44]

Mediating the intersection of the nun's chamber with the time of modern culture and history for Morgan is the notion of confraternity, a term she polemically foregrounds and recodes in *The O'Briens and the O'Flahertys* in her redefinition of female patriotism. Now rarely heard, confraternity refers to a semi-formal religious association of lay persons or a mixture of lay and clerical persons, one that is neither fully within the official hierarchy nor fully without it but something in between. It achieved visibility in British discourse in the 1820s when it took on a specifically Catholic and Irish resonance, as associations like sodalities of the Sacred Heart sprang up in parishes throughout Ireland in tandem with the stepped-up agitation campaign for emancipation by Daniel O'Connell and the Catholic Association.[45] Such associations prompted profound misgivings in the British press, which typically perceived them as operating not simply in service of the political campaign being openly waged in Ireland by the Catholic Association but, in a more sinister way, on behalf of a covert campaign by the recently restored Society of Jesus to consolidate papal power and undermine the United Kingdom.

The confraternity thus takes its place among gothic tropes like the nun's chamber delineating a suspect Catholic body in the Protestant English imagination. So the *Quarterly Review*, reporting on Ireland in 1828, declared that the Sodality of the Sacred Heart of Jesus would be just "one of those fanatical and mystical societies so common in Italy" were it not for the fact that the Jesuits used it when their order was abolished as a way of perpetuating their influence and preparing for their return. To clinch the point, the reviewer cites in (heavily ironic) evidence Morgan's recently published novel: "In fact, in proportion as that order has regained power, so has the Sodality increased; and this much is known even to Lady Morgan; for in a strange farrago of ignorance, licentiousness, and jacobinism, lately published by her, called 'The O'Briens and the O'Flahertys,' in some of the very few intelligible sentences we could discover in the whole four volumes, she alludes to this fact as one which cannot be disputed."[46]

The reviewer no doubt has in mind a chapter titled "The Confraternity" in which Murrough O'Brien (voicing some of his author's own suspicions of Catholicism) confirms that the informal religious community of Cong, where he recuperates from typhus after the death of his father, is under direct Jesuit influence and part of a concerted attempt to revive the influential order. He mounts an extended attack on the order, and claims that it has in fact never really been suppressed. If their colleges have been closed, he argues, "yet they have always maintained their congregations, their confraternities and their secret affiliations, religious and laical" (368). Abhorring confraternities as reactionary sites, O'Brien aligns himself with the secular and more radically inflected notion of "confederacy," pitting his progressive confederacy with the United Irishmen against his misguided father's regressive affiliation with the confraternity at Cong. At the same time, however, the actual practice of the male confraternity – its hospitality, mildness, and generosity – proves greatly restorative to his much tried spirit, and in the end O'Brien departs with real regret from a community that now appears to him as "the amiable confraternity" in spite of its political and religious doctrines, which he continues to despise (379).

The hero's conflicted response to his experience in Cong derives from the way in which Morgan uses the confraternity as a doubled figure in the novel: at once suspect site and utopian space. The utopian dimension is my primary concern here. The very fact that the association has no particular name – a point made early in its description – helps to set up its role as embodiment of the principle of sociality. A loose, ad hoc group of strangers of different nationalities and professions, the members of the confraternity are referred to locally as "the religious gentlemen of Cong," and in the area they become "known only by the good they did" (352). Hence they define themselves not through the a priori of a proper name announcing allegiance to a system or order but by practical acts that respond to the immediate context of those around them. In a way that recalls the feminine project of "practical piety" advocated by Hannah More and other public women of the period,[47] the confraternity takes advantage of the range of skills among its diverse members to provide medical aid, agricultural advice, and soup kitchens, along with excellent French cooking that soon wins over the "bluest protestants in Galway, the most kiln-dried high churchman of Mayo." Indeed the Protestant Bishop of the diocese proves anxious to examine "the tenets and the table of a confraternity, whose pastry almost excused their popery" (353).

Serving as an informal connector in the volatile and highly polarized local contexts of Ireland in 1798, the confraternity both is and produces community. And in aligning confraternity with community to cement its utopian function (much as "confederacy" moves into contrastive view to make the political point of its reactionary side), Morgan stresses the personal and voluntary nature of the act that creates community. The "little community" at Cong, the narrator observes, is one "whose members were neither separated from the world by vows, nor led into it by ambition; but who retired to live in purity, to love God above all things, and their neighbours as themselves" (354). Significantly, for all its retired nature, it remains linked to the motors of world historical forces, evidencing "ties and interests, which were not all centred in the remote and romantic site to which they had retired" (354). Nor, as we have seen, does the choice to "live in purity" mean living abstemiously and outside the body, but it does mean a scrambling of gender codes.

The men of Cong actively move into the feminine sphere of benevolence, where the nurturing of bodies assumes priority (cooking, visiting, healing, and so on). In this way they converge with the female confraternity run by Beavoin O'Flaherty in the neighbouring Abbey of Moycullen, a religious community she is quick to identify as "a confraternity of no particular religious order: we are at least, as yet, subject to no rules" (502). But Morgan introduces a telling difference: the male confraternity is cast as a residual society in a way the female confraternity is not. The genial men of Cong read only pre-Enlightenment texts, shudder at revolution, and spend a great deal of time rehearsing outdated debates. As O'Brien wryly notes: "The names, bandied from mouth to mouth are not D'Alembert, Diderot, Condorcet, Voltaire or Volney; but Heinsius, Scaliger, Balzac, Vaugelas and Voiture" (370). By contrast, the Abbey of Moycullen is presented as thoroughly attuned to the forces of modernity, its femininity continuous with modern rationality even as it exceeds it. Beavoin O'Flaherty stresses her active efforts to turn regressive energies to progressive use. She takes special pride in the fact that under her rule "nothing here . . . recalls the unaccommodated, slovenly devotion of the old establishment of Mary, John, and Joseph: education is here going on upon a liberal plan, to fit woman for the useful, blessed duties that belong to her sex, as wife and mother" (521). Her reforms extend beyond those of women's education, taking in the reactivation of the local mill ("no longer a mere feature of picturesque desolation"), as well as improvements to the peasant cabin ("no longer a part of the soil, out of which it rises"). But the reformation of Catholic women remains her main concern, a reformation that seeks to move them into the rational space that Morgan, like Wollstonecraft and other liberal feminists of the period, understood as the space of equality and freedom.[48]

But to attach this project to the confraternity was to remove it from its liberal-rational roots, to render it semi-secret and equivocal. While a confraternity is not strictly a secret society, it was conventionally linked with such associations in the Protestant British imagination,[49] and Morgan herself consistently attaches it – and her heroine – to fugitive spaces of disguise and secrecy. It is no accident that when Beavoin O'Flaherty enters the novel at the masquerade ball discussed earlier, she is shrouded in a heavy garment identified as typical of the "confraternities of Italy" (321). At one point in their slippery conversation, Murrough observes that her gender keeps her from membership in the secret United Irishmen, and to this she tartly replies: "Women have been members of societies, quite as secret, and much more discreet" (326).[50] Such a remark, flippant enough, has a serious edge, drawing attention to the way in which Morgan increasingly begins to ponder what we might call the politics of secrecy: the unsettling power of secrets to drain confidence from the apparent and the known. Georg Simmel again provides a useful gloss. In his important meditation on the subject in "Secrecy," he argues that secrets discompose because they introduce "the possibility of a second world alongside the manifest world; and the latter is decisively influenced by the former."[51] From *O'Donnel* on, Morgan's fictions have been predicated on this destabilizing sense of a secret "second world" not just alongside but obscurely affecting a first world, confusing the clarity of its linear models of historical flow.

The interest in confraternities in *The O'Briens and the O'Flahertys*, however, points more specifically to an interest in the secret society as a counter-space that blocks the desire of the state (or, more generally, of ideology) to render social space consonant, indeed to produce society itself as consonance. Simmel notes that secret societies generally arise when new ideas and values develop "against the resistance of existing powers," but he further notes that they are equally adept at protecting decaying ideas and values, so that the constitutive feature of a secret society is not its conservative or radical bearings but the fact that it is always in a "struggle against the overwhelming pressure of central powers."[52] The crucial implication is that even though secret societies are themselves generally temporary, they have deeply unsettling effects because their very possibility contests the monopolizing ambition of any center. As Simmel remarks, the members of a secret society are always conscious of it as a *society*; hence they appear as a threat to society in general quite apart from their specific political content: "Simply by being units, these groups compete with the principle of centralization which alone wishes to have the prerogative of fusing individuals into a unitary form."[53]

The whole of nineteenth-century Ireland, Willa Murphy has suggested, may usefully be understood as a secret society. This is not so much because of the proliferation of actual secret societies in the period but because of the way in which secrecy and silence made for the strategic opening of "alternative spaces for enacting social and political power" on colonial ground, thereby turning the Irish landscape into what Murphy calls "a gothic text . . . intricately pleated and disguised, in which nothing is as it seems."[54] Morgan made femininity an integral part of this gothic text, so placing it in disruptive relation to the consolidating functions of gender being promulgated in more domestic genres of the period. Removing her national heroine from the family interior, she attached her to shadowy and temporary associations with obscure, international connections wherein one could exploit the opening between branch and center/principal and agent to practice a politics of the interim. In the end, this politics was to prove more feminist than national or civic. Increasingly, Morgan began to pry apart the categories of gender and nation in her later career and to assign them opposing historical trajectories, as the question of women in history came more and more to compel her attention. By the time of *The O'Briens and the O'Flahertys*, a project that began as a reading of the colonial nation through a stabilizing femininity in *The Wild Irish Girl* has become a reading of femininity through the destabilizing trope of the colonial nation.

In the course of this transfer the nation itself comes to figure as an impasse or closure from which feminine energies seek a certain exit. Toward the end of *The O'Briens and the O'Flahertys* Beavoin O'Flaherty advises Murrough O'Brien to leave the country, informing him that his latest political pamphlet has attracted the attention of the government. As for herself, she declares, "I cannot, like you . . . act for Ireland, – write for her – die for her! But I will do more, *I will live in Ireland*" (527). This she calls the "purest proof of patriotism," but in the event she does not remain in Ireland for much longer. Her abbey, the site of her patriotic social experiment, is invaded by the military and destroyed, and she herself moves on and out to Paris. "Of the Abbey of Moycullen," we are told, "nothing but its ruins remain" (552). Where Morgan's national tale of Ireland ends in the impasse of such ruins, however, that of the eccentric Tory Charles Robert Maturin begins here. Crossing Morgan's travel plot with the resonant period topos of ruin in *The Milesian Chief*, Maturin transformed the national tale into Irish Gothic, producing a heretic reading of history that (like Morgan's feminist reading) skewed the conciliatory project of the genre. It is to his narrative innovation that I now turn.

CHAPTER 4

The shudder of history: Irish Gothic and ruin writing

> In Rome there are many distinguished men concerned only with discovering new relationships between history and the ruins.
>
> Germaine de Stael *Corinne* (1807)

> Ruin, as with earthquake shock, is here.
>
> Anna Laetitia Barbauld *England in Eighteen Eleven* (1812)

Charles Robert Maturin's little-known *The Milesian Chief* (1812) moved the national tale plot established by *The Wild Irish Girl*, along with Stael's performing heroine, into a limit zone, producing itself as a limit text in the process and inaugurating the genre known as Irish Gothic or Protestant Gothic.[1] "If I possess any talent," Maturin wrote in the Dedication to this novel, "it is that of darkening the gloomy, and of deepening the sad; of painting life in extremes, and representing those struggles of passion when the soul trembles on the verge of the unlawful and the unhallowed."[2] The significant point of the passage is not so much extremity as negativity: this is a writing that recognizes itself as a form of undoing and that is drawn to the peculiar space of negation signalled by the privative: "unlawful," "unhallowed."[3] It is entirely characteristic that Maturin's reading of *Corinne* – in contrast to that of Morgan – concentrates on the desolate second half of the novel. Morgan was attracted to the first part of Stael's text with its prominent motif of female performance, and she rewrote the notion of performance in pragmatic-feminist terms as a setting of screens behind which potential spaces for action could be cleared, as well as exits secured. But Maturin's Tory imagination concentrates on the dark second half of Stael's text in which the main action is a relentless contraction: a stripping away of the cosmopolitan heroine's imaginative, intellectual, sexual, and physical powers under the influence of overwhelming romantic passion. Transferring this negative action to the western edge of Ireland, Maturin charged it with contemporary historical and political point, and established Irish

Gothic as a genre in sardonic and critical relation to dominant forms of historical understanding in the period.

The Milesian Chief takes full advantage of the standard travel trope of Ireland as a place that bypassed the protocols of modern coherence yet lay within "modern eyes": "the most wild and incredible situations of romantic story are hourly passing before modern eyes" (I: v). To underline the point of "hourly passing," Maturin sets the novel in very recent time, its central event being a (fictional) rebellion in the hinterland *after* the rebellions of the United Irishmen in 1798 and Robert Emmet in 1803, to both of which the text makes explicit reference. To this place and into this event he transports the "modern eyes" of his cultivated Anglo-Italian artist-heroine, Armida Fitzalban, removing her from Italy (where she has been adored and indulged) to the remote Irish estate purchased some years ago by her father, Lord Montclare. Resentful of her exile and lacking an audience, she finds herself powerfully but reluctantly drawn to Connal O'Morven, Irish patriot and scion of the degraded Celtic family that once owned the same land, who inhabits a ruined tower on its border with his embittered and increasingly deranged grandfather. A tense, passionate, ultimately doomed romance ensues, in the course of which Armida renounces her art, her rank, and her respectability (not to mention her engagement to an English army officer) to follow Connal as his "wandering companion" when he leads a small group of followers into a rebellion of whose hopelessness he is all too aware. Enmeshed in this central romance is a complicated gothic plot of property and greed and family betrayal, along with a subsidiary love story with homoerotic overtones that involves Connal's younger brother, Desmond, who finds himself in love with a young man (Endymion). Predictably enough, Endymion turns out to be a young woman (Ines), but – in a twist on the standard cross-dressing motif – Endymion does not know himself to be female, having been raised as a son by the ruthless mother he/she unknowingly shares with Armida. The novel concludes with the execution of Connal, an event accompanied by an operatic flurry of spectacular deaths on the part of the rest of the principals: Desmond throws himself into the line of fire; Ines expires of madness nearby; and Armida, having taken poison some time earlier, silently clasps the corpse of Connal until she too dies some hours later.

Heightened and melodramatic, this extravagant plot makes clear that in this text there are no ways out (no *Ausgang*). And the claustrophobic effect has a great deal to do with how Maturin understands his Staelian intertext as a ruin text, as much as a tragic romance or national tale.[4] Stael's love story flourishes among the ruins of Rome ("the land of tombs") to which Corinne acts as guide and interpreter, ushering the British hero around the Forum, the Colosseum, the seven hills, and so forth. The classical ruins of Rome in *Corinne* generate two main ruin sentiments which are attached to two related but not-quite-parallel forms of humanism. On the one hand, classical ruins serve to confirm a cosmopolitan humanism that posits an enduring and universal human "spirit," although such confirmation typically inheres less in the monumental Grand Ruins than in the sudden appearance of a broken column or a half-wrecked bas-relief in the middle of the modern city. Fragments like these, we are told, "remind you that there is an eternal power in man, a divine spark, and that you must never grow weary of lighting it in yourself and of rekindling it in others."[5] On the other hand, the vestiges of antiquity allow for a nostalgic turn to a heroic national past away from the mean-minded and utilitarian present. "We live in an age when self-interest alone seems to determine all of man's acts," laments Corinne, detailing modernity's assault on the positive social values she associates with the categories of "empathy," "emotion," and "enthusiasm." She concludes: "It is pleasanter to dream of those times of dedication, sacrifice, and heroism that used to be, and that have left honorable traces upon the earth."[6]

Classical ruins in *Corinne* thus sustain the notion of "the human" in a way that can underpin either a cosmopolitan universalism or a nostalgic nationalism. But "wild" colonial ruins like those in *The Milesian Chief* cut across the notion of "the human," throwing humanist models of memory and the past into crisis and, along with them, cosmopolitan and nationalist forms of historical understanding. Suggestively, Maturin's first readers saw his gothic fictions not simply as exorbitant, morally dubious, and somehow foreign – his novels "bear no trace of the rich and pregnant simplicity of English genius," remarked the *Eclectic Review*[7] – but as disconcertingly un- or inhuman. "His language, however," writes the *London Magazine* in 1821, "is almost the only symptom which he deigns to give of ever having either studied, or associated with, humanity. He glories in caverns – falls in love with goblins – becomes naturalized amid ruins, and revels in the grave."[8] To underscore Maturin's exteriority, we note, the reviewer presents him as impervious to the fears that help establish what lies on *this* side of the human. Where ordinary persons fear and tremble, Maturin by contrast "revels" and "glories," at home in deathly and alien spaces of rocks and broken stones. Ruins are not simply one among other such spaces – simply another item in a list of "haunts," as in the reviewer's catalogue – but their epitome, for they pose the very question of human making and doing and thinking, in short, the question of "the human" as enterprise.

Ruins have triggered this question at least from antiquity onward, but late eighteenth- and early nineteenth-century Europe invested the salient ruin features of disintegration and abandonment with a special potency. Ruin genres proliferated – poems, paintings, antiquarian writings, travels – as did what we might term "ruin effects," as in picturesque gardening (fake ruins) and tourist sites (protected ruins). Oddly enough, despite the striking ubiquity of ruins in gothic fiction, neither the romantic gothic novel in general nor Irish Gothic in particular has been much discussed as a form of period ruin writing. Gothic genres are typically approached as ideological structures of cultural feeling, forms of displacement and projection on the part of specific social formations; hence they are understood in terms of a politically inflected psychoanalytic logic and recuperated into critical discourse as allegory and psychodrama. "Protestant Gothic," writes Terry Eagleton, summing up the prevailing view, "is the political unconscious of Anglo-Irish society, the place where its fears and fantasies most definitively emerge."[9] The twisted tales of guilt and usurpation and terror characteristic of nineteenth-century Irish Gothic, as even the brief outline of *The Milesian Chief* offered above confirms, provide ample warrant and rich material for such a reading.[10] But I want to approach Maturin's "dark romance" – to use the period term – from a rather different angle, less as unconscious psychic production than as conscious discursive intervention.

This is not to deny its tormented inward turn nor to discount the powerful pull of fantasy and unreason in the genre. Indeed, gothic affect is very much the point, and the "shudder" foregrounded in the last section of the chapter works precisely to keep in play its uncanny energies and to block their too ready rationalization. But the unsettling powers released by Maturin's generic innovation, I want to argue, have as much to do with a consciously abrasive reading of modern culture as with the more subliminal workings of the Anglo-Irish psyche. To think about Irish Gothic as a form of ruin writing is thus to understand it in the first place as part of a larger public discourse and to see it as an active and critical participant in an ongoing debate in early nineteenth-century Europe about memory, identity, and the past.

MEMORY IN THE RUINS

In a suggestive meditation on late enlightenment ruins in *The Invention of Liberty*, Jean Starobinski identifies two main ruin sentiments tied to two different moods of memory in the eighteenth century. The first is the familiar aesthetic sentiment of poetic melancholy (Starobinski titles his chapter "Melancholy Among the Ruins"), generally associated with ancient ruins whose origins are forgotten. Such ruins – in contrast to more recent ruins – assume their significance not as traces of human projects but as signs of the obliteration of human memory (the memory of earlier human intentions, of the initial constructive moment). Thus when Byron's Childe Harold contemplates the "nameless" ruins of Rome, he insists on the way they elude identification: "Temples, baths, or halls? / Pronounce who can; for all that Learning reap'd / From her research hath been, that these are walls –."[11] Ruins like these, Starobinski says, "represent oblivion," and impress on the faculty of memory its own failure as "ineffectual reminiscence, the . . . helpless effort of memory."[12] In this mood one contemplates the ruin and remembers only that one *has* forgotten, and this is the mood that usually activates the perennial *ubi sunt* theme of the transience of human (and in particular imperial) days and ways: "Behold the Imperial Mount! 'Tis thus the mighty falls," (*Childe Harold*, IV: cvii)

In apparent paradox, the same mood of memory may also set out deliberately to intensify rather than moralize oblivion, as in the act of visual abstraction that produced the topos of ruins-by-moonlight reproduced in countless ruin paintings and poems in the early decades of the nineteenth century.[13] Where the *ubi sunt* theme contemplates ruination (to this extent keeping concrete process in view), ruin nightscapes either efface process by transforming crumbling stones into a new whole (a structure) or seek to transcend it altogether. Byron's highly popular ruin poem is once again exemplary, transforming the "enormous skeleton" of the Colosseum into a "magic circle" under the light of the rising moon, which "shines serene but doth not glare" (IV: cxliv). In earlier and even more famous lines than those of Byron, Walter Scott helped set the nineteenth-century fashion for visiting ruins by moonlight, and produced probably the most quoted ruin tag in English in the entire century: "If thou would'st view fair Melrose aright, / Go visit it by the pale moonlight."[14] The verse that follows the familiar couplet explicitly turns Melrose Abbey from a ruined building ("the ruins grey" exposed by "the gay beams of lightsome day") into an interior ruin painting of glimmering silver and black arches:

> When the broken arches are black in night,
> And each shafted oriel glimmers white;
> When the cold light's uncertain shower
> Streams on the ruined central tower;
> When buttress and buttress, alternately,
> Seem framed of ebon and ivory;
> When silver edges the imagery,
> And the scrolls that teach thee to live and die;
> When distant Tweed is heard to rave,
> And the owlet to hoot o'er the dead man's grave,
> Then go – but go alone the while. (2: 3–15)

No longer a scene of ruination, this is a ruin scene and a deeply melancholy one, shot through with intimations of death and (as in the case of Byron) attached to a singular subjectivity in its solitude: "but go alone the while." With its attraction to broken things and pessimistic sense of historical time, the cult of ruins has been typically understood as part of the picturesque, but the examples of Scott and Byron suggest that its nightscapes draw as well on a rather different aesthetic.[15] In contrast to picturesque seeing, which is intimately tied to the details and textures of objects even when its compositions leave boundaries undefined,[16] moonlight seeing elides detail to focus on line and shadow, moving the perceiving sensibility more fully into the obscure zone of the sublime with its always imminent threat of the collapse of mental faculties.

Such collapse, however, is typically warded off by the activation of the second moment of memory in the ruins identified by Starobinski. The negative first moment, he argues, prompts a countering turn to the positive powers of memory, to its reconstructive energies which may override the very gaps to which the ruin testifies. It is not incidental that the depiction of Melrose Abbey as a contemporary ruin painting is rapidly followed by an elaborate description of its interior (also at night) when it was a working abbey. The opening lines of this second description set the tone and establish the contrast: "The darkened roof rose high aloof / On pillars lofty and light and small: / The key-stone, that locked each ribbed aisle, / Was a fleur-de-lys, or a quatre-feuille" (2: 96–99). And so on, for several stanzas. Melrose, reduced to a shadowy skeleton structure as the subject of a ruin painting, is filled in – restored, we might say – when it assumes its role as part of a *narrative* of places and times. "It is well known," Starobinski observes, "that historians have found their vocations while contemplating ruins,"[17] and he recalls the notable instance of Edward Gibbon musing among the ruins of the Capitol and arriving at the idea for his great history. Walter Scott's own huge and hugely influential output – ballads, romances, historical novels, antiquarian works, even his scholarly editions – can well be seen as a complex form of ruin writing, motivated by the desire to preserve (as he puts it in the Postscript to *Waverley*) "some idea of the ancient manners of which I have witnessed the almost total extinction."[18] Faced with ruin – a condition of "almost total extinction" – Scott seeks to transform it, in a characteristic Romantic move, at once into history (i.e., to recuperate the structures of intelligibility that begin to dissolve in the scene of the ruin) and into relic (i.e., to restore to the chronotope of the nation the aura stripped by the ruin). Like the negative moment of memory in this period, then, the positive moment of memory is at least double-sided, linked both to the cognitive ambitions of an increasingly professionalized form of historical knowledge (archival, archeological) and to the national, not to say imperial, desires with which it was at the same time infused.[19]

The key point for Starobinski is that at the end of the eighteenth century the figure of the ruin focalized a contest between the melancholy and solitary pleasures of negative memory (the poetry of ruins) and the more bracing outward-moving energies of the historical imagination (the history of ruins), and in this contest history won out. Its demystifying method of investigation and inventory gradually de-poeticized the ruin. "In Rome," Corinne reports, "there are many distinguished men concerned only with discovering new relationships between history and the ruins."[20] But the boundary line between the two modes was never very firm. The text Starobinski cites as pivotal in the victory of history, for instance, is Volney's influential *The Ruins; or, A Survey of the Revolutions of Empires* (1791), which assimilates ancient ruins to eighteenth-century political theory. But the rationalist Volney draws heavily on the conventions of the ruin poem, as in his much quoted Invocation (which we will encounter again below): "Solitary ruins, sacred tombs, ye mouldering and silent walls, all hail! To you I address my Invocation. While the vulgar shrink from your aspect with secret terror my heart finds in the contemplation a thousand delicious sentiments, a thousand admirable recollections."[21] And poetic melancholy lingers in his text even after the philosophical "survey" proper begins.

In an important sense, these two memory genres are less rivals than complements, for both converge in their desire to stabilize the unstable site of the ruin. In their different ways both the meditative-aesthetic and the analytic-historical approach to the ruin attempt to settle the questions unsettled by the presence of ruins. As an indeterminate mixture of culture and nature in constant, if largely imperceptible, metamorphosis, a ruin is a heterogeneous material fact incorporating various modalities of time but foregrounding the downpulling energies of natural process. When a building crumbles, writes Georg Simmel in an important gloss on "The Ruin," "merely natural forces begin to become master over the work of man."[22] For Simmel, anxious to incorporate the ruin into the idiom of nineteenth-century German idealism, this undoing of the work of the human mind and will is not a simple reversal or disintegration into formlessness. A ruin is "not a mere heap of stones" but a "new form" in which natural and human forces change places and powers, nature now using the human work as expressive material, much as it itself had previously served as material for the human work. In a classic high Romantic argument, Simmel presents a "nature" and a "spirit" that exist in contradictory and complex relationship, at once locked in antagonism ("original enmity") and sharing a metaphysical "common root" (260). They work dialectically, participating in the mobility of the two antagonistic "world potencies" Simmel terms "the striving upward and the sinking downward." These find momentary synthesis in the site of the ruin, whose significance lies in the fact that here divergent energies work "serenely together" (263).

For Simmel, then, the primary mood of the ruin is "peace" – or so he insists, reiterating the term throughout the essay. As he explains, this mood derives from the spirit's sense of "returning home" through the ruin to a "peaceful unity of belonging," a unity prior to the bifurcations and differentiations that constitute the dialectical process of history-making. But this metaphysical return "home" is at the same time a sharp turn away from the homes of human culture and history. "Expressing this peace for us," Simmel writes, "the ruin orders itself into the surrounding landscape without a break, growing together with it like tree and stone – whereas a palace, a villa, or a peasant house, even where they fit perfectly into the mood of the landscape, always stem from another order of things and blend with that of nature only as if in afterthought" (263). To put it the other way around (as Simmel himself is reluctant to do), the ruin defines human culture and history as "another order" from that of nature, an "afterthought." Hence the "peace" generated by the ruin depends on a break with the way in which consciousness ordinarily knows itself and, more particularly, on a recognition of its own affinity with an order alien to human orders. In this sense, the scene of the ruin becomes quite literally inhuman. It is in order to return it to the circumference of the human that Simmel – like his Romantic-era predecessors – seeks to make the ruin signify, to bring it within what Wordsworth in a rarely read Scottish ruin poem suggestively terms "the compass of distinct regard."

The phrase appears in Wordsworth's "Address to Kilchurn Castle, Upon Loch Awe," one of the poems included in the "Memorials of a Tour in Scotland, 1803." Coming upon a ruined medieval castle whose "fierce beginnings" have been softened and subdued over the years of its "calm decay," the speaker addresses the ruin:

> Shade of departed Power,
> Skeleton of unfleshed humanity,
> The chronicle were welcome that should call
> Into the compass of distinct regard
> The toils and struggles of thy infant years![23]

The records and dates of chronicle are all the more "welcome" because the ruined castle, for all its "silence" and "calm decay," sends out unsettling intimations, the winds producing "sounds . . . / Ambiguous, neither wholly thine nor theirs" (lines 4–5). To bring the ruin within the "compass of distinct regard" is to assimilate it to discursive mental constructs and so to achieve purchase for the subjectivity whose dissolution the ruin both obscurely threatens at the moment of actual encounter and clearly predicts as a future condition. Repeatedly, ruin texts of the period attempt to move ruins within such "compass": to find the law of the ruin. So Volney brings to bear on the ruins of Palmyra his Enlightenment reading of social structures and natural law; Stael, as we have seen, reads the vestiges of ancient Rome through a liberal aesthetic that affirms an undying "divine spark" in humankind; while Friedrich Schiller (to whom we will return) writes out the human hand altogether to transform "monuments of ancient times" into "simple nature" at the beginning of his landmark meditation on modern historical consciousness in *On the Naive and Sentimental in Literature.*[24]

But the scene of colonial ruin, abrasive and knotted, moves destruction rather than "calm decay" into the foreground and unsettles such literary-philosophic projects, reattaching the ruin to history and releasing more aggressive energies that impinge more heavily on the present. As Luke Gibbons has argued, Irish ruins in particular resisted assimilation into standard romantic tropes of ruin, standing as they did as emblems both of the reiterated bursts of violence and invasion over the centuries and of the ongoing process of ruination on Irish soil.[25] Travel writing of the period typically distinguished between ancient ruins like the famous round towers of Ireland, whose provenance was unknown or uncertain, and more recent historical ruins to which names and acts could be attached, such as the buildings destroyed by Oliver Cromwell's troops in the late seventeenth century. Cromwell was in fact a favourite target, his very name a byword for the destruction of Irish culture and a trigger for dark humour about the nature of the Irish picturesque. Noting how the numerous ruins of abbeys and castles enhanced the "pictorial effect" of Irish landscape, for example, the pioneer Anglo-Irish folklorist Thomas Crofton Croker, recorded a generic anecdote:

> To whom shall I dedicate my prints? once asked a publisher, about to produce some Irish views: – the reply was, If your dedication is prompted by gratitude, I know of no one more deserving it than Oliver Cromwell, whose cannon has made so many dilapidated buildings for you.[26]

Nor was Irish fiction of the period notably hospitable to the picturesque aesthetic of ruin even when it relied on picturesque effects in its own narrative representations. Morgan's *Florence Macarthy* is exemplary, opening with a debate on ruins that critiques the melancholy and literary pleasures of the ruin when transposed into the context of Ireland.[27] What especially rankles in Irish fiction is the impersonal and universal temporality that dominates most ruin genres. Thus Michael Banim's tale of the 1798 rebellion, *The Croppy* (1828), makes a special point of the fact that the monastery at New Ross was "destroyed by puritanical hatred more than by the gradual touch of time," observing that Cromwell "anticipated time in destroying the pile";[28] while Morgan's own tale of 1798, *The O'Briens and the O'Flahertys*, as we saw in the last chapter, closes on a note of ruination, featuring in its final pages the military invasion and wrecking of the Abbey of Moycullen of which "nothing but its ruins remain."[29]

"These recent ruins," commented Thomas Moore in 1823, "tell the history of Ireland even more than her ancient ones."[30] But even ancient ruins could be harnessed for present political (usually nationalist) purpose, as in the trope of the ruined abbey prominently featured in nineteenth-century nationalist iconography.[31] In the nationalist appropriation of the Romantic motif, the passive site of picturesque affect becomes active and menacing, a metamorphosis so well established by the second decade of the century that Moore himself makes it central to the mock national tale and parody of the civic tour which frame his *Memoirs of Captain Rock* (1824). The preface to these "memoirs" is written by the supposed editor, who is a caricature of both the ignorant English traveller and the imperializing missionary, having come to Ireland under the auspices of a Protestant missionary society to effect "the conversion and illumination of the poor benighted Irish."[32] At one point he visits a clerical friend in Roscrea, where he is disconcerted to find his host barricading the house every night and clearly prepared for armed defence. In the vicinity there stands a celebrated ruined abbey ("much resorted to by romantic travellers") which the traveller longs but fears to visit in the proper moonlit setting (x). One night, however, emboldened by whiskey, he ventures forth, but on passing through the portals of the ruin finds himself suddenly surrounded by "some hundred of awful-looking persons – all arrayed in white shirts, and ranged in silent order on each side" (xi). A comic moment, it nonetheless activates the dynamic of dislocation characteristic of the national tale, as the anticipated touristic scene of melancholy and solitary pleasure morphs into a threatening site of local assembly and militancy, and jolts the hapless visitor off course. As in the case of his more serious counterparts in the national tale, the encounter prompts the visitor to a new view of Ireland. Giving up his original evangelizing mission, he becomes the editor of the fierce counter-reading of Irish history proffered by Captain Rock, the rebel leader encountered in the ruin.

In *The Milesian Chief*, too, an encounter with a rebel in the ruins will prove transformative, as Maturin activates the discursive matrix of early nineteenth-century ruin writing to inaugurate Irish Gothic as a critique of both Enlightenment cosmopolitanism and Romantic nationalism. The tense romance of Armida Fitzalban and Connal O'Morven at the heart of Maturin's narrative is importantly a struggle over the meaning of ruins. Armida, raised amid vaguely reassuring classical ruins, exemplifies a cosmopolitan sensibility that intuitively turns to a comparatist mode to make sense of things, and lives easily in a flat chronotope in which different places and times are assembled on the same plane. Fittingly, her primary performative genre is the synchronic and reproductive genre of tableau. The opening pages of the novel detail a series of such tableaux in which Armida enacts a variety of roles, each the representation of a literary figure or type (e.g., Niobe, the oriental muse) and each carefully staged in spaces saturated with references to the tradition of high European art. From this tradition she draws her models and materials, so much so that her art appears spun out of a self-referential system in which terms refer back to other terms within the same order. With little sense of either personal or national history, Armida herself lives in – and as – simile, having been taught "to sing like a muse, dance like a grace, compose like a Sappho, and declaim like an Aspasia" (I: 4). She dresses in antique Grecian style, and orders her lyre to be made "from the model of one found in Herculaneum" (I: 125). Replication defines both her person and her art: she attracts every eye at public assemblies in Italy because she "gives so exquisite a resemblance of some classical model," while in Paris she is applauded as a performer "who revived all the images of classic beauty . . . recalled all the wonders of the classic fables" (I:8, 35).

Imbued with the late Enlightenment poetry of ruins, Armida understands ruin only as representation, incorporating ruin paintings into her own performances as backdrops for the display of her own sensibility. Her first tableau, for instance, draws the eye to a view of the ruins of Persepolis ("the spectral grandeur, the prostrate dignity of antiquity"), ruins whose scale suggests "the work of super-human hands, and the haunt of the spirits of former ages" (I: 11). Performing as the Grecian muse somewhat later, she is set off by a painting of Athens that includes "almost every ruin of classic celebrity" (I: 15). And when she first hears the story of the dispossessed O'Morvens upon arrival in Ireland, she immediately assimilates it to familiar ruin genres, conjuring up "the romantic spirit . . . that comforts itself in being compelled to inhabit ruins by tracing among them the remains of ancient palaces" (I: 52).

In transporting this figure to the Irish hinterland, Maturin presents it very much as the "sentimental" modern subjectivity famously defined by Friedrich Schiller, which treasures its own self-consciousness and technical powers (Armida prides herself on her knowledge of the "science" of music) even as it envies the unselfconscious "naive" forms of being it has posited outside itself, precisely in order to envy their "quiet functioning from within themselves."[33] Among such forms Schiller includes "many products of distant antiquity" (along with "children," "animals," and "childlike races"), and he argues that such forms generate a special pleasure, moral rather than aesthetic, because "[t]hey *are* what we *were*; they are what we *should become* again" (21–22). The key point for a reading of *The Milesian Chief* is the degree to which this sentimental pleasure translates a felt sense of lack – Armida experiences a "chasm of the soul" very early in the text (I: 28) – into the necessary condition of a progressive modernity. If it is the case, as Schiller argues, that naive forms recall "what eludes us, but for which we are called upon to struggle," it is even more the case that they confirm their own obsolescence in doing so. As he notes: "*In ourselves* we see a merit which they lack but which they can either never possess, like the unreasoning, or only if they travel on the same path *as us*, like children. They therefore provide us with the sweetest enjoyment of our humanity as an idea" (22).

Armida's sentimental response to the sound of native Irish music is paradigmatically modern in this way. When she hears this music for the first time in the "tremulous" harp of an aged bard, she finds herself strangely moved despite the defective instrument and feeble performance: "Armida forgot all science while she listened to him, and felt the effect of the scenery united with the sound" (I: 63). A music that appeals "from rules to the heart," it is likened to the irresistible "inarticulate cry of infancy," and the scene concludes with the refined Armida ("nursed in the classic elegance of Italian melody") weeping as she listens to "the rude song of the Irish bard" (I: 63–64). Such a moment is clearly fuelled by a "bardic nationalism" that confirms rather than dislodges the model of the sentimental and the naive. Indeed Maturin typically intensifies its logic, but he does so less to bolster the notion of "naive" authenticity (although this certainly comes into play) than to hollow out the authority of the "sentimental" modern move of cosmopolitan figures like Armida. Nor is his focus simply on the self regard of the sentimental move (a familiar charge in the period) but, more interestingly, on its role as the deflection of a certain "naive" anguish. In his text, that is, the naive is no longer temporally distanced into "what we *were*" or "what we *should become*" but appears as the ever-present possibility of radical destabilization within the modern subject.

A telling moment occurs in the novel's central ruin episode in which Connal takes Armida to the ruined abbey that serves as the O'Morven burial ground. As he rows her over to the site, he begins to hum a mournful song. "Armida started from the feeling it inspired," the narrator reports, "and hastened to a subject of conversation like those upon which she could once speak with eloquence." What follows is a frenetic exercise in the comparatist method of ethnological discourse, in many respects perhaps the quintessential "sentimental" discourse of the period: "She spoke of the rosary of the Biscayners, of the vesper-hymn of the Italian mariners, and of the chromatic chorus of the Chinese boatmen. Then she mentioned the proceleusma of the ancients, and the high antiquity of naval music, of which she traced the origin to an imitation of the sounds that haunt the sea-shore" (I: 181–82). And Armida continues in this vein for another half a page. It is precisely this comparatist move that Connal O'Morven blocks, rebuking her a few pages later explicitly on the matter of sentiment and native ruins.

Himself reared in a ruined Gaelic tower, symbol of a stolen inheritance, Connal operates well outside the fluid horizontal plane of Armida's cosmopolitanism, defining himself in terms of a single patrilineal line and an ever-depleting heritage shaped by continual reiteration of the original moment of loss. The ruined abbey to which he takes Armida is the focus at once of his sense of ancestral pride and his sense of waste, bearing the obscure "traces" of his family's "regal ornaments" but now awaiting only the deaths of "a feeble old man, and two unknown young ones, to close on the last of the race" (I: 178). Various ruin texts converge on this elaborate ruin sequence (including Scott's famous lines on Melrose, which Connal quotes at one point), but the main intertext is Volney's *The Ruins*. Linked to Armida it stands for cosmopolitan abstraction, when she quotes the famous opening of his invocation in French, ironically in an attempt to convince Connal that she is "touched by local feeling" while gazing at the ruins holding the remains of his ancestors: "*Je vous salue, ruines solitaires*" (I: 186). Connal immediately stops her, and delivers an impassioned denunciation of the whole genre of the poetry of ruins in which Volney's address participates: "The nameless ruins . . . which are supposed to commemorate greatness now unknown, and virtues that have no other memorial; ruins amid which fancy sits down at leisure to dream of what its tenants might have been; such may suggest an abstract and indefinite melancholy – a melancholy without passion and without remembrance." But here in this place, he tells Armida, there is "a local genius . . . I feel who lies below" (I: 186–87).

Rejecting the ritual of citation attached to the cosmopolitan ruin-event, Connal refuses the modern sentimental move: its abstraction of the particular into idea. "Even when it mourns a real loss," explains Schiller in speaking of elegy, "it must first reform it into an ideal one."[34] Suggestively, he turns to Ossian to illustrate how the "experience of particular loss" can be extended to "the idea of a general transience," and he pictures the bard, "moved and pursued by the picture of omnipresent ruin," flying up to the heavens "to find there in the course of the sun an image of the infinite."[35] For Schiller, outward materials and forms are, as he puts it, "always indifferent"; only when transformed into idea can they achieve literary status or, much the same thing for Schiller, human meaning. But for a figure like Connal outward materials and forms are always resonant, filled with a "remembrance" that is as much somatic as mental and emotional: "I feel who lies below." He is intent on maintaining the ruin as specific and abrasive: an active material reminder and remainder in the present. Connal may try to reconcile himself to his bitter lot by visiting the graves of his ancestors, but this is not the same thing as collapsing the ruin itself into the grave-to-which-all-must-descend. Throughout he insists on the ruin (to cite Dominick LaCapra's useful distinction) as the scene of particular historical "loss" rather than general transhistorical "absence," the product of distinctive historical trauma rather than universal processes or structures.[36]

This resistance to the poetry of ruins is a resistance not just to erasure of or indifference to the particularity of Ireland's history but to its removal from the category of history altogether by cosmopolitan and metropolitan models. "A country that excites no recollections can have no power over the mind, but from its weakness," Armida asserts, speaking of Ireland: "the tomb of Achilles inspired Alexander with the conquest of the east, and amid the ruins of Rome Gibbon conceived the idea of the history of its falling empire." As in the earlier debate over Volney, Connal disputes her sense of terms: "And I too have recollections . . . on this spot my ancestors were princes and their descendant has not where to lay his head" (III: 119–20). Connal's notion of the "recollection" that makes for history (as opposed to an undifferentiated "past") is a specifically nationalist one, rooted in a reading of local space as native place. In contrast to Armida, for whom the "local" is simply the spot in which one finds oneself at a particular moment and who moves easily between national borders, Connal cannot bear the thought of leaving "my native land." This clashing sense of "recollections" powerfully surfaces when Connal, preparing himself for emigration to America, mourns that this is "the last time I shall tread this ground and say this is my native land." "But there are other lands, and climates more bright and benign," replies Armida, and she weaves a fantasy of Italy as the land of sun where they can be happy. "I never can be happy out of Ireland," cries Connal, and his outburst unsettles her by revealing how deeply his subjectivity is grounded in national feeling. Over "a mind so national," Armida fears, she has little chance of gaining the "entire influence" she desires (III: 118–19).

Maturin's sympathies clearly lie with the "national" rather than cosmopolitan mind, but this opponent of the Union was an equal opponent of nationalist separatism, and he makes Connal a reluctant rebel, one whose reason tells him that Ireland cannot succeed as an independent nation and who pursues his rebellious course out of an archaic sense of loyalty and duty to the past in the person of his fiercely nationalist grandfather. "I listened to the harp and the legend till I believed them true as inspiration," he tells Armida, casting his youthful commitment to armed resistance as grounded in delusion and illusion (III: 50). If Maturin uses the native bardic moment to expose the hollowness of high European cosmopolitanism, once he moves into narrative focus the rebellion that is its outcome, he increasingly defines the bardic moment in terms of an outdated feudal structure of patriarchal loyalty whose price is paid by the bodies of those invested in it, including in the end the degraded body of Connal himself.

Connal's failed rebellion, graphically represented in these volumes, indicts a nationalism attached to a regressive chronotope of the original or idyllic national moment. Grounding itself in the desolated native place, the nationalist subjectivity suffers its own melancholy of the ruin and produces its own entrapping form of nostalgia: "I must wither on a solitary rock," Connal laments, "unknown, unremembered, watching the fall of ruins that once were the seat of my ancestors, and . . . almost wishing those ruins would fall on me and crush me" (I: 222–23). Governed by the attempt to restore the "once" of Gáelíc possession not only does he find his own personal time taking on a suicidal shape but he turns the land and lives around him to repeated ruin. Maturin's harrowing presentation of the rebellion is at once a fearful indictment of rebellion as folly and horror and a stark depiction of history as the suffering of those outside power whether in colonial-imperial or vestigial native forms.

To indict Irish nationalism as feudal is to make a predictably conservative ideological point in the period, but what distinguishes *The Milesian Chief* is the way in which it pushes through the particularity of an ideology to achieve a broader political resonance by undercutting the whole notion of history as piety on which all nationalist models, whatever their particular location or politics, depend. In the desperate night marches, hand-to-hand battles, desolate caves, and trackless moors of the rebellion chapters, the sustaining values of patriotic history (e.g., loyalty, valour, just claim) give way as bodies, as well as buildings, are repeatedly brought to literal ruin, suffering dissolution, metamorphosis, and scattering. Bodies are hanged, wounded, beaten, and starved; above all, from young children to old men, they die. Significantly, the bitter price of history as patriotic piety is voiced primarily by women. One gaunt and heartbroken follower of the O'Morvens, carrying the dying child who is the last of the male members of her own family (all dead in the O'Morven cause), declares "I can go on no longer." But the standard sentiment of the scene is broken when she suddenly shrieks out: "Oh God! . . . I would sell him to the soldiers that would give a morsel of food" (III: 101–02). Even more bitterly, another mother responds to Connal's request for food for his starving and mad grandfather by telling him "I have food enough" and then taking him to the corpse of her son, killed in battle the previous day: "There is the feast I promised you: you may devour him yourself, for that is all you have left me to give you. There, gnaw his bones, but leave his heart to his mother" (IV: 120). A macabre moment exploiting the fuzzy line between literal and metaphoric meaning, the woman's statement functions as an act of downpulling, puncturing the idealizing moves of nationalist myth-making by reducing them to brutal inhuman effects. Maturin's whole presentation of the insurrection stresses the breakdown of human community in all senses: the failure of acts of rescue and succour, the transformation of language into curse and shriek, the proliferation of acts of betrayal, revenge and lust.

On this terrain historical experience turns gothic, and both cosmopolitan and nationalist forms of historical understanding give way. What finally joins cosmopolitan and nationalist models of history, despite their divergence, is that both assimilate the past to the present through a thought of continuity and coherence that opens out onto the possibility of a capacious or more just future. Cosmopolitan history projects a surmounted past (ruins as ruin paintings) to establish the freedom of its own moment, freedom being understood in its Schillerian sense as the wound of self-consciousness that paradoxically expands human potential. Nationalist history, for its part, projects a persistent past (the repeated return to the ruin) to recover for the present degraded moment the possibility of a future shaped by the authentic native, rather than inauthentic colonial, past. Cutting across both in *The Milesian Chief* is the pulse of gothic history (the shudder of the ruin) that jolts the present, and renders the past not in terms of rational continuity (i.e., persistence, surmounting) but in the unpredictable, stochastic rhythm of an *insistence* through which one glimpses a future narrowed by fear.[37]

THE SHUDDER OF THE RUIN

Gothic anxiety, Ian Duncan notes in relation to English domestic gothic of the period, encodes and defuses "a middle-class subject's anxious intuitions of historical powers which are ostensibly alien to it – located in past and foreign scenes – and yet claim possession of it."[38] Maturin's Irish Gothic intensifies such anxious intuitions through a shudder that brings them "home" from the remote settings of Radcliffean gothic, ratcheting up the level of discomfort always characteristic of the discourse on Ireland. The shudder frames Armida's entry into the country. When she considers the contrast between the desolate landscape of Ireland and "the sunny regions of Italy, or the cultivated fields of England," she feels she is moving in "a new world." But this "new world" generates no anticipatory exhilaration. On the contrary: "She shuddered at the idea of becoming the inhabitant of such a country; and she thought she felt already the wild transforming effect of its scenery" (I: 55). To feel the future "already" and to feel it as "wild" transformation rather than continuation (or even change) is to move into the collapsed temporality of the shudder wherein tenses give way and trajectories become obscure. Under its pressure the rationalities of modern subjectivity (and the modern nation) are thrown into crisis.

A corporeal event, the shudder registers through the convulsive tremor of the body the impact of something outside but near at hand: a pushing away of something that is pushing in. Hearing a sound from his harp that he has not himself struck, the blind old bard of the O'Morvens "shuddered: he dropped the harp." And he underscores the point of invisible but very palpable presence: "The hand of the dead is on my harp!" (II: 100). In the scene of the shudder something hovers over rather than haunts or counsels the present. "Fury hovers in the heart of the ruins, and old unexpiated crimes threaten to recoil upon our own destiny," writes Starobinski.[39] Where to haunt is to infuse present time with spectres of the past – to make it spectral[40] – to hover is to impend on this time, to fill it with the sense of an energy very close by, ready at any moment to cut in.[41] It is at such moments that one shudders, struck by the apprehension of a future from elsewhere which seeks to thrust one's own time off course ("to recoil upon our own destiny," as Starobinski puts it).

Crucially, the shudder is not simply a matter of involuntary somatic response but a function of cerebral processes. What makes it telling is the degree to which it involves a mental power: Armida, we recall, "shudders at the *idea* of becoming the inhabitant of such a country," and Armida's female companion on her ordeals refuses food at one stage because she "shuddered *to think* the purchase of [the food] might have been some brave man's life" (II: 217; italics added). In gothic territory, those mental powers of reflection and projection that produce and maintain internal equilibrium on classical ground turn to disequilibrium and become themselves fearful. As Corinne puts it, voicing the classical effect: "seeing the eternal mobility of man's history, you learn to take the events of your own day calmly; in the presence of so many centuries which have all undone the work of their predecessors, you feel somewhat ashamed of your own agitation."[42] But the mobility of Irish history "throws" Armida precisely into agitation, and she increasingly figures as a convulsive body: falling, quivering, fainting. She thus recalls the conventional body of sensibility, well established in European fiction, but this is the body of sensibility turned hysterical, its convulsions and lapses no longer the sign of modern virtues but the mark of a vulnerability in modern consciousness. When Pamela's body gives way, physical collapse makes visible the persistence of the inner (moral and psychic) personal identity that constitutes "Pamela." But Armida finds herself asking: "Am I Armida Fitzalban?" (II: 14).

Under the extremity of her experience in Ireland, the negativity always present in Armida's melancholy cosmopolitan mind turns in on that mind and dissolves its constructive and regulative powers. That negativity, evocatively described by Laurence Goldstein as "the strange death-dance of thought occasioned by ruin," surfaces almost immediately upon arrival when Armida conjures up a series of ruin scenarios on first hearing about the O'Morvens.[43] As noted earlier, she readily imagines the dispossessed O'Morvens as possessors of a reassuringly "romantic spirit" consoling itself among the ruins by "tracing" the outlines of what used to be there. But this elegiac note soon yields to a more gothic and disturbing tone when she calls to mind the spirit of Alfonso the Good in *Castle of Otranto* as it "stalks amid its ancient seat till it smells beyond it, and stands forth amid the fragments dilated and revealed, terrifying the intrusion of modern usurpers." Quickly, Armida shifts back to a more assimilable scene, this time featuring a young man clinging with "romantic attachment, with ancient duty" to an aged relative as he wastes his own youth "on a comfortless and fallen ruin" (I: 52–53). At stake in this sequence is the sense of the past as a stable unit of that which has, precisely, passed. The "romantic spirit" that traces the outline of the ruins or that clings to them with ancient duty may recognize the past as definitive of its own moment, but agency remains in the present with an individual subjectivity that engages in acts of virtue and knowing ("tracing"). By contrast, the gothic image shifts agency to the past, which now "stalks" the modern world and exceeds it rather than allowing itself to be passively "traced" by it.

This second, dark ruin scenario bears importantly on Armida's dramatic first meeting with Connal. As Armida and her father approach the former seat of the O'Morvens in their carriage, Ireland takes shape as complex ruin, a land "brown, stony, and mountainous" on which it seems the sun never shone, "as if it lay for ever under the grey and watery sky":

> Yet Armida could descry on one of the boldest promontories . . . a pile of buildings, which at first, from its dark grey hue and giant massiveness, seemed like a part of the rock it stood on. A solitary tower or two, perched on a bare rock, and a few islands near the shore, appeared to be contending for their existence amid the loud and restless war of waters. (I: 54–55)

The pile gradually turns into a castle, "a rude, shapeless, wide-spreading structure, the work of different ages" with broken arches and a courtyard "strewn with fragments." At the cry of the deracinated O'Morvens, the horses bolt and gallop down the steep incline. Just as the carriage is about to plunge over the cliff, an imposing male figure springs out from the rocks and seizes Armida, who responds with terror at his intervention: "Her imagination full of terror, she thought that the Irish prince was rushing forward to seize and dash her from the precipice; and as the figure approached she screamed aloud to him to spare her life." Her senses fail, and when she recovers consciousness, she faintly recollects "a tall figure bending over her" (I: 58). The anticipation of Bram Stoker's more famous Irish Gothic text is not incidental: the vampiric motif persists throughout Maturin's narrative, which constantly presents Connal as a very large figure bending over Armida's prone body. He functions, we might say, as the very materialization of the gothic hover, and in this vampiric figure the shudder of fear conjoins with the sexual shudder of desire to wrench Armida from her cosmopolitan moorings in moments of terrifying ambiguity, repeatedly bringing her to a state of collapse.

As the gothic side of the notion of sympathy so central to the national tale (see Chapter 3), the shudder depends, like the sympathetic tear, on the somatic-imaginative capacity of projection. It depends, that is, on the capacity of the individual subject to exceed itself both in the sense of entering into the zones of others (the Smithian spectator) and in the sense of receiving impulses from them (Humean "communication"). But what distinguishes the shudder and makes it weird is its temporality. Sympathy works spatially as a crossing over into another object, a flow of feeling across space that confirms the synchrony of the sympathetic subjects. One impulse catches or adjusts to another impulse, so that sympathy carries with it the assurance that, to some extent at least, those involved in the scene of sympathy inhabit the same kind of space-time. By contrast, the shudder involves anticipating or registering another time in present time, cutting it into the current moment, so that it exposes an asynchrony of beings or cultures or histories.

The act of anticipation itself, of course, is central to the *memento mori* theme of ruin writing: I/you too will one day be as is this ruin. But something more than the generic imperative tends to drive those writers who concentrate on imagining their own world as a ruin rather than dwelling on a past that has come to ruin. The poet in Byron's celebrated ruin poem deploys the familiar generic move, for example, when he urges in Athens, "Look on its broken arch, its ruin'd wall" (*Childe Harold*, II: vi); but Stael's Corinne, wandering through Rome, takes a special pleasure in reducing St. Peter's to ruin: "As she drew near, her first thought was to picture the building as it would be when its turn came to fall into ruin, an object of admiration for the centuries to come. She imagined the columns now standing, half lying on the ground, the portico shattered, the vault open to the sky."[44] Closer to home, Anna Laetitia Barbauld notoriously turned England into a ruinscape in her sage poem *Eighteen Hundred and Eleven* (published around the same time as *The Milesian Chief*), which warns England against its pursuit of military and commercial gains during the Napoleonic wars. Hers is an apocalyptic stance: "Nor distant is the hour . . . / Ruin, as with earthquake shock, is here."[45] Offering a lengthy deconstruction and evacuation of English space, the poem projects a time when the powerful and confident imperial seat will be known only "By the gray ruin and the mouldering stone" (line 124). It presents an England become a heritage site for dutiful tourists from North America (who continue, incidentally, to visit "Melrose by the pale moonlight") and a place of forgetting for its few inhabitants. London itself is a waste space (crumbling turrets, broken stairs, a sedge-clogged Thames, etc.) whose only life is museum life, the names that resonate with active energy in the now of Barbauld's writing having become musty reminders of a remote history.

More elaborately than most ruin texts, *Eighteen Hundred and Eleven* thus imagines the present as a future past, and so highlights the way in which ruin writing typically loosens the hold of the indicative tenses (is, was, will be) to release more strange and speculative tenses: this will have been, this may well not be, this could have been, and so on. On the one hand such tenses open up utopian and satiric possibilities that confirm the powers of mind in the present (as in Barbauld's poem, for example, or Volney's well-known text); on the other, they disorient precisely those powers (as in *The Milesian Chief* or *The O'Briens and the O'Flahertys*). At stake in either case is the sense of the future. The gothic power of the shudder, which is always anticipatory even though prompted by the recoil of the past, lies in its rendering eerie the very notion of the future as premise. In the realm of the shudder the rational notion of the premise, which sustains the historian's sense, is turned inside out: no longer a future that follows from the present, it becomes a future that slips out of the present, transformed into something to be feared and repelled. Suggestively, the second shudder in Maturin's arrival scene comes when Armida and her father hear the piercing cry of the dispossessed O'Morvens: "Lord Montclare and his daughter shuddered, and scarcely thought themselves safe within their castle" (I: 57). Generating their shudder is the visceral sense of an unwanted future made present, a peculiar sensation nicely captured in Armida's formulation later in the text when the sight of the rebel army makes her "shudder at the idea of such men being encountered" (III: 88).

Maturin's extended arrival sequence helps to identify the fear lying at the heart of the gothic ruin: it is the fear of an improper death. Every organism, Freud asserts in *Beyond the Pleasure Principle*, seeks "to die only in its own fashion," and it tries to ward off whatever threatens to short-circuit the proper route to that proper death.[46] The gothic ruin not only threatens such short-circuit but confuses the distinction between proper/improper on which the notion of a meaningful death (and life) depends, for cultures as much as for individual persons. Such confounding potentially inheres in all ruins, as we have seen; hence the constant urge to argue that the endings they signal were somehow proper. But the gothic ruin is peculiarly charged with the energy of unnatural death as classical ruins are not. Irish gothic ruins – especially after 1798 – all the more so. "Have you no chill, no shudder . . . passing this spot?" asks a predatory Irish rebel named Brennan, as he leads Armida through a series of places that have witnessed aberrant deaths on the way to what he expects to be her own unnatural death at the hands of the old Milesian Chief himself, Connal's deranged grandfather (III: 152). The grandfather, conflating Armida with Elizabeth I, indeed attempts to bayonet her to death, setting up yet another traumatic rescue scene.[47]

The desire for a natural death in a vivid Ascendancy memoir of the summer of 1798 in Wexford helps to gloss gothic scenes such as these. Jane Adams' "Private Narrative of the Rebellion of 1798," which Thomas Crofton Croker appended to his folkloric travel text, *Researches in the South of Ireland* (1824), is a series of letters detailing the experience of Adams during the most intense period of the Wexford rising. "I fear we are in a most alarming situation," the text opens. "We have just had dreadful accounts from Naas – the rebels have defeated and killed

Captain Swayne, of Youghall."[48] As the sister of an outspoken Orange clergyman and a woman on her own responsible for a sick father and two children, Jane Adams had good reason to fear. In rapid succession, her house was trashed by insurgents, she and her family were briefly jailed, and her Orange brother (increasingly raving) narrowly escaped the massacre of prisoners at Wexford Bridge. Throughout this time Adams herself seems to have been in a constant state of nervous agitation, even convulsion (at one point she falls into screaming fits), but at the same time, she found herself filled with an unusual strength. When she sets out to get her brother out of jail, for instance, she states that she had not lain down on a bed the night before, "but I felt as if nothing had power to tire me; I could not eat a bit, and my thirst was not to be satisfied" (365). Significantly, her deepest longing during this period is that her father die a "natural" death: "How often did I wish my dear father laid quietly by her [i.e., the dead mother], so much did I dread his being murdered" (362). And a few pages later she writes: "I should have rejoiced at seeing him [her father] sinking into a quiet *natural* death" (364). Her sense of "natural" sequence and order thoroughly shaken, not least by her own "unnatural" way of being in this moment, Adams clearly yearns for signs of the continuing existence of ways of happening familiar to her: "a quiet *natural* death." As historical energies from outside her field of cognizance suddenly erupt into her view, threatening the possibility of a world quite literally turned around (Adams reports that the peasants expect to "change places" with the gentry), the categories by which she has oriented herself abruptly tilt. If in the end balance seems to be restored (she and her family emerge safely from Wexford), the hysterical tone of the text, some of which was written well after the events, testifies to a harrowing sense of colonial history as threateningly unfinished.

Armida Fitzalban knows no Irish history and remains indifferent to it. When told that insurrection has broken out and that British soldiers have set fire to the tower of the O'Morvens, which is now a heap of "burning ruins," she is aware only that the troops are led by her English fiancé Wandesford: "Ignorant of the distracted state of Ireland, she did not comprehend the rest" (II: 132). Nonetheless, she registers the impact of the history of which she remains ignorant not only on specific occasions, as when the old Milesian chief attempts to kill her, but also more generally and radically as the sudden, disorienting transposition to a limit zone where (as in the real-life instance of Jane Adams) she loses her hold on her proper self and its familiar civilized powers: "I try to write, but I cannot put together one distinct sentence. I try to speak, but I utter only frightful and inarticulate cries" (III: 21). Early in her sojourn in Ireland she had written with a certain gratifying self-dramatization that "I appear to have reached the limits of human existence," casting herself as an enchantress who has "gone beyond her own circle, and dreads to raise the spirits she can no longer govern" (I: 88, 89). But metaphors of extremity and loss of control turn disconcertingly literal, as Armida loses her creative and intellectual powers and eventually ends up alone on an island off the west coast of Ireland for several months, waiting to hear the outcome of the rebellion. Here she leads so attenuated an existence that she often finds it "hard to credit my own existence" (III: 122). Natural sounds, she writes to a friend in a series of ghostly letters she never expects to be received, are all that remind her of "the living world," but even these appear phantasmatic traces rather than actual signs:

> the winds and waters are all that remind me of existence, and even they seem only like the echo of the similar sounds in the living world: this apparent extremity of the creation seems like the extremity of life; they who have reached it appear to feel as if death was past, and there was nothing more to do or to suffer. (III: 123–24)

Pushed to the edge of Europe and suspended between life and death, Armida inhabits Ireland as a space without clear horizons, where death becomes dangerously attractive as the only promise of "perfect and perennial security" (III: 131).

The gothic work of *The Milesian Chief* is summed up in such a moment. Over and over again, at the level of its own narrative practices as well as at the level of plot and figure, it undoes horizons. "Every living thing," Nietzsche writes in his well-known meditation on the uses of history, "can become healthy, strong and fruitful only within a horizon: if it is incapable of drawing a horizon . . . it will wither away feebly or overhastily to its early demise."[49] Nietzsche's point is that it is as crucial for nations and individuals to forget as it is for them to remember in order for meaningful action to be possible. The important thing, of course, is to forget "at the right time," as well as to remember "at the right time."[50] But the stabilizing sense of a "right time" cannot begin to take shape in a ruinscape such as that of *The Milesian Chief.* Ruins in general, themselves manifestations of dissolution, dissolve horizons in their turn, blurring the lines that allow for the clarity of distinction and action ("a line which distinguishes what is clear and in full view from the dark and unilluminable," as Nietzsche puts it). But rankling colonial ruins block the satisfying drift that such dissolution can induce, along with any move to sublime transcendence.

To live in their presence is to enter what Armida's female companion calls "that sick and hopeless state of mind in which we seem no longer to know good from evil, in which characters change before us like figures in a dream, and the landmarks of life appear to be removed from their places" (II: 145). Markers disappear; textures erode. Armida herself puts it perhaps most memorably when she laments the loss of her imaginative powers: "But now my imagination is gone: an object without dimensions and without colour seems to occupy my mind's eye" (II: 170–71).

As it brings its protagonists to the non-redemptive *Liebestod* of its final pages, *The Milesian Chief* establishes Irish Gothic as a skeptical turn on the rational and humanist inflections of late Enlightenment forms of history (cosmopolitan, revolutionary, nationalist). Less a counter-history in the sense of "another telling" of national time than heretic history, it exerts pressure on the historical form itself by pushing its narrative to where the memory and reason that sustain historical understanding begin to undo themselves. Maturin's dark romance thus releases a negativity that potentially inhered in the national tale from the outset as a genre that revolved in an unstable interspace instead of either inhabiting an orthodox zone or constituting an alternative space. This negativity, generally submerged in the more optimistic and rational modes adopted by Edgeworth and the early Morgan, was intimately tied to the liminal status of a post-Union sensibility that could not live readily between the national and political lines being drawn up in the period.[51] So it is not surprising that when a newly confident Catholic nationalism took over the national tale in the final heated stages of the Emancipation drive in the 1820s, it challenged the whole notion of an interspace and brought the "clamour" of Irish agitation to bear more directly on British public discourse.

CHAPTER 5

Agitated bodies: the Emancipation debate and novels of insurgency in the 1820s

It is difficult to judge of the numbers of the rebels, they appear in such crowds and so little order.

Brigadier-General John Moore, Wexford, 23 June 1798

"And when *will* they grow quiet, Sir?"
"When, indeed, General."

John Banim *The Anglo-Irish of the Nineteenth Century* (1828)

Responding to stepped-up Irish political agitation in 1824, an exasperated reviewer in the *Literary Chronicle* complained that Irish Catholics, led by "that hot-headed lawyer, Daniel O'Connell," were "perpetually clamouring." The specific object of the clamor was Catholic Emancipation, but the reviewer is in no doubt that were emancipation to be gained, the Irish would "next day clamour for a separation from England."[1] Clamor thus marks the endemic mode of Irish political being, an old charge but one that took on a distinctive edge in the 1820s. In this decade Ireland once again became a prominent site of turbulence and anxiety in British discourse, as it suffered severe economic distress and famine; witnessed renewed agrarian militancy under the name of Captain Rock, along with increased sectarian violence; and – most immediately to the point for civic discourse – saw the innovative and formidable campaign for full civil rights spearheaded by O'Connell and the Catholic Association. The Association's barrage of petitions, speeches, pamphlets, motions, and meetings combined with its extraordinary organization of the Catholic masses in the Irish countryside to produce a new Irish politics. This new mass politics mounted an effective challenge to the gentry politics of Westminster and Dublin Castle, in the process achieving a significant constitutional victory and itself becoming a model for later out-of-doors campaigns such as the Anti-Corn Law League in both Ireland and Great Britain.[2] Neatly underscoring its pivotal and paradigmatic role, the OED leads off its illustration of agitation in the political sense ("to keep a political or other object perpetually under discussion so as to impress on the public mind") with an example from the Irish emancipation campaign: c.1828, Marq. Anglesey (to Irish Deputation): If you really expect success, *agitate, agitate, agitate.*[3]

The O'Connellite agitation of the 1820s altered the modality of the Irish question in British public discourse. If, as Chapter 3 argued, the early national tale shifted Ireland from the English space of the "case" (a situation to be determined by those outside) into the Anglo-Irish space of the "claim" (a subject seeking rights), the final drive for emancipation in the 1820s pushed the claim into an Irish space of "demand" (an authoritative asking). To demand is to speak with authority, to command obedience rather than to declare title to a right and await settlement. Irish Catholics, formerly cast in the abject posture of the colonial "cringe" or "crouch," quite literally changed the tone of their address and thereby signalled their successful entry into what Slavoj Žižek calls the "properly political" moment. The "elemental gesture of politicization," Žižek argues, is that by which "the part of society with no properly defined place" identifies itself with "the whole" (e.g., the democratic nation) or "the principle of universality" (e.g., the principle of equality) professed by the established social order but which it conspicuously fails to embody.[4] The important point in relation to the emancipation campaign is that this gesture destabilizes the social order not just by exposing its fissures and calling it to account but by demanding that the excluded group "be heard on equal footing with the ruling oligarchy or aristocracy." At stake is never only the particular demand (even if it is often convenient for both sides to pretend that such is the case) because political struggle, as Žižek puts it, is "never simply a rational debate between multiple interests but, simultaneously, the struggle for one's voice to be heard and recognized as that of a legitimate partner."[5]

The Catholic Association's tactics of agitation were thus directed not simply at securing the specific measure of removing the remaining civil disabilities of Irish Catholics but at achieving legitimacy for what O'Connell liked to call "the public voice" of Ireland, a new middle-class voice that assumed prominence in the early years of the century by displacing that of elite Catholics on the one hand and winning a remarkable resonance among the Catholic peasantry on the other. In directing the articulation of this "public voice," O'Connell was highly sensitive to the power dynamics at work in different acts of public enunciation. He (temporarily) abandoned the practice of submitting annual petitions to parliament, for instance, on the grounds that it doomed the

Irish to the permanent role of supplicants: "We have only to behave ourselves as petitioners; to be very temperate, and mild, and forbearing; to avoid all agitation, and to be most respectful and submissive, and we shall be allowed the mighty privilege of continuing petitioners and cadets during our existence."[6] Significantly, when he did revive petitioning, he transformed it from a ritual of formal request to an act of assault: "They [i.e., the Catholic Association] would petition week after week, as if those who had the power persisted in refusing to remove the fetters, their ears should, at least, be dinned with the clanking of their chains" (*Select Speeches*, II: 224). By presenting specific petitions on the full range of Catholic grievances rather than restricting themselves to a general petition on the issue of emancipation, as had previously been the custom, the Catholic Association ensured there was a steady stream of Irish paper directed to Westminster: "We shall never cease petitioning, nor shall a week pass that our case shall not come before them in some shape, until justice is obtained" (II: 400). The sheer fact of reiteration – "the efficacy of repeating, and repeating, and repeating again," as O'Connell put it earlier in his career (II: 11) – effected a change in genre, transforming the "time of petitioning" (in the words of the *Edinburgh Review*) into the "time for demanding": "The time for petitioning may soon end, as it did with America, and the time for demanding begins [*sic*]."[7]

When language moves into the temporality of demand, it loses its distance and its moderation; harnessed for purposes of agitation, it casts off the protocols of rational and gentlemanly discourse. O'Connell himself was routinely charged with "demagoguery," shorthand for a language outside that of a liberal politics of consensus, balance, and decorum. Evaluating O'Connell's career, William Lecky was to stress the drawback of the "defiant and . . . overbearing tone" adopted by O'Connell to propel Irish Catholics out of their habitual stance of inferiority. This tone lost its force, he remarks, when transferred to a parliamentary chamber where "gentlemanly moderation," spiced with "well-bred, pungent raillery," was the dominant accent.[8] Certainly, O'Connell's political goals themselves remained firmly within the frame of constitutional politics. As with Edgeworth and Morgan, his conceptual political roots lay in eighteenth-century Enlightenment thought, and his speeches continually invoked "rational liberty," "constitutional reform," and "public opinion" while denouncing more radical or revolutionary forms of thought and action. But he meshed this civil model with a post-revolutionary political intuition fully alert to the power of bodies and words outside the official orders of discourse and rule. Herein is the key to the potency of his experiment with the Catholic masses and to the profound unease it generated in official circles. "Whatever little [Irish Catholics] had gained," he urged in a speech to an aggregate meeting of the Catholic Association in 1824, "they had gained by agitation, while they uniformly lost by moderation. The last word was repeated so often, that he was completely sick of it" (II: 299).

Refusing the moderate word of reason, which made him "sick," O'Connell championed the aggressive word of agitation. For him, as for Bakhtin, language was a dialogic field of social struggle, and his speeches and writings typically represent it as a thick medium in which words force their way through and against other words. In O'Connell's hands words assume palpability, and public words in particular appear as forms of quasi-physical pressure, bursts and flows of energy directed at obdurate others. "You must I repeat *force* your question on the Parliament," he writes to the leader of the British Jews, Isaac Lyon Goldsmid in September 1829. "You ought not to confide in English liberality. It is a plant not genial to the British soil. It must be *forced*. It requires a *hot-bed*."[9] This is the abrasive (rather than often celebrated ludic or heteroglossic) side of the Bakhtinian word, the word oriented to an anticipated answer. Parliamentary ears are to be "dinned" by constant petitioning, and Catholic applications to be conveyed in "a voice of thunder, whose roaring will force attention when asking for the rights of man and privileges of Christians" (II: 400–01). Such assault came under predictable attack as hollow and useless (not to mention vulgar) "bullying," prompting a fierce debate on the value and status of O'Connell's tactics. Morgan, for one, leaped to a spirited defence in the final stages of the emancipation campaign when she inserted a sardonic footnote in *The O'Briens and the O'Flahertys* on the subject. Recent Irish history, she points out, has shown that "the Tory faction (calling itself the State) *has been bullied* and *may be bullied*; and that, as it never has granted any thing to justice or generosity, the turbulence of the catholic agitators is not quite as groundless, or devoid of policy, as their opponents affect to imagine."[10]

Like *The O'Briens and the O'Flahertys*, most Irish novels of the 1820s were explicitly part of the "*hot-bed*" of the emancipation drive, and it is by no means incidental that this decade witnessed the entry of Catholic writers into a hitherto Protestant field with the publication of *Tales of the O'Hara Family* (1825) by the O'Connellite Banim brothers. Nor is it incidental that this was the decade that established the Irish novel as a separate generic category in the British literary sphere. It is not simply, as Jacqueline Belanger has recently confirmed, that Ireland became more prominent as a novelistic subject in the 1820s;[11] it is that novels from Ireland in the previous decade – Edgeworth's reformist fictions, Morgan's national tale, Maturin's weird gothic – had been treated in the reviews primarily as manifestations of a general fictional impulse. Certainly they were seen as importantly Irish and shaped by "national character," but they were not understood in relation to a "school" or "tradition" of national fiction. From the mid-1820s on, however, survey and review articles begin to appear under titles like "Irish Novels" (Thomas Moore, *Edinburgh Review*, 1826); "Irish Romance," (T. N. Talfourd, *New Monthly Magazine*, 1827); "National Tales of Ireland" (F. D. Maurice (?), *Westminster Review*, 1828); "Novels Descriptive of Irish Life," (T. H. Lister, *Edinburgh Review*, 1831). An Irish *line* of fiction begins to be defined, one not yet firmly in place and inevitably marked by politics, so that the Irish novel emerges in the periodicals (by comparison with the English line) as immature and not quite literary. "Irish novelists have uniformly given a party cast to their fiction," flatly states the *Athenaeum* in 1828, declaring that "not one able Irish romance" from Edgeworth's *The Absentee* to Michael Banim's *The Croppy* has been free from political ends. What this means, the reviewer concludes, is that so long as Irish writers continue "to use the imagination solely for writing supplements to the newspapers, so long will it be evident that Ireland and Irishmen are not what they ought to be."[12]

The question of what Ireland "ought to be" and what fiction "ought to do" in relation to it fuelled the production and reception of Irish writing in the volatile literary field of the 1820s, when a Thomas Moore could continue to produce soothing, nostalgic verses on "Erin" for English drawing rooms even while composing what Seamus Deane terms "a rebel view of Irish history" in *Memoirs of Captain Rock* as part of the push for emancipation.[13] With a title alluding to the militant Rockites of the early 1820s, Moore's ironic counter-history signals its timeliness from the outset and presents itself as a direct intervention in current debate. The signal is reinforced by the equally timely travel frame mentioned in the last chapter, which mocks the notorious "second Reformation" that prompted Protestant missionaries to come over to Ireland to convert the Catholics. Moore's hapless English missionary not only completely fails in his Irish mission but, in the reversal characteristic of the national tale, concludes that "it is the rulers, not the People of Ireland, who require to be instructed and converted."[14]

British reviewers were not in general much persuaded of this argument. What bothered them about Moore's text was less its anti-English reading of history, which could be readily dismissed as "falsifications," than the kind of readership it implied. "Those to whom his book is addressed," *Blackwood's* claims, "are more likely to look to the colouring, than to the truth of the narrative."[15] Even as it puts down Moore's readers, the reviewer's dismissive gesture registers the way in which his narrative operates outside rational and cognitive protocols. This is what makes it an "inflammatory volume" for *Blackwood's*, and other reviewers struck similar notes of concern: the *British Review* judged the book "most pernicious," while the *British Critic* accused it of having no other object than "goading [Ireland] into madness and crime."[16] In the evaluation of Irish texts like the *Memoirs of Captain Rock*, the rhetorical and pragmatic axes of the narrative occupy the foreground, underlining the way in which Irish fictions of the period were generally understood as living their real life outside the covers of books and inside the public questions they engaged and activated. So Sydney Smith, who for his part commended Moore's "agreeable and witty book" in the *Edinburgh Review*, used the occasion mainly to urge once again the argument for emancipation, although he assumes (or affects to assume) the inevitable failure of rational appeal: "the measure will never be effected but by fear."[17] More radical journals tended to make less of the measure itself, as in the obscure and short-lived *Ghost of the Rushlight* from Belfast, which praised Moore's mock-history but repudiated emancipation as "only a subordinate measure, and one which of itself could do little good."[18]

Irish novels of the 1820s were thus immediately caught up in an active and wide public controversy as they had not been when Edgeworth and Morgan inaugurated the national tale as a way of directing British attention to Ireland. During this decade the Irish thread wove itself into British culture in more salient and intense fashion, prompting Walter Scott to joke in early 1829 (when the parliamentary debate over emancipation was in its final days) that if he was to recover his financial situation, he had to pray for quiet times: "for how can men mind their serious business – that is, according to Cadell's views – buying Waverley novels when they are going mad about the Catholic question?" More seriously, he notes that he can postpone deciding what to do about the manuscript of *Anne of Geierstein*, unfavourably reviewed by Ballantyne, because "the book cannot be published, at any rate, during the full rage of the Catholic question."[19] Within Irish fiction itself the pole of English address became more strained, discursive relations increasingly testy and prickly. "To what purpose, it may be asked, are these bitter recollections revived?" Morgan asks, as she opens the footnote on "bullying" in *The O'Briens and the O'Flahertys* cited earlier. "Certainly neither to irritate nor insult the English nation, from whose justice and good sense Ireland has so much to expect" (63). Shot through with irony, her gesture of conciliation rapidly undoes itself, releasing the barely repressed resentment that had always simmered within it.

This is not to say that the later national tale and cognate genres like the Irish historical novel renounced either the set to English eyes or the attempt at reconciliation. But the political agitators' sense of demand underwrote their tone, and locutionary relations established by the narratives as often blocked as enabled sympathetic attachment. Michael Banim's *The Croppy: A Tale of the Irish Rebellion of 1798* (1828) is a striking example. The novel includes several addresses to English readers, ostensibly deferring to English sensibilities but in effect underscoring their inadequacy for a reading of Irish novels. When the narrator reports the imposition of martial law in Ireland in March 1798, for instance, he addresses the reader as a member of an enlightened nation "long familiar with liberty and independence, – long delivered from despotism." This concession to English self-imagining, however, is turned back on the reader, as enlightenment becomes incomprehension when confronted with "our facts": "It is therefore with some doubts of even the capability of the minds of Englishmen to receive our facts, that we proceed to mention in what manner the trampled down men of our country were, in many instances, driven into the toils which were coolly set for them by mongrel legislators neither Irish nor English" (II: 37–38).

Banim's targeting of normative English reading is even more explicit later in the text when he interrupts his narrative to introduce an odd metacritical scenario in which a "tyro-critic" whispers to an indolent reader on a sofa of the excesses of this very novel. This scenario launches a repudiation of English literary norms by way of an insistence on the very different historical trajectories of Ireland and England: "We do not pourtray the minds, the hearts, the habits, the manners, or the acts of a tranquillized and a happy people; least of all do we pourtray the quiet and passionless decorum which can only result from a well-knit, long-confirmed, prosperous, and perhaps selfish state of society" (III: 58). Thus banishing the normative English novel of manners, he turns on the critic himself to negate his charge of "extravagance," and ends by impatiently dismissing the critic's "washy, water-colour taste" (III: 59). This moment roused at least one real-life critic to reply. Reprinting the entire passage in the *Westminster Review*, the reviewer (who was likely F. D. Maurice) embarked in turn on a defence of English critics: "Now, at the risk of being stigmatized as tyro-critics, we must tell our somewhat combative author that he has equally mistaken the nature of the charge to which he is liable, and the persons who make it."[20] So marked by charge and counter-charge, more or less serious, the interchange between Irish writers and the British literary field refused to settle, agitating the public sphere and threatening to displace, if not replace, its norms of discourse and models of self-understanding.

Thus even as the Irish were being brought "home" into the United Kingdom with the removal of Catholic disabilities – "This is the real year from which the Irish Union ought to run," exultantly proclaimed the *Edinburgh Review* in March 1829[21] – their entry further estranged home space. Ireland's fearful "great body" meant that incorporation was not necessarily assimilation or, as had been hoped, pacification, and Ireland was to remain a persistent sore spot on the domestic body politic. As it deliberately inflamed this sore spot in the 1820s, this chapter will argue, the Irish agitation campaign shook up public genres of history and political discourse, deranging their composure and destabilizing the ethos of distance that underpinned their norms of detachment and impersonality. At the same time, the very insistence of this agitation shut down certain cultural and national spaces ambivalently opened by borderland genres like the national tale. In *The Anglo-Irish of the Nineteenth Century* by O'Connell's literary follower John Banim, to which I turn in the final section, the national tale was subjected to demand, and it unravelled in the process.

FORMS OF INSISTENCE

At one point in the frame narrative of Moore's *Memoirs of Captain Rock*, the would-be English missionary finds himself sharing space in the Limerick Coach with an odd character wearing green spectacles and a wig who, he later discovers, is the feared rebel leader Captain Rock himself. As they travel through the countryside, this figure offers a running commentary on the misrule of Ireland and the bitterness of its historical memory. When they pass the town of Kildare, he directs special attention to "the still existing traces of that ruin and havoc, which were produced by the events of the year 1798" (viii). Novels of the 1820s began to activate these "still existing traces," returning to view the smouldering topic of 1798 as one that resonated into the unsettled present. Even as the novels, like the emancipation campaign in general, were careful to distance themselves from insurrectionary violence and radicalism, they kept this insurrectionary past in explicit play. Theirs was a crossed political gesture, pointing at once to domestication and to inflammation. In these fictions,

1798 emerges not only as a memory to be appropriated and defused, as has often been argued, but also and more aggressively as a volatility to be *raided* for the political work of the 1820s.

The topic of 1798 was by no means discursively invisible before the 1820s. The United Irishmen rebellion had moved rapidly into literary representation, producing a flurry of memoirs, ballads, analyses, and other texts shortly after its suppression.[22] But in Irish fiction itself it had remained for the most part a troubling undercurrent in the first two decades (with the arguable exception of Maturin's *Milesian Chief*), appearing as narrative episode or interpolation or showing up in paratextual space like footnotes.[23] The late 1820s, however, witnessed the appearance of a series of novels foregrounding the question of 1798, ranging from Michael Banim's pioneering account of the Wexford rebellion in *The Croppy* (1828) and Morgan's evocation of the political failure of the United Irishmen in the west in *O'Briens and the O'Flahertys* (1827) to James McHenry's focus on the outbreak in county Antrim in *O'Halloran, or The Insurgent Chief: An Irish Historical Tale of 1798* (1828) and Eyre Evans Crowe's critique of Orange practices in "The Northerns of Ninety-Eight."[24] In the zig-zag of generic interchange that constitutes the genealogy of Romantic novelistic modes, the national tale was now modulating into the novel of insurgency, folding into itself the *Waverley* model of historical fiction as it did so. (Scott himself had initially developed his influential narrative genre out of the Irish national tale.[25])

The Scott model may be summed up as the (tolerant) modern mediation of the heated differences of the (intolerant) past, and it is articulated perhaps most explicitly in James McHenry's preface to *O'Halloran.* A Presbyterian from Ulster who emigrated to Philadelphia and saw the rebellion close up as a child in Larne, McHenry had a special interest in and sympathy for the United Irishmen and their role in the north; indeed, he made something of a career of 1798, producing several narratives on the subject, including an early poem titled *Patrick* (1810). The preface to *O'Halloran* opens by extolling the patriotism, talents, and courage of the United Irishmen, along with "the generous nature of the principles for which they contended."[26] While it is clear that he remains attracted to their political program ("had . . . the designs they had formed for the advantage of the country been realised, what epithets of praise would have been considered too high for their deserts?"), McHenry sharply distinguishes his narrative from himself, defining it as an impersonal medium for the display of the opposing ideologies at war in 1798: "The United Irishmen and the loyalists are permitted to express their sentiments with equal force and freedom; the fanatical and the fierce, on either side, are painted as such; while the moderate and lenient, I hope, have ample justice done to the rationality of their views."[27] Thus located in a transparent and stable center, the authorial voice reads the past so that, as in the Waverley Novels, historical truth overlaps with (national) public good, and both are identified with a modern rationality and moderation set against political fanaticism and ferocity.

But 1798 was not part of a surmounted past in the Ireland of 1828 as was 1745, at least in Scott's reading of Scottish history, in the Scotland that saw the publication of *Waverley* in 1814. "There is no European nation, which, within the course of half a century, or little more, has undergone so complete a change as this kingdom of Scotland," Scott famously asserted in the conclusion to his first novel.[28] But the problem of history for Ireland was precisely the opposite, that it lay outside change altogether, "never advancing," as Moore's Captain Rock notes right after pointing out the traces of 1798, "always suffering – her whole existence one monotonous round of agony!"[29] On Irish terrain a plan of "neutrality" (McHenry's term) along the lines of a Waverley Novel did not appear so inevitably the transparent form of historical insight; moreover, it proved virtually impossible to implement in narrative terms. Few points of vantage presented themselves to yield the clear temporal differentiations and divisions on which depended the control of narrative distance central to Scott's authority for nineteenth-century readers. In contrast to Scott's slow-moving and capacious fictions, the novels of Irish insurgency are markedly angular, characterized by jolting shifts in angle, scene, and mode. As Tom Dunne notes, speaking of *The Croppy*, the text is marked by "frequent breakdowns and abrupt changes in direction and tone," while the narrative itself "lurches" from melodrama to comedy to horror.[30] The genteel Anglo-Irish heroine marries the wrong man, an insurgent leader (also Anglo-Irish), from whom the plot strains to keep her apart after the wedding so that she may eventually marry the right man, a loyal yeoman. A gothic subplot features her school friend, a theatricalized fallen heroine, who flits in and out of the story in disguise in Morganesque fashion, sporting rebel gear (including a pistol) but effecting benevolent acts of rescue even as she plots revenge on her faithless lover. Various other characters, including a garrulous old nurse, appear and disappear, often to no apparent purpose.

The heart of the tale is a compelling if lurid account of the Wexford rising centered on the historically symbolic site of the local forge, where pikes are sharpened and United Irishmen come to swear in recruits. This forge in turn becomes the object of a furious attack by the local yeomanry, an attack that includes the harrowing torture of the blacksmith's son. Out of this matrix, insurrection explodes. For Banim, the year 1798 is "that baleful year which . . . was doomed to witness in Ireland, such scenes of convulsion, of carnage, and of horror, as, to this day, leave a shuddering recollection among the inhabitants of our country" (*The Croppy*, 1: 123). In this approach to the insurrection, *The Croppy* is symptomatic of the novels of the 1820s which, by and large, replay the motif of fearful and fatal "convulsion" that had framed perception of 1798 in British public discourse from the beginning. The rebellion appears as an inchoate event, primarily rural, produced by the collision of a whole set of volatile and heterogeneous impulses and energies in the hot summer of that year. Foremost among these is provocation by an Orange yeomanry tacitly (or not so tacitly) supported by the government, but also prominent is incitement on the part of the revolutionary United Irishmen. Other contributing forces featured in the narratives include foreign manipulation, local grievances, peasant anger at a settler class, and the catchall of "madness" and "delusion" infecting a sorely tried people.

Most of all, the events are presented as ones for which no single or strictly rational account seems possible, so that the summer of 1798 is repeatedly figured in terms of a world suddenly spinning beyond control. "I shrink from the vortex," says an enlightened landlord in *The Croppy*, summing up the dominant view (1: 276). In this reading of the rebellion the novels of the 1820s run counter to current readings, which stress by contrast the rationality of 1798 as a planned revolt. In particular, they have restored to prominent view the role of the United Irishmen, which had been significantly obscured over the course of the nineteenth century. Concentrating on the specifically modern and rational character of the United Irishmen, recent accounts stress their micro organization, interest in political education, and resolute nonsectarianism. In short, where nineteenth-century readings tend to see a reactive, convulsive episode rooted in traditions of rural protest and marked by sectarianism, current interpretations find an active attempt to seize power driven by a modern, urban-based ideology with a republican commitment in Wolf Tone's often quoted phrase to "the common name of Irishman in place of the denominations of Protestant, Catholic and Dissenter." In current narratives of the rebellion, then, the former master trope of incoherence has been replaced by that of coherence, so that 1798 no longer appears (in the pithy formulation of the *Westminster Review*) as "that blind outbreaking of a miserable multitude."[31] Thus Kevin Whelan, for example, argues that only the failure of the crucial Dublin city plan, blocked by preemptive government action, gave the rebellion an "improvised, incoherent appearance" and veiled its actual levels of planning and execution.[32]

Such relegation of incoherence to the contingent realm of "appearance" rather than to the inherent structure of the event allows for the restoration of historical initiative and purpose to Irish political organization. But incoherence, whether contingent or essential, nevertheless remains the trait that characterizes the unfolding of 1798 for both nineteenth- and late twentieth-century commentators, and its "appearance" is worth taking seriously, not least because appearance has very real effects and matters greatly to the bodies caught up in and by it. In the novels of 1798 bodies are hanged, tortured, shot, kidnapped, and otherwise molested, but most of all they are unsettled, put into constant motion. The dominant figure of these fictions (whose central plots and characters are rarely memorable) is the scene of traversal, as refugees, prisoners, soldiers, cottiers, and others trek back and forth amidst the chops and changes of war. Spilling out of confines, milling about, and moving from place to place, especially as crowds, they signal at once the confusion of distraction (the "distracted multitude" of common idiom) and a circulation that eludes clear demarcation. "It is difficult to judge of the numbers of the rebels," wrote Brigadier-General John Moore in a dispatch from Wexford in June 1798, "they appear in such crowds and so little order."[33]

This sense of a force and an event that cannot quite be bounded infuses the chronotope of passage governing these novels. Characters from all sides keep crossing one another on the road, changing places and roles, and engaging in acts of rescue. While their motion makes the conciliatory point of meetings across lines, it also effects a simple blurring of lines not only between opposing groups but between kinds of episodes or actions – indeed, around the entire action of the insurrection itself. The point is not that there are no lines but that they are shifting and indistinct, so that 1798 emerges (to paraphrase Wittgenstein) as an event with blurred edges. This makes it hard to fix and contain, as indeed historically Cornwallis found it difficult to proclaim an end to what we now call 1798. In January 1799 he reported to the Irish Parliament in his speech from the Throne that "a spirit of disaffection still prevails in several parts of this kingdom."[34] Cornwallis was justifying the maintenance of severe martial law, but that does not in itself discount his observation, and the British press continued to note outbursts of insurgency in remote pockets of the country. The package of "Interesting Intelligence from Ireland" in the *Gentlemen's Magazine* from which I cite Cornwallis' speech, for instance, includes a report dated 15 January announcing that county Clare "has been proclaimed this evening in a state of rebellion." The immediately following report, however, dated 21 January, announces that this "insurrection" was "dressed by rumour in too formidable colours, [and] has been completely got under."[35] As a matter of rumor, remoteness, and unpredictable eruptions, the insurgency of 1798 proved difficult to grasp, an obscure and agitated scene that refused to yield a clear view or come to a definite end. As late as April 1799 the *Critical Review* states in its report on the state of Ireland: "Tranquillity is not yet restored to this country."[36]

Harnessing the mobility of 1798 for the mobilization of 1828, the novels of insurgency kept its traces before the public mind. Both *The O'Briens and the O'Flahertys* and *The Croppy* print out in full the oath of the United Irishmen, framing it in each case with a celebratory roll call of the leaders of the organization. And Banim's novel reproduces several rebel songs, including "Rise up, my poor Croppies" even as it disavows the violence of those who sang them. The pertinence of such recirculation becomes evident in his Epilogue, which asserts that while the "storm of insurrection" has blown away, "not so its effects." The effect Banim has in particular mind – the effect that allows him to close the gap between then and now – is the Union, a union achieved, he stresses, on the basis of "a promise of advantages which have not yet been conceded." Exerting the pressure of this "not yet" as he turns from his public to his private plot, Banim ostentatiously refuses the conciliatory ending conventional in the national tale. His protagonists, he records, married in 1800, thereby forming "another union, which proved happier than the national one."[37]

The novels of 1798 thus *summon* the past, specifically the insurrection, to enforce a present demand, and in so doing they draw attention to the way in which the matter of Ireland made it impossible to overlook the dependence of history (as representation of the past) on its status as an enunciation in and for the present. For British public discourse, Irish writing on the past raised in an embarrassing way the problem of historical knowledge – its purpose, its validity, its norms – at a moment when the discipline was beginning to establish itself as a modern knowledge genre devoted to impersonal and rational protocols. "A good History of Ireland is still a *desideratum* in our literature," declared Francis Jeffrey as he opened a review of John O'Driscol's *The History of Ireland* in 1827.[38] The problem, as he saw it, was that the story of Ireland generated such powerful interest that it blocked "impartiality," and the very investigation of the past that should have dispelled political and religious animosities ended up fuelling them instead by "making the history of past enormities, not a warning against but an incitement to, their repetition."[39] So caught up in the very problems from which they should have detached themselves, Irish historians betrayed both the discipline's scholarly norm and its social mandate to promote public peace.

Behind this failure for Jeffrey lay the way in which such historians understood their discourse less as truth than as debate.[40] Impelling their writing, he argued, was a sideways glance that made them anxious "far more ... to irritate and defy each other, than to leave even a partial memorial of the truth."[41] Jeffrey's distinction nicely locates two modes of history, pitting a history intent on producing "memorials" against one that produces only contention. For the first kind of history, the past is over and done with, and this makes it available to knowledge as disinterested "truth"; for the second, the past is unsettled and hence an ongoing "irritation" to the present, so that it operates in a perturbed dialogic space rather than belonging to the ideal calm of cognition. In this second mode, history is constituted less by reflection and research (although these are by no means ruled out) than by a particular mode of recollection, one we might term, paraphrasing Wordsworth, recollection in agitation.

Suggestively, Wordsworth's celebrated definition of poetic composition as originating in "emotion recollected in tranquillity" appears in the context of a discussion of the uses of meter to regulate the mental and emotional excitement produced by the reading of poetry.[42] Indeed, the Preface as a whole can be seen as a meditation on the proper arousal and regulation of excitement in a post-revolutionary culture. Wordsworth's analysis stresses that poetry excites both the mind that receives and the mind that produces it, and in each case some tempering power is required to counter the disordering potential of excitement. While he identifies the production of "excitement" as the goal of poetry, he insists that excitement must coexist with "an overbalance of pleasure" ("Preface" 739). As a harmonizing power, pleasure is necessary to ensure that poetic excitement is not "carried beyond proper bounds," for excitement in itself, Wordsworth notes, is "an unusual and irregular state of the mind; ideas and feelings do not, in that state, succeed each other in accustomed order" (739). It is because poets experience the disorientation of mental excitement *as* poets that they are all the more obliged "to take care" that the passions communicated by their work are restrained by pleasures. In their own creative moment (as they enact the deliberate swerve out of accustomed order that sets it in motion), excitement is contained by various pleasures overseen by a "Nature" whose caution Wordsworth emphasizes. As he clearly recognizes, recollection itself is an act of agitation, the poet deliberately exciting a past emotion in such a way that an emotion "kindred" to the earlier emotion gradually "does itself actually exist in the mind" (740). The important point for my purposes is that this disquieting but productive emotion, at once specular and intensely present, is a function not so much of a past that returns (repetition) as of a past explicitly summoned by the present (recollection).[43] It is to help contain this agitating impulse that Wordsworth specifies "tranquillity" as the condition for its proper activation.

In so foregrounding recollection as at once an act of consciousness and an affective charge, Wordsworth's Preface throws useful light on the debate about the writing of history in the period, especially when it came to the matter of Ireland. When recollection becomes a more strictly public act, as in the turn from poetic to historical recollection, the charge effected by recollection becomes more unbounded and volatile. History implicates readers as a collective national public and not simply as individual and generic "men" as in Wordsworth's account of poetry; nor are these readers addressed simply as recipients of an account of the national past ("this is how it was"). Rather, the recollective mode of history actively recruits readers to participate in bringing back to mind a certain past ("let me remind you"), and the risk of rousing emotions "kindred" to those being recollected has potentially graver consequences than in the case of lyric poetry. Accordingly, the requirement of tranquility becomes all the more urgent, for to recollect in agitation is to double the excitation. "We have no desire," declared the *British Critic* in commenting on Jane Adams' memoir of 1798, "to continue or revive the feelings which the recollection of that rebellion must excite." Over and over again in the period the topic of 1798 is accompanied by the vocabulary of agitated recollection: "shuddering recollection" (*The Croppy*, 1: 23); "bitter recollections" (*The O'Briens and the O'Flahertys*, 63); "rankling sting" (Trotter's *Walks Through Ireland*, 68); and "burning remembrances."[45]

Such phrases confirm the often-noted observation that in post-Union Ireland history was increasingly regarded as what Leerssen terms "unfinished business . . . a set of outstanding grievances waiting to be redressed."[46] Such a sense of the past as unclosed, as an ongoing power that might be turned to present account, prompted an understanding of history writing as neither memorializing remembrance (as in nationalist historiography) nor as impartial knowledge (as in the emerging Rankean model) but precisely – and romantically – as active recollection. Refusing to elide the scene of enunciation, Irish representations of the past offered a model of history as a pointed intersection of the horizons of past and present directed to a shaping of the horizon of the future. Formulating this point perhaps most memorably in the period was William James MacNeven, a Catholic leader of the United Irishmen himself engaged in the events of 1798: "history, or the present recollection of past events, if properly applied, would emancipate the Catholics, or, better still, the Irish."[47]

Buttressing the "present recollection of past events" and giving Irish discourse compelling purchase on the British public mind in this period was the material fact of the enormous Irish population. The resonance of 1798 in the 1820s was intimately tied up with this fact, which (like the insurrection itself) was all the more alarming because it was not clearly bounded and known. "Cabin-population swarms," reported the *Monthly Review* in commenting on the difficulty experienced by Thomas Reid in making an accurate population table for his *Travels in Ireland*: "Mr. Reid found the same difficulty which has always been experienced in Ireland, namely, of ascertaining the amount of its population."[48] Estimates of the Irish population before the 1841 census were notoriously inadequate, and O'Connell, for one, lost no chance to claim that the Irish numbers were seriously underestimated.[49] His speeches make a mantra of Irish Catholic "millions," their precise number vague and fluctuating – sometimes "five millions," sometimes "seven millions" – but always burgeoning and rapidly augmenting. Repeatedly, he hammered home that these "millions" constituted "a strength and an energy daily increasing, and hourly appreciating [its] own importance."[50] The point was not lost on the British press. By 1809 the *Edinburgh Review* was warning that "Catholic strength and wealth, it must be remembered, increases eightfold in proportion to that of the Protestants."[51] But it was not until the 1820s that the population-fact fully emerged as the menacing horizon of political discourse, as Ireland began to loom up (in a common image of the time) "like some giant figure, rising and expanding in the mist," threatening to topple the Union of which Ireland was becoming an ever more recalcitrant member.[52]

Francis Jeffrey sounds the note in his 1827 review of O'Driscol's *History of Ireland*. Unsettled by the "marvellous multiplication" of the Irish population, Jeffrey fears this "great body" will erect an Irish Catholic Republic at the very first opportunity: "the great body of the nation [will] rise in final and implacable hostility, and endeavour ... to erect itself into an independent state" (435, 439). Given the close proximity of Ireland to Britain, he finds the prospect of such a republic impossible to contemplate. The two nations, he claims, have now reached a point of stark decision: they "*must* either mingle into one – or desolate each other in fierce and exterminating hostility" (439). Since mingling is the preferred liberal alternative, Jeffrey mounts an argument for a renovated Union, but he concludes on a note of warning. "Things are fast verging to a crisis," he writes, "and cannot, in all probability, remain long as they are. The Union, in short, must either be made *equal* and *complete* on the part of England – or it will be broken in pieces and thrown in her face by Ireland" (442). The demographic dynamic thus brought with it the possibility of a reversal of the lines of force ("thrown into her face by Ireland"), as the sheer mass of Irish bodies rather than, as in the civic tour and early national tale, their sentimental potential came to lend traction to the arguments of reason. In a telling fictional moment in John Banim's *The Anglo-Irish of the Nineteenth Century*, the English-centered protagonist proposes a restoration of the anti-Catholic penal laws. "How will you stop us?" he asks the nationalist Anglo-Irish squire with whom he is debating. His interlocutor simply repeats the same words but reverses their trajectory: "HOW WILL YOU STOP US?"[53]

Population was at once Ireland's weakness and the power that gave it leverage. To English eyes the rapid rate of Irish reproduction placed the nation in a kind of surreal speeded-up natural time, a strangely accelerated temporality (rather like that of revolution) which allowed a nation outside productive modern time to press in on modern institutions and modern ways of being. All sides agreed that repetition rather than development was the structure of historical time in Ireland, although they drew different conclusions from this. When crossed with the multiplication of reproduction, however, the time of repetition (no matter its specific political inflection) received a new charge. To mesh the ever-filling space of the present with not only past but future time was to transform repetition into insistence. Reproduction spread itself out in space – the proverbial teeming landscapes of the Irish countryside – but it also stretched out in time, attaching the pressures of geography to those of history to form a new spatio-temporal figure of foreshortened proximity. Witness the "giant figure" that looms up in the *Edinburgh Review*. In this way, the repetitive temporality of Ireland's "monotonous round of agony" began to assume palpability and to appear less as futile monotone than as ever-present volatility in the space of the now. This is not to deny the way in which assimilation of Irish historical events to models of recurrence in this period served to dilute and stabilize dissonant energies, relegating them to epiphenomena of the Eternal Same. But it is to say that, even so, the time of repetition in the 1820s was a revved-up time and one very close at hand. Joined with the spatial figure of population, the repetitive form of Irish history began to bear down on the English present with a new weight.

Nor were Irish bodies simply a formidable mass "over there"; increasingly, they seemed a a fluid mass spilling over into "here." For manual workers in British cities with large concentrations of Irish immigrants, the Irish were unwanted competition in tight labour markets, and they fiercely petitioned against the granting of Catholic relief.[54] Further up the social scale elite periodicals displayed their own alarm at what the *Quarterly Review* called "the hordes of Irish emigrants who infest every district of this country."[55] Testifying to the whole sense of being impinged on by Irish affairs and bodies, *Blackwood's Magazine* (vehemently opposed to emancipation) not only printed a series of five articles on "Ireland As It Is: In 1828" but explained its decision by declaring: "at this time when the agitations of Ireland attract so much of public notice – when the Irish themselves threaten to overwhelm us by their power, while the Emigration Committee tremble lest they should overwhelm us with their poverty – we have resolved to write a short series of papers."[56] These papers were the product of William Johnston, an Anglo-Irish barrister living in London and employed in 1828 as secretary to Lord Lowther, member of Wellington's ministry and opponent of emancipation.[57] An ultra Tory who wrote extensively on Ireland for *Blackwood's* in 1828–29, Johnston offers a predictable line in his articles, arguing that the material condition of Ireland has been improving but that the pernicious politics of the Catholic Association and its allies, the "Popish priests," threaten to enslave the people and explode the empire. Any appearance of tranquility is deceptive and temporary, he warns, "a smothering of the flame which must soon burst out anew, with increased violence, unless the Catholic Association, which supplies the material of the fire, be crushed utterly, and at once."[58]

What makes these articles nonetheless striking is their vivid sense of the way in which Irish bodies ("mere animal force"[59]) encroach on English space and English politics: they swarm, threaten invasion, attack the Constitution. Johnston's is a scenario of besiegement and revulsion that anticipates, although it does not reach, the racial hysteria of the 1840s when Carlyle denounced the "hordes of hungry white savages" invading England and undermining its order.[60] Especially disturbing to his mind is the contamination of public words by the force of bodies – indeed their explicit linkage – in the new political sphere being carved out by the Catholic Association. Reserving his fiercest attack for the Association, he denounces it as "one of the greatest public nuisances that ever was permitted to exist under a regularly established government," and he execrates in particular "the Association orators," who charge their words with the "physical force which they have at command" and are themselves barely able to control "the whirlwind of wild and disaffected spirit" they have raised.[61] With his scornful reiteration of the word "orators," Johnston registers the way in which the Irish emancipation campaign, notably the figure of O'Connell, was widely seen as importing into the British political scene a suspect pre-modern oral model of public speaking that at the same time exploited modern political resources of print and publication. Refusing distance and infusing the impersonal print-ideal with the "noise" of personality and embodied speech, this hybrid model moved across generic lines and boundaries, slipping between indoors and out-of-doors, popular and print culture, statistical account, and comic anecdote to confound conventional lines of authoritative speech.

As Steven Goldsmith has pointed out, English agitation too had been bound up with "an ideal of dynamic discourse (literally, running to and fro)" since the seventeenth century,[62] and this tradition shaped figures in the period as obscure as Blake (Goldsmith's own subject) and as notorious as William Cobbett, whose polemical *A History of the Protestant Reformation in England and Ireland* (1824), incidentally, played a significant role in the agitation for emancipation on British soil. But O'Connell's oratorical words carried with them the very real potential for an immediate rupture of the Union in a way that those of others did not. If in the end it was the menacing potential of poised masses that gave purchase to those words, what made O'Connell disconcerting for public discourse in the first place was that he openly and deliberately exposed public words to the destabilizing powers of contingency and matter at a time when influential forms of both political and literary thought were attempting to secure language to more permanent and abstract forms.

William Hazlitt's 1820 essay "On the Difference Between Writing and Speaking" is a classic instance, relevant not least because it features as a centerpiece the mocking portrait of "flashy, powerful demagogue."[63] As Lucy Newlyn has pointed out, Hazlitt had an ambivalent response to orality, which itself functioned importantly as a class and political marker in the ongoing period debate over literary audience.[64] But in this essay

Hazlitt puts the case starkly: the two forms of articulation, writing and speaking, are not only incommensurate but diametrically opposed. In particular, they operate in contrasting temporalities: where writing takes time and lives in the postponed moment, speaking lives in the immediate now. From this it follows that a speaker's language is directed by the moment and to those in the same moment. "The habit of speaking is the habit of being heard, and of wanting to be heard," writes Hazlitt. He takes as paradigm "the orator," whose social and situation-dependent words are governed by the desires of the audience: "The orator sees his subject in the eager looks of his auditors" (XII: 274). By contrast, the writer, removed from face-to-face contact with an audience, is a solitary being whose language is shaped by commitment to the "sacred cause of truth." Thoughtful, deep, and original, the writer is an autonomous creature who lives outside the "glow" of sympathy on which the orator depends: "the habit of writing is the habit of thinking aloud, but without the help of an echo" (XII: 274).

The words of each reside in the body but in significantly different dimensions. Where oratorical words spill out of the orifices, writerly words (or, as Hazlitt calls them, "authorial" words) inhabit recesses of symbolic and not simply physical value, recesses from which they must be extracted with some difficulty. Authorial words, he states, do "not lie at the orifices of the mouth ready for delivery, but [are] wrapped in the folds of the heart and registered in the chambers of the brain" (XII: 279). Despite their own deep interiority and the characteristically inward turn of authors, however, these writerly words end up purged both of lowly corporeality and of individual personality as they become text. "The *personal* is to him an impertinence," Hazlitt asserts in speaking of a "true" author, "so he conceals himself and writes" (XII: 279). For Hazlitt, as for many others thinking these questions in the period, the truth of words was a function of their distance and detachment from persons.[65] On this reading, the personal necessarily appeared "an impertinence," at once an irrelevance and an offensive reduction. To identify authorial words with the contingent being and site of their production was to deny them the power and respect pertaining to universals and generalities, and this meant denying them the continuously productive and independent cultural power central to Romantic aesthetics.

So when it comes to charismatic speech – the emphatically personal and embodied speech of an orator – Hazlitt goes into rhetorical overdrive in a representation of the "flashy, powerful demagogue" as a creature "infuriated with the patriotic *mania*," heaving and writhing and swelling as he manipulates "the fierce democracy." Like a Lady Morgan in the hands of the reviewers (including Hazlitt himself[66]), the orator proves but a shallow imitation of proper authorship. When his words are translated into text ("printed speeches"), the whole performance collapses, revealing itself as but the product of gesticulation and far outside the meaningfulness of signification: "The orator's vehemence of gesture, the loudness of the voice, the speaking eye, the conscious attitude, the inexplicable dumb show and noise . . . are no longer there, and without these he is nothing" (XII: 265). Insistence on the "nothing" of the orator salvages the "something" of the author, and to secure authority for the latter Hazlitt launches a distinction (fuzzy and wishful enough) between superficial personal "manner" and profound impersonal "matter."

From their very different political positions, then, a radical like Hazlitt and an ultra like Johnston turn decisively away from public words attached to bodies, reflecting a general period suspicion of scenes of immediacy and enunciation in the post-revolutionary political sphere, when "orators" and "mobs" tended to imply one another in discomfiting scenarios of (recently remembered) reciprocity. Backed as he was by the Irish "millions," a figure like O'Connell clearly – and deliberately – played into such a scenario, and part of the fascination he generated throughout Europe at this time has to do with that fact. But what made him spooky to British (including Irish) contemporaries was the way in which he wielded his unmodern power (oratorical words, "wild" Irish bodies) in the very modern modalities of discipline and order to bring a newly effective national body onto the serious political stage. If it is a commonplace that the "teeming landscapes of Ireland . . . [were] ultimately the essential reason for the capitulation on Emancipation in 1829,"[67] those landscapes would have exerted little pressure had they remained simply "teeming." The crucial lever was their organization, parish by parish, through the collection of the Catholic Rent established by the Catholic Association. When O'Connell proposed this "penny rent" in 1824, his aim was not just to generate funds to finance a broader and more intense emancipation campaign but to lend national authority to what had hitherto been a campaign run by middle-class committees from Dublin. Such a rent, he argued before the Association, would show the people of England "that Catholic millions felt a deep interest in the cause, and that it was not confined, as is supposed, to those styled 'agitators.'"[68] The point was not lost on the former Irish secretary Robert Peel, who, as Oliver MacDonagh notes, very quickly recognized that the danger posed by the rent did not lie in the war chest it might build up but in the network it would establish in the process: "the organization by means of which it is raised may be very formidable."[69]

And so it proved. Over and over again contemporaries testify to the extraordinary sense of concentration and of controlled power in the huge O'Connellite crowds. Peel, once again, provides a suggestive articulation, writing to Walter Scott in April 1829: "We were watching the movement of tens of thousands of disciplined fanatics, abstaining from every excess and every indulgence, and concentrating every passion and feeling on one single object."[70] What clearly disturbed Peel was that this was no "raging mob" but the manifestation of a new, properly political authority in Ireland, one that superseded the government on its own ground. As Lecky long ago pointed out, O'Connell won his victory in 1829 not by increasing the number of advocates for emancipation but by "creating another system of government in Ireland, which overawed all opponents."[71] And the prospect of an effective rival system on Irish ground chilled not only long-standing Tory opponents like Peel. A former ally like Morgan soon found herself equally appalled. Watching an O'Connellite crowd in January 1831, she writes in some dread to her old friend Tom Moore: "Imagine countless thousands of the lower classes pouring through the streets, silent, concentrated, *worked* by a nod, a sign; and this, the day after a proclamation from the government forbidding *all* meetings."[72] It is a striking image: the uncanny materialization of a secret counter-order ("*worked* by a nod, a sign") so sure of itself that it now moves, a unitary body, into the public square from which it has been expressly barred.[73]

Behind Morgan's alarm lay not only an immediate fear of lower-class revolution but a longer term apprehension that in such a crowd there was no room for ambiguous and interstitial figures such as "Lady Morgan." Flushed with the success of the emancipation drive in early 1829, she had joked about attending a party of "the *débris* of the ascendancy faction," where "the Orange ladies all looked *blue*, and their husbands tried to look green."[74] By 1831, however, she was coming to realize that she might be part of that *débris* herself. For an Anglo-Irish figure like Morgan, the Connellite mobilization represented a crucial and negative modulation in national politics, one that she understood very much in terms of what Žižek has described as the passage from "politics proper" to "policing." Žižek defines this passage as the shift from a claim made by the excluded on the universalist ground of "the people" to a claim based on the more restricted and nationalist notion of "one people" or "a people." In the turn to the latter, he argues, "the momentary authentic political opening" effected by the former begins to close down.[75] While the Anglo-Irish national tale established by Morgan is a long way from the kind of radical political opening a Žižek envisions, its necessarily equivocal relation to the models of national belonging and national history being established in the period meant it operated in an interspace outside strict national identification. Such an interspace allowed both for the imagining of different constructions of the nation and for the indeterminacy of the case. But the increasingly confident discourse of nationalism released by the Catholic agitation of the late 1820s demanded identity and decision, and under its pressure the national tale was turned back on itself and dissolved. The key figure here is John Banim to whose *The Anglo-Irish of the Nineteenth Century* I want to turn by way of conclusion.

UNDOING THE NATIONAL TALE

Published anonymously in the latter stages of O'Connell's emancipation campaign, *The Anglo-Irish of the Nineteenth Century: A Novel* (1828) rewrites the national tale as a refusal of the very cultural category that had enabled the genre: the hyphenated Anglo-Irish. Working out of the standard travel-and-education plot established by Morgan and Edgeworth, the novel focuses on a young Anglo-Irish aristocrat named Gerald Blount, who has been raised in England where he has not only learned to despise the Irish and identify himself with the English but also become convinced that anglicization is the proper course for Ireland as a whole as well. In volume II, this figure inadvertently "falls" into the country itself thanks to a shipwreck, and there he undergoes a series of encounters with, among others, sleazy Ascendancy types, half-threatening Rockite rebels, patriot Protestant landlords, and (not least) a trio of capricious Morganesque heroines.[76] A fundamental change of mind ensues, confirmed by the conventional marriage with a woman committed to living in and for Ireland. Banim, however, is not much interested in tracing this familiar plot of political *Bildung*;[77] what primarily attracts him to the national tale is the opportunity it offers to constitute the Anglo-Irish themselves as a quasi-anthropological object of study. The very title of the text points less to a fiction – indeed the subtitle has to clarify this status ("A Novel") – than to an ethnographic analysis, so that its narrator occupies the position of an enlightened modern eye surveying a peculiar culture ("the Anglo-Irish"). This Ascendancy culture thus becomes aligned with those archaic societies such as "the native Irish" typically featured in proto-anthropological discourses of the period. In biting scene after biting scene, the "curious" manners and mores of this group are displayed and their "superstitions" exposed, as in the puncturing of Ascendancy fears of lower-class Irish militancy when guests at a Dublin dinner party fall into a panic at the sound of "clashing" in the street, a sound that proves to be the product of "mockery" by a crowd of mischievous ragged boys who deliberately set in motion some noisy cans and kettles in order to excite the anxieties of the gentry (II: 272–89).

From its opening pages, which consist of a lengthy debate on Ireland, the novel takes a predominantly analytic shape, assuming the form of both a problem (the question of Ireland) and a case study (the case of the Anglo-Irish as part of that problem). Its pages are crammed with discussion, argument, and disputation, including several scenes of debate on Irish matters set in England, along with an extended representation of a heated contest between Daniel O'Connell and Richard Lalor Sheil in Dublin on the tactics of Catholic petitioning. Narrative itself is highly attenuated, almost an afterthought, as Banim pursues the Connellite argument for a Catholic Ireland "free and national" (III: 132). Importantly, this is no longer an Ireland characterized primarily as a negative site of grievances to be redressed (such redress, presumably, then bringing it into the fullness of the United Kingdom) but an Ireland that understands itself as a positive entity and seeks, in the words of a nationalist Protestant landlord, "to work out its own resources" (III: 121). "Since we plainly see that Ireland *cannot* be made English," the same character asserts, "suppose we just allow her to make herself what she is every day becoming in spite of us – Irish?" (III: 120). Calling on the population-fact, he stresses that the "real people" of Ireland, as opposed to the "sojourning strangers" in the land, now have the numbers "to form a great nation"; moreover, he adds, in an allusion to the failed project of the United Irishmen, these numbers are now consolidated into a fully united body: "they are at last united, firm; . . . united by a riveting of every link of the social chain; united in religion, – or at least their fellow-countrymen who join them *in purpose*, care nothing for the difference, – and above all, Sir, they are – United Irish" (III: 121). In the hands of this body lies the future, and those Anglo-Irish who resist identification with it may go or stay as they please, for their actions no longer matter: "They have spurned every opportunity of getting on along with the Irish people . . . and now the Irish people will get on without them; ay, and worse than that; shake them off, and leave them behind on the course" (III: 124).

Unusual as is such blunt argument in British fiction of the period, the innovative force of Banim's text lies not so much in direct discourse of this kind than in the way that its nationalist commitment to a unified national body pushes it toward a psycho-ethnographic anatomy of a collective cultural psyche. In Banim's reading, the Anglo-Irish live out a pathological condition, trapped in a derelict psyche whose only rescue from absolute disintegration is abandonment of the hyphen that distinguishes it. "What a name you've all got!" exclaims an English friend of the hero, "English-Irish, or Anglo-Irish; why you make yourselves out nothing at all" (III: 3). Lacking the anchor of a single name, these hyphenated beings drift in profound unconnection around the places they inhabit, at once spurned by the country of original ancestry – "detached and forgotten brethren among the bogs and fastnesses of another country," as Banim puts it in prefatory remarks to *The Boyne Water*[78] – even as they themselves spurn their Irish duties and roots. Thus doubly derelict, the Anglo-Irish gentry are permanently dislocated, and the novel presents them very much as emigrés in both England and Ireland. In England, for example, they revolve in their own circle, as do the Anglo-Irish students at Cambridge with whom Gerald Blount associates, flinching from the contamination of "Irish uproar" in immigrant neighbourhoods but unable to stop talking about the shameful land they repudiate. In a real sense, however, they are emigrés from nowhere; hence the great play with name and title and identity in the novel, where all three slide about in bewildering fashion.[79] Theirs is a radically destabilized subjectivity, or, more accurately, a personality so destabilized that it can hardly be said to constitute a subjectivity at all.

Through relentless pressure on and disorientation of his hero, Banim subjects this personality to a demand for location. In a way reminiscent of Morgan, he articulates this demand most tellingly in a scene of aggressive feminine speaking. Shortly before the journey that unexpectedly lands him in Ireland, Gerald encounters an unknown young woman, apparently French, in a cemetery in Paris. "You are quite English, of course, Sir?" the woman assumes. "Not quite," he replies. She then runs through various possibilities of national allegiance, and when she comes to "Irlandois," he offers the same reply: "Nor quite Irish, either." This reply triggers an outburst:

> 'What! neither Dutch, German, Italian, Spanish, Scotch, nor yet English-quite, nor Irish-quite? Have you a country at all, Sir? . . . or, perhaps, since you are not English-*quite*, nor Irish-*quite* . . . perhaps we must call you by that doubtful title which people who *have* a country laugh at – you are English-Irish, Sir?" (II: 22–23)

When Gerald confirms that this "doubtful title" is indeed his preferred identification, she immediately brings to bear the language of the claim: "The title gives you no claim to one country or the other; and every man ought to claim one country to stand by against all the world" (II: 23–24). Her eliding of national and gender identity ("every man ought to claim one country") foregrounds the degree to which the model of nationality as a "claim" seeks to implicate it in the body, to render it inherent and quasi-biological, not (as Gerald himself would have it) simply an "accidental tie" or a matter of personal choice.

The skewed gender relations in the text signal confused national identities. Gerald's narrative in particular makes the point that to remain in the hyphen is to operate outside the stabilizing parameters of possession, claim, and action proper to masculinity: one must "*have*" a country, and assert its claim against all others. To live in the ambiguity and equivocation of the "not quite" is to lose the clarity and vitality that give men purchase in the world, so it is entirely fitting that when Gerald lands in Ireland, he finds himself carried about by women and repeatedly placed in situations that bewilder and disorient his powers of perception and interpretation. "Am I under some nervous delusion?" he wonders at one point, "or is there a duplicate face of every face in the world?" (III: 152). Ever more ready to jettison the hyphen, by the end of the novel he is poised to adopt the simplicity and singularity of becoming "mere Irish." Banim thus radicalizes the critique of Anglo-Irish irresponsibility and sleaziness that had been part of the national tale from the beginning, taking as his target not typical figures within the denomination (e.g., the absentee landlord, the corrupt Ascendancy toady) but the very denomination itself. Presenting the Anglo-Irish as an anachronism in the modern Connellite nation wherein lies the Irish future, he sets out to bring them within the new national union, a union only tenuously and ambivalently located within the larger Union that O'Connell himself would soon seek to repudiate. As he does so he directs the national tale out of the unhomely space of the hyphen into the homely space of identification, moving into the center terms of belonging ("native," "real," "home"), which begin to replace those of mediation. But the very obsessiveness of the play with national nomenclature in the text – "half Irish," "mere Irish," "English-Irish," "purely English," and so on – bespeaks an anxiety about the determination of national identification in the uneven and divisive terrain of the United Kingdom.[80] The hyphen of Anglo-Irish, as Eagleton reminds us, had always been a peculiarly indeterminate sign: "In the end, it is a question of whether the hyphen of 'Anglo-Irish' is bridge or impasse, linkage or sign of contradiction – an enabling passage between terms or an aporia."[81] To forestall such questions and stabilize the concept of the nation Banim sought to banish it altogether.

The implications of this gesture were not lost on Sydney Morgan. In an address "To the Reader" prefacing a book of essays titled *The Book of the Boudoir* in 1829, Morgan considered her role as Irish writer after the passage of the Catholic Relief Bill for which she had so long campaigned. She presents herself as surrendering with a certain relief the role of national author, which she now characterizes as having meant an uncongenial exercise of bitterness and sarcasm for one of her own cheerful temperament. At the same time she fears (not entirely seriously), that she will now be reduced to writing books for boudoirs like this one or albums for ladies' drawing rooms. What she sensed, rightly enough, was that "[a]mong the multitudinous effects of catholic emancipation, I do not hesitate to predict a change in the character of Irish authorship."[82] The extent of that change escaped her purview, much as full recognition of the implications of Irish claim eluded her understanding, but she knew well enough that the conjunction of politics and fiction that had sanctioned her own form of female civic authorship was the function of a very specific historical contingency. When she looked back on the period that witnessed the emergence of the national tale forty years after the publication of *The Wild Irish Girl*, she observed that in certain epochs "*nationality*, both as principle and a watchword, does good service. Such was the epoch when the Wild Irish Girl was written, and the Irish melodies were sung; but that time is past."[83] Morgan was engaging in some special pleading at this point, justifying her removal from Dublin to London, but at the same time she was also registering an insight into the obsolescence of cultural forms.

She wrote these words in 1846 as she prepared a revised edition of her landmark novel for Colburn's Standard Novels, an edition whose title page interestingly identifies it as "*The Wild Irish Girl.* By Sydney Owenson. Edited by Lady Morgan." Even as it conveniently distances her from the embarrassing effusions of her younger self, the divided signature attests to her persistent wariness of unitary bodies and single names. Rereading the enthusiasm of Owenson through the skeptical lens of Morgan, she exploits the slippage of female names sanctioned by the gender code to remain within a hyphenated space governed by models of interaction rather than convergence. But her own national tale was now a curiosity, even to herself, its energies having modulated in different ways into the cultural nationalism of a Young Ireland on the one hand and a less prominent feminist "undercurrent" of fiction and history on the other. On the stage of public discourse the Irish – and Daniel O'Connell – continued to agitate, and the English continued to be agitated. But by the 1840s discursive authority had decisively shifted from the late-Enlightenment liberalism underpinning the national tale, and Irish enunciation was moving to new locations, leaving behind even the celebrated Agitator himself. One case had closed, and another (as is the way with cases) had begun. At the same time the moment of civic and discursive opening represented by the "incomplete union" of Great Britain and Ireland in the early decades of the nineteenth century continued to reverberate in important ways for the rest of the century.

As a crucial fault line within the newly created compound of the United Kingdom, the problem of Ireland in Romantic-era Britain points not only to the inescapably unsettled nature of British public discourse in the period but also to the way in which that discourse pivoted less on the glamor of antimony (the Other, the sublime) than on the more mundane frictions of discomfort and agitation. Disordering the metropolitan discursive field, the persistent irritant that was the Irish question operated at the level of subsurface, that level of culture, discourse, and consciousness where the separations that mark what lies "above" and what lies "below" mingle and become permeable. To return this question to the matrix of British Romanticism is thus to bring into sharper view the workings of this often overlooked stratum in cultural formation and to argue, more generally, for the historical agency and productive value of the indistinct and the indeterminate within the discursive negotiations of civic culture in the period.

Notes

INTRODUCTION: THE AWKWARD SPACE OF UNION

1 Benedict Anderson, *Imagined Communities: Reflections on the Origin and Spread of Nationalism*, rev. edn. (London: Verso, 1991).
2 Clifford Siskin, *The Work of Writing: Literature and Social Change in Britain 1700–1830* (Baltimore: Johns Hopkins University Press, 1998), 85–86. Leith Davis has shown how even within the relatively more stable unit of Great Britain, the union of Scotland and England was a continuing site of discursive contestation throughout the eighteenth and early nineteenth centuries, *Acts of Union: Scotland and the Literary Negotiation of the British Nation 1707–1830* (Stanford: Stanford University Press, 1998).
3 See, for example, the readings of Ireland as England's unconscious in Terry Eagleton, *Heathcliff and the Great Hunger: Studies in Irish Culture* (London: Verso, 1995) and Declan Kiberd, *Inventing Ireland: The Literature of the Modern Nation* (Cambridge, Mass.: Harvard University Press, 1995). Eagleton also has some suggestive pages on the Union as "replete with ironies, paradoxes, backfirings, unintended effects" (136), but he regards it as finally a merely constitutional matter remote from the realities of colonial power in Ireland.
4 Paul Magnuson, *Reading Public Romanticism* (Princeton: Princeton University Press, 1998). On the public sphere, see the classic text by Jürgen Habermas, *The Structural Transformation of the Public Sphere*, trans. Thomas Burger (Cambridge, Mass.: MIT Press, 1989).
5 Katie Trumpener, *Bardic Nationalism: The Romantic Novel and the British Empire* (Princeton: Princeton University Press, 1997).
6 Mary Jean Corbett, *Allegories of Union in Irish and English Writing, 1790–1870* (Cambridge: Cambridge University Press, 2000). Corbett's is one of the few studies to direct attention to Ireland as part of a problematic United Kingdom.
7 Lord George Gordon Byron, "Roman Catholic Claims Speech," *The Complete Miscellaneous Prose*, ed. Andrew Nicholson (Oxford: Clarendon Press, 1991), 41.
8 Opinions changed so radically and quickly that within five years, for example, the powerful Ascendancy figure of John Foster, one of the most vociferous antagonists of the Union, had become a firm supporter; meanwhile William Pitt, English architect of the Union, who resigned in 1801 over the king's adamant refusal of any Catholic relief, returned to office in 1804 a

determined opponent, speaking against the Catholic petition introduced by Henry Grattan in the House of Commons in 1805.

On the political history of the Union, see the series of articles by S. J. Connolly in *A New History of Ireland*, vol. v: *Ireland Under the Union, I (1801–70)*, ed. W. E. Vaughan (Oxford: Clarendon Press, 1989). See also Thomas Bartlett, *The Fall and Rise of the Irish Nation: The Catholic Question 1690–1830* (Dublin: Gill and Macmillan, 1992); G. C. Bolton, *The Passing of the Irish Act of Union: A Study in Parliamentary Politics* (London and Oxford: Oxford University Press, 1966); W. J. McCormack, *The Pamphlet Debate on the Union Between Great Britain and Ireland, 1797–1800* (Dublin: Irish Academic Press, 1996); Oliver MacDonagh, *Ireland: The Union and its Aftermath*, rev. edn. (London: Allen & Unwin, 1977).

9 Kevin Whelan, *The Tree of Liberty: Radicalism, Catholicism and the Construction of Irish Identity 1760–1830* (Notre Dame: University of Notre Dame Press, 1996), 129.

10 On the French connection (which was crucial to English readings of Ireland in this period), see Marianne Elliott, *Partners in Revolution: The United Irishmen and France* (New Haven: Yale University Press, 1982).

11 Coleridge, *The Morning Post* (15 Jan. 1800, 22 Jan. 1800), *The Collected Works of Samuel Taylor Coleridge*, vol. III, pt. 1 *Essays on His Times in The Morning Post and The Courier, I*, ed. David V. Erdman (Princeton: Princeton University Press, 1978), 107, 120.

12 See Joep Leerssen, *Remembrance and Imagination: Patterns in the Historical and Literary Representation of Ireland in the Nineteenth Century* (Notre Dame: University of Notre Dame Press, 1997), chap. 1.

13 John Banim, *The Anglo-Irish of the Nineteenth Century: A Novel*, 3 vols. (London, 1828), II: 101.

14 Coleridge, *Essays on His Times*, 121. By 1814, Coleridge's tone on Irish matters had taken on a more decidedly sectarian edge (e.g., "To Mr. Justice Fletcher," *The Courier*, 6 Dec. 1814, rpt. in *Essays on His Times, II*, vol. III, pt. 2 404–09). The alteration testifies as much to the rapidly altering meanings of Ireland and Union in the period as it does to Coleridge's own developing conservatism.

15 Bartlett, *Fall and Rise*, 261.

16 On how political power is founded in the binding together of people through promises and mutual pledges, see Hannah Arendt, *On Revolution* (New York: Penguin, 1965).

17 Francis Jeffrey, "Pamphlets on the Catholic Question," *Edinburgh Review* 11 (Oct. 1807): 125.

18 Sydney Smith, "Parnell's *History of Irish Popery Laws*," *Edinburgh Review* 13 (Oct. 1808): 77.

19 "Newenham's *View of the Circumstances of Ireland*," *Monthly Review* 68 (May 1812): 195. For an example of high official interest, see Lord Grenville's *Letter from the Right Honourable Lord Grenville to the Earl of Fingall* (London, 1810).

20 James MacIntosh "Wakefield's *Ireland*," *Edinburgh Review* 20 (Nov. 1812): 363.

21 In a related but more general argument about the importance of political process, Slavoj Žižek has recently identified the "metaphoric elevation" of an excluded part into the sign of the whole as the definitive move of "politics proper," "A Leftist Plea for 'Eurocentrism'," *Critical Inquiry* 24 (Summer 1998): 988–1009.
22 Jeffrey, "Pamphlets on the Catholic Question," 125.
23 Tadhg Foley and Seán Ryder (eds.), *Ideology and Ireland in the Nineteenth Century* (Dublin: Four Courts Press, 1998), 7. Michael McKeon similarly observes that Ireland made it difficult to sustain the pastoral discourse of imperial Britain in "The Pastoral Revolution," in *Refiguring Revolutions: Aesthetics and Politics From the English Revolution to the Romantic Revolution*, ed. Kevin Sharpe and Steven N. Zwicker (Berkeley: University of California Press, 1998), 286.
24 Bourdieu's entire analytic effort is animated by this assumption, but see in particular pt. 1 of *In Other Words: Essays Towards a Reflexive Sociology*, trans. Matthew Adamson (Stanford: Stanford University Press, 1990). I take my epigraph from p. 54 of this text.
25 *An Address, to the Irish People*, *The Complete Works of Percy Bysshe Shelley*, ed. Roger Ingpen and Walter E. Peck, 10 vols. (New York: Gordian Press, 1965), v: 232, 229. Richard Holmes argues that this non-violent Godwinian rhetoric contends in the pamphlet with a more violent dream of global revolution, *Shelley: The Pursuit* (London: Penguin, 1987), 120–21.
26 Shelley, *Address*, 246.
27 In relation to this second pamphlet, Kenneth Neill Cameron comments: "After actual contact with the Irish situation, his understanding of its essential issues and needs had sharpened," *The Young Shelley: Genesis of a Radical* (New York: Macmillan, 1950), 147–48.
28 *The Letters of Percy Bysshe Shelley*, 2 vols., ed. Frederick I. Jones (Oxford: Clarendon Press, 1964), I: 268.
29 In a letter to Elizabeth Hitchener on 26 January 1812, Shelley wrote: "I have been busily engaged in an address to the Irish, which will be printed as Paine's works were, and pasted on the walls of Dublin," *Letters* I: 238–39.
30 Mikhail Bakhtin, "The Problem of Speech Genres," *Speech Genres & Other Late Essays*, trans. Vern W. McGee; ed. Caryl Emerson and Michael Holquist (Austin: University of Texas Press, 1986), 91, 95.
31 Magnuson, *Public Romanticism*, 37.
32 As Wolfgang Iser notes, the concept of representation is so closely identified in our critical thinking with mimesis that its performative sense has been largely overlooked. His own emphasis falls on the Aristotelian notion of representation as the performance of a potential rather than on the speech-act sense I am activating. See "Representation: A Performative Act" in *The Aims of Representation: Subject/Text/History*, ed. Murray Kreiger (New York: Columbia University Press, 1987), 217–32.
33 Maurice Merleau-Ponty, "The Spectre of a Pure Language," *The Prose of the World*, trans. John O'Neil; ed. Claude Lefort (Evanston: Northwestern University Press, 1973), 3.

34 The most extensive and complex discussion of the national tale appears in Trumpener's *Bardic Nationalism*, chap. 3. Suggestive commentary is also included in Miranda J. Burgess, *British Fiction and the Production of Social Order 1740–1830* (Cambridge: Cambridge University Press, 2000), chap. 4; Gary Kelly, *Women, Writing, and Revolution, 1790–1827* (Oxford: Clarendon Press, 1993), chap. 5; and Nicola Watson, *Revolution and the Form of the British Novel, 1790–1825: Intercepted Letters, Interrupted Seductions* (Oxford: Clarendon Press, 1994), chap. 3.

35 Spearheaded by Marilyn Butler's landmark *Maria Edgeworth: A Literary Biography* (Oxford: Clarendon Press, 1972), the revival of critical interest in Edgeworth has produced not only monographs and articles but a new 12-volume collected edition, *The Works of Maria Edgeworth*, ed. Marilyn Butler and Mitzi Myers (London: Pickering and Chatto,1999/2000). On her Irish writing in particular, see Corbett, *Allegories of Union*, chaps. 1 and 2; Butler's Introduction to her edition of *Castle Rackrent and Ennui* (London: Penguin, 1992); Seamus Deane, *A Short History of Irish Literature* (Notre Dame: University of Notre Dame Press, 1986), chap. 4; Brian Hollingworth, *Maria Edgeworth's Irish Writing: Language, History, Politics* (New York: St. Martin's Press, 1999); Vera Kreilkamp, *The Anglo-Irish Novel and the Big House* (Syracuse: Syracuse University Press, 1998), chap. 2; and Mitzi Myers, "'Completing the Union': Critical *Ennui*, the Politics of Narrative, and the Reformation of Irish Cultural Identity," *Prose Studies* 18 (1995): 41–77, along with her "'Like the Pictures in a Magic Lantern': Gender, History, and Edgeworth's Rebellion Narratives," *Nineteenth-Century Contexts* 19 (1996): 373–412.

36 Terry Eagleton gives Morgan prominent and sympathetic space in *Heathcliff and the Great Hunger*, 177–87, as does Katie Trumpener in *Bardic Nationalism*, chap. 3. The first critical edition of *The Wild Irish Girl* has recently appeared, edited by Claire Connolly and Stephen Copley (London: Pickering and Chatto, 2000), as has a new edition of *The Missionary* edited by Julia Wright (Peterborough, Ont.: Broadview Press, 2002).

37 I discuss the latter point in *The Achievement of Literary Authority: Gender, History, and the Waverley Novels* (Ithaca: Cornell University Press, 1991), chap. 2.

38 See in particular Mellor, *Mothers of the Nation: Women's Political Writing in England, 1780–1830* (Bloomington and Indianapolis: Indiana University Press, 2000). The relative critical profiles of Edgeworth and Morgan are reflected in a recent collection of essays on *Women, Writing and the Public Sphere 1700–1830*, ed. Elizabeth Eger *et al.* (Cambridge: Cambridge University Press, 2001), which includes a discussion of Edgeworth but none on Morgan. The same situation obtains in an earlier collection on female authorship edited by Dale Spender, *Living By the Pen: Early British Women Writers* (New York: Teachers College Press, 1992).

39 Sir Walter Scott, "General Preface" (1829), *Waverley*, ed. Claire Lamont (Oxford: Oxford University Press, 1981), 352.

40 Sydney Morgan, Preface to *O'Donnel*, rev. edn. (London, 1835), viii.

41 For a development of this argument, see Chapter 2.

42 Pertinent to my argument is Homi K. Bhabha's influential revision of binary models of alterity through notions of ambivalence, hybridity, and in-betweenness; see in particular *The Location of Culture* (London and New York: Routledge, 1994).
43 Whelan, *Tree of Liberty*, 35.
44 Patrick J. O'Farrell, *Ireland's English Question: Anglo-Irish Relations 1534–1970* (London: B. T. Batsford, 1971), 17.
45 Charles Robert Maturin, *The Wild Irish Boy* (London, 1808), v.
46 John Banim, *The Boyne Water, A Tale, By the O'Hara Family* (London: 1826), xxiv.
47 Michel de Certeau, "Conclusion: Spaces and Practices," *Culture in the Plural*, trans. Tom Conley; ed. Luce Giard (Minneapolis: University of Minnesota Press, 1997), 145.

1 CIVIC TRAVELS: THE IRISH TOUR AND THE NEW UNITED KINGDOM

1 John Carr, *The Stranger in Ireland* (London, 1806), 2; James Hall, *Tour Through Ireland; Particularly the Interior & Least Known Parts*, 2 vols. (London, 1813), 1: 153. Nineteenth-century Irish travels have recently become more accessible. See, for example, the following collections: Andrew Hadfield and John McVeagh (eds.), *Strangers To That Land: British Perceptions of Ireland From the Reformation to the Famine* (Gerrards Cross: Colin Smythe, 1994); John P. Harrington (ed.), *The English Traveller in Ireland: Accounts of Ireland and the Irish Through Five Centuries* (Dublin: Wolfhound Press, 1991); Glenn Hooper (ed.), *The Tourist's Gaze: Travellers to Ireland, 1800–2000* (Cork: Cork University Press, 2001). See also the earlier collection by Constantia Maxwell (ed.), *The Stranger in Ireland: From the Reign of Elizabeth to the Great Famine* (London: Cape, 1954).
2 Seamus Deane, "Virtue, Travel and the Enlightenment" in *Nations and Nationalisms: France, Britain, Ireland and the Eighteenth-Century Context*, ed. Michael O'Dea and Kevin Whelan (Oxford: Voltaire Foundation, 1995), 283.
3 W. J. McCormack stresses that the very obsession with "incomplete union" points to the general investment of the Romantic period in notions of completion and wholeness, *Ascendancy and Tradition in Anglo-Irish Literary History from 1789 to 1939* (Oxford: Clarendon Press, 1985).
4 Joep Leerssen rightly argues that Irish travel writing, which emerged as an English genre, remained one well into this period. See *Mere Irish & Fíor-Ghael: Studies in the Idea of Irish Nationality, its Development and Literary Expression Prior to the Nineteenth Century* (Amsterdam: John Benjamins Publishing Company, 1986), 83–84.
5 The civic role of the tour is underlined by William Shaw Mason's inclusion of "Tourists" as a separate category in the bibliography of works on Ireland he began to compile for Robert Peel during the latter's tenure as chief secretary to Ireland (1812–19), *Bibliotheca Hibernicana: Or A Descriptive Catalogue of a Select*

Irish Library Collected For the Right Hon. Robert Peel (1823; rpt., Shannon: Irish University Press, 1970).

6 Carr, *Stranger*, 75.

7 [Maria and Richard Lovell Edgeworth], "Carr's *Stranger in Ireland*," *Edinburgh Review* 10 (Apr. 1807): 40. Marilyn Butler reprints much of this review as an appendix to her edition of Maria Edgeworth, *Castle Rackrent and Ennui* (London: Penguin, 1992). In a valuable overview of English images of nineteenth-century Ireland, Seamus Deane presents travels as part of a discourse of inspection and tourism, "The Production of Cultural Space in Irish Writing," *boundary 2* 21 (Fall 1994): 117–44. See also Glenn Hooper, who stresses travels and epistemological power, "Stranger in Ireland: The Problematics of the Post-Union Travelogue," *Mosaic* 28 (Mar. 1995): 25–47.

8 Leerssen, *Remembrance and Imagination*, 38.

9 J. C. Curwen, *Observations on the State of Ireland*, 2 vols. (London, 1818), I: vi.

10 Hall, *Tour Through Ireland*, II: 229.

11 *Ibid.*, 229–300.

12 *Ibid.*, 301. On the way in which the cultural began to be pitted against the economic in this period, see Seamus Deane, *Strange Country: Modernity and Nationhood in Irish Writing Since 1790* (Oxford: Clarendon Press, 1997). Deane understands the Union as largely a project to reconcile cultural and economic spheres.

13 Hall, *Tour Through Ireland*, II: 302.

14 Trumpener, *Bardic Nationalism*, chap. 1.

15 For a reading of the Union that stresses, by contrast, the degree to which it was perceived as a fresh start allowing for the construction of "a restorative narrative of Anglo-Irish cooperation," see Glenn Hooper, "Stranger in Ireland," 25–47.

16 Edward Wakefield, *An Account of Ireland, Statistical and Political*, 2 vols. (London, 1812), I: vii, vi.

17 [John Gough] *A Tour in Ireland. In 1813 & 1814*. By An Englishman (Dublin, 1817), 120. I will continue to refer to the author as Gough (a Quaker with a bookshop in Dublin) because the tour is generally listed under his name. But see C. J. Woods' argument that the author was more likely an obscure Englishman named John Alexander Staples, "The Authorship of *A Tour in Ireland in 1813 & 1814*," *Notes and Queries* 34 (1987): 481–82.

18 John Bernard Trotter, *Walks Through Ireland, in the Years 1812, 1814, and 1817* (London, 1819), 595.

19 *Ibid.*, 54.

20 Edgeworths, "Carr's *Stranger in Ireland*," 75.

21 Seamus Grimes (ed.), *Ireland in 1804* (Dublin: Four Courts Press, 1980), 47. Published by Richard Phillips (who also published Carr and *The Wild Irish Girl*), the tour originally appeared as a thirty-six-page pamphlet called *Journal of a Tour in Ireland &c. &c. performed in August 1804. With Remarks on the Character, Manners, and Customs of the Inhabitants* (London, 1806).

22 Hall, *Tour Through Ireland*, I: 54, 113; II: 17.

23 Curwen, *Observations*, II: 181.
24 Christopher Morash argues that after the great famine of midcentury, the disease metaphor became the more prominent motif. Although it features in early nineteenth-century discourse on Ireland as well, the favoured metaphors are those like "wound" or "distraction," which stress a temporary or occasional condition. See Morash, *Writing the Irish Famine* (Oxford: Clarendon Press, 1995).
25 Review of John Gamble's *A View of Society and Manners in the North of Ireland*, *Gentleman's Magazine* 89 (Jul. 1819): 51.
26 Anne Plumptre, *Narrative of a Residence in Ireland During the Summer of 1814, and That of 1815* (London, 1817), 310–13. In one of the few commentaries on Plumptre's tour, Glenn Hooper also makes a point of her unease at this juncture, "Anne Plumptre: An Independent Traveller," *Gender Perspectives in Nineteenth-Century Ireland*, ed. Margaret Kelleher and James H. Murphy (Dublin: Irish Academic Press, 1997), 129–39. For an overview of Plumptre's life and writings, see Deborah McLeod's introduction to Plumptre's novel, *Something New: Or, Adventures at Campbell-House* (Peterborough, Ont.: Broadview Press, 1996).
27 Harrington, *English Traveller*, 9.
28 *Narrative*, v. Plumptre had published *A Narrative of a Three Years' Residence in France, 1802–5* in 1810.
29 George Cooper, *Letters on the Irish Nation: Written During a Visit to That Kingdom in the Autumn of the Year 1799* (London, 1800), ix. Even a full generation after Union, Thomas Crofton Croker feels compelled to construct his opening paragraph around the same motif: "Intimately connected as are the Sister Islands of Great Britain and Ireland, it is an extraordinary fact that the latter country should be comparatively a terra incognita to the English in general," *Researches in the South of Ireland* (London, 1824), 1.
30 Curwen, *Observations*, I: 7.
31 *Letters*, xiii. Cooper's lengthy preface testifies to the heightened self-consciousness of the Irish tour at the turn of the century, but the volume itself (despite its subtitle) gives little sense that Cooper ever visited Ireland. His is one of the most abstract and formal tour-texts of the period, offering a standard application of late eighteenth-century stadial history and unusual only in the virulence of its almost Elizabethan contempt for the native Irish.
32 James Glassford, *Notes of Three Tours in Ireland, In 1824 and 1826* (Bristol, 1832), iii.
33 Curwen, *Observations*, I: 8.
34 Thomas Reid, *Travels in Ireland in the Year 1822, Exhibiting Brief Sketches of the Moral, Physical, and Political State of the Country* (London, 1823), 149.
35 [James MacIntosh], "Wakefield's *Ireland*," *Edinburgh Review* 20 (Nov. 1812): 347.
36 James Chandler, *England in 1819: The Politics of Literary Culture and the Case of Romantic Historicism* (Chicago and London: University of Chicago Press, 1998), 114.

37 On dates in travel texts, see Stuart Sherman, *Telling Time: Clocks, Diaries, and English Diurnal Form, 1660–1785* (Chicago and London: University of Chicago Press, 1996), chap. 5.

38 See Johannes Fabian, *Time and the Other: How Anthropology Makes Its Object* (New York: Columbia University Press, 1983).

39 See note 21 above.

40 Cooper, *Letters*, 36–37.

41 Review of Curwen, *Observations on the State of Ireland*, *British Review* 12 (Aug. 1818): 71. The motif of Ireland as anomaly was standard in the period, and it continues to reverberate in critical analysis, as in the title of David Lloyd's recent *Anomalous States: Irish Writing and the Post-Colonial Moment* (Durham, N.C.: Duke University Press, 1993).

42 Chandler, *England in 1819*, 209.

43 Reid, *Travels*, 335.

44 *Letters From the Irish Highlands* (London, 1825), 57. This anonymous tour is listed by the National Library of Ireland as written by Henry Blake and his family, who were returned absentees with an estate in the far west of Ireland. Maria Edgeworth mentions "the family of Blakes of Renvyle" as authors of this text in her long travel letter to her youngest brother, published as *Tour in Connemara and the Martins of Ballinahinch*, ed. Harold Edgeworth Butler (London: Constable & Co., 1950), 4.

45 Wakefield, *Account*, 376.

46 T. R. Malthus, "Newenham and Others on the State of Ireland," *Edinburgh Review* 12 (Jul. 1808): 336–55. Malthus' articles on Ireland are reprinted in Bernard Semmel (ed.), *Occasional Papers of T. R. Malthus on Ireland, Population, and Political Economy* (New York: Burt Franklin, 1963).

47 Travel writers also turned to the population-fact to buttress the argument for emancipation, often citing the enormous discrepancy between Catholic and Protestant populations in Ireland. An Irish Presbyterian army surgeon named John Gamble, for example, devotes his Conclusion to an urgent appeal for Catholic Emancipation, noting the "unnatural state of Ireland" in which one million relative newcomers enjoy all privileges while four million find themselves "rejected, dreaded and distrusted," *A View of Society and Manners, in the North of Ireland, in the Summer and Autumn of 1812* (London, 1813), 385. For more on the population-fact and the emancipation debate, see Chapter 5.

48 Ironically, Malthus, often regarded as a catastrophist, rejects the catastrophic scenario for Ireland that was in fact to play itself out in the great famine of the 1840s: "Although it is quite certain that the population of Ireland cannot continue permanently to increase at its present rate, yet it is as certain that it will not *suddenly* come to a stop" ("Newenham," 345).

49 Curwen, *Observations*, II: 180.

50 Trotter, *Walks*, 55.

51 Julia Kristeva, *Powers of Horror: An Essay on Abjection* (New York: Columbia University Press, 1982), 4.

52 Carr, *Stranger*, 361–62.
53 Kristeva, *Powers of Horror*, 3.
54 Hall, *Tour Through Ireland*, I: 188. A prominent motif in the writing on Ireland, the pig is a creature of the threshold, as Peter Stallybrass and Allon White stress in their influential *The Politics and Poetics of Transgression* (Ithaca: Cornell University Press, 1986), 44–59.
55 Reid, *Travels*, 153.
56 J. H. Andrews, "Land and People, c.1780," *A New History of Ireland*, vol. IV: *Eighteenth-Century Ireland*, ed. T. W. Moody and W. E. Vaughan (Oxford: Clarendon Press, 1986), 264.
57 Hadfield and McVeagh, *Strangers to That Land*, 252.
58 [James Mill], "State of Ireland," *Edinburgh Review* 21 (Jul. 1813): 342.
59 Curwen, *Observations*, I: 181–84.
60 Class difference enters the equation here as well as national difference, and for some readers it is the primary term. See, for example, Elizabeth Kowaleski-Wallace on Maria Edgeworth's fascination with how lower-class Irish lived in their bodies, *Their Fathers' Daughters: Hannah More, Maria Edgeworth and Patriarchal Complicity* (New York: Oxford University Press, 1991), 159–66.
61 Thomas Campbell, *A Philosophical Survey of the South of Ireland, In a Series of Letters to John Watkinson, M.D.* (London, 1777), 144–45.
62 Carr, *Stranger*, 266, 268.
63 At one point, for example, Young comments that although he has heard the potato "stigmatized as being unhealthy," the "well-formed, vigorous bodies" and numerous children of the Irish make it difficult "to believe them subsisting on an unwholesome food," *A Tour in Ireland 1776–1779*, 2 vols., ed. A.W. Hutton (Shannon: Irish University Press, 1970), II: 43.
64 Rev. Thomas Erlington, *A Sketch of the State of Ireland, Past and Present* (Dublin, 1808), 31–32.
65 Frances Bartkowski, *Travelers, Immigrants, Inmates: Essays in Estrangement* (Minneapolis: University of Minnesota Press, 1995), 21. On intertextuality in travels, see also Susan Stewart, *Crimes of Writing: Problems in the Containment of Representation* (New York: Oxford University Press, 1991; Durham, N.C.: Duke University Press, 1994).
66 "Domestic Literature," *New Annual Register* 27 (1806): 337.
67 "Carr's *Tour in Holland and Germany*," *Edinburgh Review* 10 (Jul. 1807): 272.
68 Carr's habit of quotation was one of the main targets of Edward Dubois' satire, *My Pocket Book; or, Hints for "A Ryghte Merrie and Conceitede" Tour, in Quarto: To be Called "The Stranger in Ireland," in 1805* (London, 1807). Even modern readers are struck by Carr's extensive quotation. Trumpener, for instance, finds that his Irish tour "comes close to plagiarism," *Bardic Nationalism*, 56.
69 "Carr's *Caledonian Sketches*," *Quarterly Review* I (Feb. 1809): 182–83. The review was written with William Gifford.
70 Travel writing at once confirms and complicates Clifford Siskin's argument in *The Work of Writing* that "writing" in the extended sense (the whole

complex of writing/print/silent reading) was received as a potent new technology in the eighteenth century, one that required "taming" through regulatory institutions like the reviews and regulatory notions like the Author.

71 Marilyn Butler, "Distinction in the Early Nineteenth-Century Novel," *Modern Language Quarterly* 58 (Dec. 1997): 481. I discuss the relationship between the critical reviews and travel writing at greater length in "Mobile Words: Romantic Travels and Print Anxiety," *Modern Language Quarterly* 60 (Dec. 1999): 451–68.

72 [Sydney Smith], "Heude's *Voyage and Travels*," *Edinburgh Review* 32 (Jul. 1819): 114. Travel writing is thus assimilated to what Mary Poovey calls "the problematic of the modern fact": the valuation, largely derived from the Enlightenment, of both observed particulars and systematic knowledge. But Poovey also notes, in her discussion of Samuel Johnson's Scottish tour, that the informal genre of travels may allow for some revision of the assumptions sustaining the modern fact, *A History of the Modern Fact: Problems of Knowledge in the Sciences of Wealth and Society* (Chicago and London: University of Chicago Press, 1998), 249–63.

73 [Henry Brougham], "Porter's *Travels in Russia and Sweden*," *Edinburgh Review* 14 (Apr. 1809): 170.

74 Edgeworths, "Carr's *Stranger in Ireland*," 43.

75 Carr, *Stranger*, 230.

76 Gamble, *A View*, v.

77 Mikhail Bakhtin, *The Dialogic Imagination*, trans. Caryl Emerson and Michael Holquist; ed. Michael Holquist (Austin: University of Texas Press, 1981), 33.

78 "Trimmer on the State of Agriculture in Ireland," *Monthly Review* 68 (May 1812): 310.

79 [John Wilson Croker], "Mason's *Statistical Account of Ireland*," *Quarterly Review* 13 (Apr. 1815): 76.

80 "Newenham's *View of the Circumstances of Ireland*," *Monthly Review* 67 (Apr. 1812): 356.

81 "Wakefield's *Account of Ireland*," *Monthly Review* 71 (Jun. 1813): 153.

82 On the shift between analytic and narrative modes in travel writing, see Dennis Porter's discussion of "plotless" and "plotted" texts in *Haunted Journeys: Desire and Transgression in European Travel Writing* (Princeton: Princeton University Press, 1991). The double-structured discourse of ethnography has recently come under a great deal of scrutiny. See, for example, the useful collection edited by James Clifford, *Writing Culture: The Poetics and Politics of Ethnography* (Berkeley: University of California Press, 1986).

83 For more on this point, see Ina Ferris, "The Question of Ideological Form: Arthur Young, the Agricultural Tour, and Ireland," in *Ideology and Form in Eighteenth-Century Literature*, ed. David Richter (Lubbock: Texas Tech University Press, 1999), 140–43.

84 Hooper, "Stranger in Ireland," 41.

85 Trumpener, *Bardic Nationalism*, 57.

86 I am thus reading travel writing in terms of a literary pragmatics that would place the genre within what Ross Chambers, drawing on French postmodernism, calls "opposition" (which works within the structure of power) rather than "resistance" (which challenges the legitimacy of a particular power-system). See his *Room for Maneuver: Reading the Oppositional in Narrative* (Chicago and London: University of Chicago Press, 1991).

87 Harrington, *English Traveller*, 22.

2 PUBLIC ADDRESS: THE NATIONAL TALE AND THE PRAGMATICS OF SYMPATHY

1 Thomas Moore, "Irish Novels," *Edinburgh Review* 43 (Feb. 1826): 372. For a useful survey of Irish fiction in the first two decades of the century, see Jacqueline Belanger, "Some Preliminary Remarks on the Production and Reception of Fiction Relating to Ireland 1800–1829," *Cardiff Corvey: Reading the Romantic Text* 4 (May 2000). <http://www.cf.ac.uk/encap/corvey/articles/cc04_n02.html. (The publisher has used its best endeavors to ensure that the URLs for external websites referred to in this book are correct and active at the time of going to press. However, the publisher has no responsibility for the websites and can make no guarantee that a site will remain live or that the content is or will remain appropriate.)

2 Daniel Corkery, *Synge and Anglo-Irish Literature: A Study* (Cork: Cork University Press, 1931), 8, 6.

3 Eagleton, *Heathcliff*, 201.

4 Joep Leerssen, "On the Treatment of Irishness in Romantic Anglo-Irish Fiction," *Irish University Review* 20 (1990): 257.

5 *Ibid.*, 258. See also Vivian Mercier, who argues that the shape of Anglo-Irish writing up to 1848 was "dictated by readers in Great Britain" in his "English Readers: Three Historical Moments," *Irish Writers and Politics*, ed. Okifumi Komesu and Masaru Sekine (Gerrards Cross: Colin Smythe, 1990), 5.

6 I draw loosely on Alexander Welsh's notion of narrative as the *making* of representations in the sense both of making quasi-legal truth claims and of the rhetorical marshaling of language on behalf of a specific person or group: "To make a representation usually means representing the facts on someone else's behalf – there can be a slippage in the idiom itself, from representing the facts to representing a client," *Strong Representations: Narrative and Circumstantial Evidence in England* (Baltimore and London: Johns Hopkins University Press, 1992), 9.

7 Maria Tymoczko, "Two Traditions of Translating Early Irish Literature," *Target* 3, no. 2 (1991): 207–24.

8 When it comes to the question of translation, commentators are divided. For two contrasting recent perspectives, see Lawrence Venuti (ed.), *Rethinking Translation: Discourse, Subjectivity, Ideology* (New York: Routledge, 1992), and Sanford Budick and Wolfgang Iser (eds.), *The Translatability of Cultures:*

Figurations of the Space Between (Stanford: Stanford University Press, 1996). See also the influential anthropological rethinking of translation in James Clifford and George E. Marcus (eds.), *Writing Culture: The Poetics and Politics of Ethnography* (Berkeley: University of California Press, 1986).

9 *The Complete Works of William Hazlitt*, 21 vols., ed. P. P. Howe (London: Dent, 1930–34), IV: 68. Hazlitt's immediate point is that the French gained more by making their language the language of high official culture in Europe than by all their conquests.

10 Michael Cronin, *Translating Ireland: Translation, Languages, Cultures* (Cork: Cork University Press, 1996), 95. See also David Lloyd, who argues for translation as minor writing in those cases where it does not return to "the originating moment of the original," *Nationalism and Minor Literature: James Clarence Mangan and the Emergence of Irish Cultural Nationalism* (Berkeley: University of California Press, 1987), 22.

11 Robert Tracy, "Maria Edgeworth and Lady Morgan," *Nineteenth-Century Fiction* 40 (1985): 1–22. This article is reprinted in his *The Unappeasable Host: Studies in Irish Identities* (Dublin: University College Dublin Press, 1998), 25–40.

12 This is not to suggest that all such readings converge on the same point. Where Corbett, for example, sees Morgan's novel as manipulating the affective powers of romance on behalf of a modern (hegemonic) form of colonial authority (*Allegories of Union*, chap. 4), Claire Connolly argues for a more problematic relationship between the marriage plot and imperial politics in the introduction to her edition of *The Wild Irish Girl* (London: Pickering and Chatto, 2000), xxv–lvi. For readings of the novel that highlight, in different ways, the question of desire and politics, see Ian Dennis, *Nationalism and Desire in Early Historical Fiction* (London: Macmillan, 1997) and Leerssen, "How *The Wild Irish Girl* Made Ireland Romantic," *Dutch Quarterly Review of Anglo-American Letters* 18 (1988): 209–27. On the national tale as imperial romance more generally, see also Deane, *Strange Country*, Trumpener, *Bardic Nationalism*, Watson, *Revolution and the Form of the British Novel*. Mitzi Myers challenges the imperialist model in a spirited defence of Edgeworth, "Goring John Bull: Maria Edgeworth's Hibernian High Jinks versus the Imperialist Imaginary," *Cutting Edges: Postmodern Critical Edges in Eighteenth-Century Satire*, ed. James E. Gill (Knoxville: University of Tennessee Press, 1995), 367–94.

13 Bakhtin, *Dialogic Imagination*, 282.

14 Niilo Idman, *Charles Robert Maturin: His Life and Works* (Helsingfors: Helsingfors Centraltryckeri, 1923), 70.

15 *Ibid.*

16 Idman's reading recalls Lyotard's notion of the "reply" in "Lessons in Paganism" as a turning of the tables and rearranging of narrative positions. See *The Lyotard Reader*, ed. Andrew Benjamin (Oxford: Blackwell, 1989), 122–54.

17 Franz Kafka, *Tagebücher*, ed. Max Brod (New York: Schocken Books, 1948), 150. The notion of the small nation is also foregrounded by Patrick Rafroidi,

who aligns Morgan with the democratic Judaic model of small-nation nationalism, *Irish Literature in English: The Romantic Period (1789–1850)*, vol. 1 (Gerrards Cross: Colin Smythe, 1980). In different ways both Morgan and Maturin ostentatiously played out the role of being-minor (young, small, obscure), deliberately drawing attention to the lack of conventional public authority to underwrite their venture into authorship. This gesture of minority of course served less to establish their modesty and timidity than to highlight their boldness and unconventional disregard for norms of literary authority. Margaret Russett offers a suggestive account of the way in which various legal, social, and literary sense of "minor" shaped the literary field of the period, *De Quincey's Romanticism: Canonical Minority and the Forms of Transmission* (Cambridge: Cambridge University Press, 1997).

18 Moore, "Irish Novels," 359.

19 Some critics have preferred a broader definition of the national tale. Gary Kelly, for instance, presents it as part of an attempt in the aftermath of the Revolution to build a new national consensus in Britain, *English Fiction of the Romantic Period 1789–1830* (London: Longman, 1989), chap. 3, and Miranda Burgess argues for a conservative "British national tale" spearheaded by Austen in *British Fiction and the Production of Social Order*, chap. 4.

20 There were Irish novels before Edgeworth, as Siobhán Marie Kilfeather has amply demonstrated, but none was understood either in its own time or later as launching a distinctive national or regional thread within British fiction. For eighteenth-century Irish novels by women, see Kilfeather, "'Strangers at Home': Political Fictions by Women in Eighteenth-Century Ireland" (Ph.D. diss., Princeton University Press, 1989).

21 *The Wild Irish Girl*, ed. Claire Connolly and Stephen Copley (London: Pickering and Chatto, 2000), 255. I cite this edition, which includes the "Prefatory Address" as an appendix, unless otherwise noted.

22 *Ibid.*

23 Although Edgeworth was writing *Ennui*, whose narrative is closer to Morgan's definition of the national tale, in 1803–05 (well before the publication of *Wild Irish Girl* in 1806), the novel itself was not published until 1809.

24 Morgan, *O'Donnel*, rev. edn., ix.

25 T. H. Lister, "Novels Descriptive of Irish Life," *Edinburgh Review* 52 (1831): 411–12.

26 On the national tale and travel writing, see also Trumpener, *Bardic Nationalism*, 142–46.

27 The point is even stronger when one recalls that the quotation from *Romeo and Juliet* cited by Mortimer in fact reads, "bide the encounter of *assailing* eyes [italics added]," *Romeo and Juliet* I.i.210.

28 In an interesting reading of the novel, Vivien Jones places it within a feminist interrogation of masculine libertinism in the period, and she assimilates the satiric view of Horatio to this genre, foregrounding not the novel's plot of travel but the feminine act of waiting (an immured young heroine

awaits rescue), "'The Coquetry of Nature': Politics and the Picturesque in Women's Fiction," *The Politics of the Picturesque: Literature, Landscape and Aesthetics Since 1770*, ed. Stephen Copley and Peter Garside (Cambridge: Cambridge University Press, 1994), 120–44.

29 *Florence Macarthy: An Irish Tale*, 4 vols. (London, 1818), II: 236–44. At the time of the novel's publication, typhus fever had in fact been raging in Ireland.

30 *Castle Rackrent and Ennui*, 186.

31 Kelly's argument, made over a series of publications, is usefully summed up in *English Fiction of the Romantic Period.*

32 On the role of feminine energies in *Ennui*, see Mitzi Myers, "'Completing the Union': Critical *Ennui*, the Politics of Narrative, and the Reformation of Irish Cultural Identity," *Prose Studies* 18 (1995): 41–77.

33 On romantic nationalism and femininity, see Angela Keane's recent *Women Writers and the English Nation in the 1790s* (Cambridge: Cambridge University Press, 2000).

34 Luke Gibbons, "Romanticism, Realism and Irish Cinema," in *Cinema in Ireland*, ed. Kevin Rockett, Luke Gibbons, and John Hill (London: Croom Helm, 1987), 206. By contrast, Joep Leerssen's important reading of *The Wild Irish Girl* stresses its investment in notions of national essence, "How the *Wild Irish Girl* Made Ireland Romantic."

35 Gibbons, "Romanticism, Realism," 204–10.

36 [Ellen O'Connell Fitzsimon], "Irish Novels and Irish Novelists," *Dublin Review* 4 (Apr. 1838): 496. Published in London and aimed at English readers, the *Dublin Review*, founded by Nicholas Wiseman and Daniel O'Connell, made Catholicism its cause, so that it occupied a position in the public discourse on Ireland similar to that of the national tale.

37 Hazlitt, "On Going a Journey," *Complete Works*, VIII: 185.

38 "The Stranger," *The Sociology of George Simmel*, trans. and ed. Kurt H. Wolff (Illinois: The Free Press, 1950), 402.

39 A stranger may also be someone who simply passes by a group, as in James Buzard's account of the tourist as a "passing stranger," but the national tale activates the potential of encounter in the act of traversal. See Buzard, *The Beaten Track: European Tourism, Literature, and the Ways to Culture, 1800–1918* (Oxford: Clarendon Press, 1993), chap. 1.

40 Daniel Dewar, *Observations on the Character, Customs, and Superstitions of the Irish* (London, 1812), 23, 61.

41 Thomas Moore, *Memoirs of Captain Rock, the Celebrated Irish Chieftain, with Some Account of His Ancestors*, Written by Himself (London, 1824), 244.

42 Corbett offers a suggestive account of the usually overlooked father's plot in the novel, *Allegories of Union*, 64–68.

43 Maria Edgeworth, *The Absentee*, ed. W. J. McCormack and Kim Walker (Oxford: Oxford University Press, 1988), 129.

44 James Clifford, "Traveling Cultures," in *Cultural Studies*, ed. Laurence Grossberg *et al.* (New York: Routledge, 1992), 96–116.

45 Julia Kristeva, *Strangers to Ourselves*, trans. Leon S. Roudiez (New York: Columbia University Press, 1991), 17.

46 As the ardent mutual gazes highlighted in the novel suggest, not all looking implies detachment and control, but the play of seeing and hearing in this pivotal scene certainly recalls the distinction Susan Stewart makes in her discussion of travel writing between the separating function of the gaze (aestheticism) and the implicating function of the dialogic (ethics), *Crimes of Writing*, chap. 6.

47 Michel de Certeau, "Ethno-Graphy: Speech, or the Space of the Other: Jean de Léry," *The Writing of History*, trans. Tom Conley (New York: Columbia University Press, 1988). See also Robert J. C. Young on "colonial desire" in *Colonial Desire: Hybridity in Theory, Culture, and Race* (New York: Routledge, 1995).

48 My reading of Smith and Hume draws in particular on John Mullan, *Sentiment and Sociability: The Language of Feeling in the Eighteenth Century* (Oxford: Clarendon Press, 1988), and Adela Pinch, *Strange Fits of Passion: Epistemologies of Emotion, Hume to Austen* (Stanford: Stanford University Press, 1996).

49 Adam Smith, *The Theory of Moral Sentiments*, ed. D. D. Raphael and A. L. Macfie (Indianapolis: Liberty Fund, 1982), 22.

50 David Hume, *A Treatise of Human Nature*, ed. L. A. Selby-Bigge (Oxford: Clarendon Press, 1973), 576.

51 *Ibid.*, 592.

52 Fiona Robertson suggests that Maturin's reversal of gender makes Ireland more tragic and less assimilable than in Morgan's novel because the country is now linked to serious, male power, *Legitimate Histories: Scott, Gothic, and the Authorities of Fiction* (Oxford: Clarendon Press, 1994), 219.

53 *The Milesian Chief: A Romance*, 4 vols. (London, 1812), 1: 57.

54 The title of Mary Louise Pratt's influential study sums up much of current postcolonial thought on the eye, *Imperial Eyes: Travel Writing and Transculturation* (London and New York: Routledge, 1992). The role of the eye in the picturesque has also been much discussed. For a good sense of the debate about the picturesque, see Stephen Copley and Peter Garside (eds.), *The Politics of the Picturesque* (Cambridge: Cambridge University Press, 1994); see also Kim Ian Michasiw's important rejoinder to critique of the picturesque, "Nine Revisionist Theses on the Picturesque," *Representations* 38 (1992): 76–100.

55 Morgan, "Prefatory Address," *Wild Irish Girl*, 256. Moore took as his model for the *Melodies* an early volume by Morgan, *Twelve Original Hibernian Melodies, with English Words, Imitated and Translated, from the Works of the Ancient Irish Bards* (1805), which contains melodies she took down from her Irish-speaking father, Robert Owenson (MacEoghain), and supplemented with English words.

56 I cite the Oxford edition, *Wordsworth: Poetical Works*, ed. Thomas Hutchinson and Ernest De Selincourt (London: Oxford University Press, 1969). "The Solitary Reaper" (along with "Tintern Abbey") is something of a *locus classicus* for new historicist readings of Wordsworth. See, for example, Peter Manning, *Reading Romantics: Text and Context* (New York: Oxford University Press, 1990), chap. 11.

57 Jean-Jacques Rousseau and Johann Gottfried Herder, *On the Origin of Language*, trans. John H. Moran and Alexander Gode (Chicago and London: University of Chicago Press, 1966), 11.
58 *Ibid.*, 9.
59 Mikhail Bakhtin and P. N. Medvedev, *The Formal Method in Literary Scholarship: A Critical Introduction to Sociological Poetics*, trans. Albert J. Wehrle (Cambridge, Mass.: Harvard University Press, 1985), 103.
60 Hazlitt, *Works*, VIII: 185
61 *Ibid.*, 188.
62 Johannes Fabian, *Time and the Other: How Anthropology Makes Its Object* (New York: Columbia University Press, 1983), 162.
63 I draw on the influential notion of "recognition" as articulated by various thinkers in recent years from Charles Taylor to W. J. T. Mitchell. Fabian uses this notion to frame a suggestive recent meditation on the question of identity, "Remembering the Other: Knowledge and Recognition in the Exploration of Central Africa," *Critical Inquiry* 26 (1999): 49–69.
64 The phrase appears in "Lady Morgan–Her Publisher, &c," *Literary Gazette*, 6 Oct. 1821, p. 640. On Morgan's theatricality, see Mary Campbell, *Lady Morgan: The Life and Times of Sydney Owenson* (London: Pandora, 1988); Seamus Deane, *A Short History of Irish Literature*; Tom Dunne, "Haunted by History: Irish Romantic Writing 1800–50," in *Romanticism in National Context*, ed. Roy Porter and Mikulás Teich (Cambridge: Cambridge University Press, 1988), 68–91; Terry Eagleton, *Heathcliff and the Great Hunger*, 77–87. On Edgeworth as interventionist, see in particular Myers, "'Like the Pictures in a Magic Lantern': Gender, History, and Edgeworth's Rebellion Narratives," *Nineteenth-Century Contexts* 19 (1966): 373–412.
65 Maria Edgeworth, *Ormond*, ed. Claire Connolly (London: Penguin, 2000), 259.
66 *Memoir of Maria Edgeworth with a Selection from her Letters* ed. Frances Edgeworth (privately printed, 1867), III: 259.
67 For the reception of Morgan's fiction under the dubious category of "female reading" versus proper "feminine writing," see my discussion in *The Achievement of Literary Authority*, chap. 1.
68 *Lord Byron's Selected Letters and Journals* ed. Leslie A. Marchand (Cambridge, Mass.: Belknap Press, 1982), 256.
69 Claire Connolly has uncovered the controversy surrounding the publication of *The Wild Irish Girl* in Dublin, widely understood to have been triggered by newspaper articles written by the future Tory luminary and *Quarterly* reviewer John Wilson Croker, " 'I accuse Miss Owenson': *The Wild Irish Girl* as Media Event," *Colby Quarterly* 36 (2000): 98–115.
70 Colburn was angered by reviews of Morgan's *The O'Briens and the O'Flahertys*, and started up the *Athenaeum* as a new venue for literary commentary. In her 1863 biography, Julia Kavanagh remarks how the "strange animosity" to Morgan was "the means of raising one of the critical authorities of this day–the 'Athenaeum'," *English Women of Letters: Biographical Sketches*, 2 vols. (London, 1863), II: 298.

71 Edgeworth had used the name Crawley for a corrupt agent in *Ennui*, but it is the idea of a clan of Crawleys that lies behind Thackeray's appropriation of the satirical moniker in *Vanity Fair*.
72 *Edinburgh Monthly Review* 1 (Jun. 1819): 655.
73 "My Reviewers," *The Book of the Boudoir*, 2 vols. (London, 1829) I: 302; *Letter to the Reviewers of "Italy"* (London, 1821), 8.
74 Kavanagh, *English Women of Letters*, II: 296.
75 Morgan, *Absenteeism* (London, 1825), 111.
76 Morgan, *France* (London, 1817), vii.
77 Morgan, *Letter to the Reviewers*, 5–6.
78 *Ibid.*, 6.
79 Frank Donoghue *The Fame Machine: Book Reviewing and Eighteenth-Century Literary Careers* (Stanford: Stanford University Press, 1996), 4.
80 Morgan, *France*, vii.
81 [John Wilson Croker and William Gifford], "France, by Lady Morgan," *Quarterly Review* 17 (Apr. 1817): 263.
82 Jon Klancher has analyzed the making of different reading audiences in the period in his landmark, *The Making of English Reading Audiences, 1790–1832* (Madison: University of Wisconsin Press, 1987). My point is the reluctance to give up the idea of a singular "public," even as the participants in the debate were quite aware of the stratification of different "publics."
83 Review of *Florence Macarthy*, *British Review* 13 (May 1819): 483.
84 "Lady Morgan – Her Publisher," 640.
85 Review of *Florence Macarthy*, *British Review*, 483.
86 [Horatio Townsend], review of *Tales of the O'Hara Family*, *Blackwood's Edinburgh Magazine* 24 (Oct. 1828): 469.
87 Stewart, *Crimes of Writing*, 122.
88 Dennis, *Nationalism and Desire*, chap. 2. A revealing moment in Morgan's memoirs preserves the response of Lady Abercorn when the author sent her, as requested, a design for the gold bodkins for fastening hair known as "glorvinas": "I received the Glorvina this morning, which I do not very much admire, and as *I do know* you do not mind trouble, I sent it back to you, and wish you would ask the man wthat [*sic*] he would one for me of Irish gold, with the shamrock on the head in small Irish diamonds, which I think would look very well," *Lady Morgan's Memoirs: Autobiography, Diaries, and Correspondence*, ed. W. Hepworth Dixon and Geraldine Jewsbury, 2 vols. (London, 1862), I: 411–12.
89 Morgan, *O'Donnel* (1814; rpt., New York: Garland, 1979), 177. I cite the 1835 revised edition only for the preface.
90 Deane, *Short History*, 97.
91 Jeanne Moskal argues that even as Morgan constructed her literary authority along masculine lines, she at the same time invoked the conventionally feminine role of advocate in another's cause, "Gender, Nationality, and Textual Authority in Lady Morgan's Travel Books," in *Romantic Women Writers: Voices and Countervoices*, ed. Paula R. Feldman and Theresa M. Kelley (Hanover: University Press of New England, 1995), 170–93. On the tensions of women

and authorship in the period more generally, see Sonia Hofkosh, *Sexual Politics and the Romantic Author* (Cambridge: Cambridge University Press, 1998).

92 Ernest Gellner, *Nations and Nationalism* (Ithaca: Cornell University Press, 1983).

3 FEMALE AGENTS: REWRITING THE NATIONAL HEROINE IN MORGAN'S LATER FICTION

1 Sydney Morgan, Preface, *Patriotic Sketches of Ireland* (London, 1807), x.

2 Harriet Guest has analyzed the complex relations between domestic norms and women's patriotism in the period, *Small Change: Women, Learning, Patriotism, 1750–1810* (Chicago and London: University of Chicago Press, 2000). See also Keane, *Women Writers and the English Nation in the 1790s* and Mellor, *Mothers of the Nation.*

3 [Christian Isobel Johnstone], "Lady Morgan's Princess," *Tait's Edinburgh Magazine*, n.s., 2 (Feb. 1835): 113.

4 Kavanagh, *English Women of Letters*, II: 342.

5 *Ibid.*, 344.

6 Michel de Certeau, "Spatial Stories," *The Practice of Everyday Life*, trans. Steven Randall (Berkeley: University of California Press, 1984), 117–19.

7 Hepworth Dixon and Jewsbury (eds.), *Lady Morgan's Memoirs*, II: 75.

8 More attention is now beginning to be directed to this international line of women's fiction; see, for example, Deidre Lynch, "The (Dis)Locations of Romantic Nationalism: Shelley, Staël, and the Home Schooling of Monsters," in *The Literary Channel: The Inter-National Invention of the Novel*, ed. Margaret Cohen and Carolyn Dever (Princeton: Princeton University Press, 2002), 194–224.

9 *Lady Morgan's Memoirs*, I: 325.

10 [Johnstone], "Lady Morgan's Princess," 113. For early Stael-Morgan references, see the reviews of *Ida of Athens* in *British Critic* 33 (May 1809): 525, and *Annual Review* 7 (1809): 589.

11 Ellen Moers, *Literary Women: The Great Writers* (New York: Oxford University Press, 1976), chap. 9. Deidre Lynch reads *Corinne*, along with Morgan's *Ida of Athens*, as a "transnational" novel rather than as a national tale, but her argument that this cosmopolitan genre resisted Burkean nationalist identity-discourse usefully complements my own. See Lynch, "Domesticating Fictions and Nationalizing Women: Edmund Burke, Property, and the Reproduction of Englishness," *Romanticism, Race, and Imperial Culture, 1780–1834*, ed. Alan Richardson and Sonia Hofkosh (Bloomington: Indiana University Press, 1996), 40–71.

12 Germaine de Stael, *Corinne, or Italy*, trans. and ed. Avril H. Goldberger (New Brunswick: Rutgers University Press, 1987), 25.

13 Martin Thom, *Republics, Nations, and Tribes* (London: Verso, 1995), 182, 242. Thom's main point, however, is that Stael's disillusionment with the republic led to an increasing valorization of the ineffable tribe-nation.

14 Kelly, *Women, Writing, and Revolution*, 178.

15 Mona Ozouf stresses Stael's lack of nostalgia for the past and her distinctively modern conviction that it is always possible to break away from one's given condition, *Les Mots Des Femmes: Essai Sur La Singularité Française* (Paris: Fayard, 1995), 132–41.
16 Morgan, *The O'Briens and the O'Flahertys* (London: Pandora, 1988), 334.
17 See Bhabha, "DissemiNation: Time, Narrative, and the Margins of the Modern Nation," in *Location of Culture*, 139–70.
18 Morgan *The Princess; or the Beguine*, 3 vols. (London, 1835), I: 22.
19 The heroine of Johnstone's own national tale, *Clan-Albin* (1815), not so incidentally, is an eminently rational and enlightened being.
20 My notion of "elsewhere" draws on Luce Irigaray's well-known comment that women can play the generic gender role because they exist "elsewhere" than in the scene where they "mime" what is expected of them, but I shift it from her psycho-ontological register into a more socio-historical one, *This Sex Which Is Not One*, trans. Catherine Porter (Ithaca: Cornell University Press, 1985), 152.
21 "Women's Time" (1979), *The Kristeva Reader*, ed. Toril Moi (New York: Columbia University Press, 1986), 188–216.
22 Morgan, *O'Donnel*, rev. edn., ix.
23 *Woman and Her Master* (1840; rpt., Westport, Conn.: Hyperion Press, 1976), 21.
24 Morgan, *The Princess*, I: 323.
25 Bourdieu, *In Other Words*, 9.
26 *Edinburgh Monthly Review* 1 (Jun. 1819): 661.
27 These lines initially appeared in the concluding stanza to Hemans' "Corinne at the Capitol," and they are reiterated in the epigraph to "Woman and Fame." Interestingly, Morgan's biographer, Geraldine Jewsbury, makes a point of the contrast between Hemans and Morgan: "No two persons could have been more entirely opposed to each other in their nature, taste, and character, than Lady Morgan and Mrs. Hemans. With all her celebrity, Mrs. Hemans shrank from publicity, to which Lady Morgan had been inured, until it had become her second nature," *Lady Morgan's Memoirs*, II: 271.
28 "The O'Briens and the O'Flahertys," *New Monthly Magazine* 20 (Dec. 1827): 498.
29 *Literary Gazette*, 3 Nov. 1827: 707.
30 Julia Wright rightly sees the novel as a critique of "antiquarian nationalism," "'The Nation Begins to Form': Competing Nationalisms in Morgan's *The O'Briens and the O'Flahertys*," *ELH* 66 (Winter 1999): 939–63.
31 For the historical and cultural layers in early nineteenth-century Ireland, see William J. Smyth, "A Plurality of Irelands: Regions, Societies and Mentalities," in *In Search of Ireland: A Cultural Geography*, ed. Brian Graham (London: Routledge, 1997), 19–42.
32 Trumpener has drawn particular attention to how gothic temporalities in the national tale challenged the Enlightenment model of national evolution underwriting other narrative forms in the period, notably Scott's historical novel, in *Bardic Nationalism*, chap. 3.

33 For a decade at the very end of the sixteenth century, Hugh Roe O'Donnell (who spent several years in his youth imprisoned in Dublin Castle) waged war against the English. He was defeated in 1601, a defeat that completed the Tudor conquest of Ireland. Morgan had originally planned to make this O'Donnell the subject of her novel, but abandoned the plan when she realized that his story was too bitter for her liberal purposes. As she put it in her Preface to the first edition: "when I fondly thought to send forth a dove bearing the olive of peace I found I was on the point of flinging an arrow winged with discord" (x). The embedded text is the trace of this earlier, discordant story.

34 Such narrative moments thus function as what Anne Fogarty calls "spectral Irelands," "Imperfect Concord: Spectres of History in the Irish Novels of Maria Edgeworth and Lady Morgan," in *Gender Perspectives in Nineteenth-Century Ireland*, ed. Margaret Kelleher and James H. Murphy (Dublin: Irish Academic Press, 1997), 116–26.

35 Trumpener, *Bardic Nationalism*, 153.

36 Especially after the publication of *Florence Macarthy*, with its author-heroine, critical charges of narcissistic self-projection noticeably stepped up. See, for example, the reviews of *Florence Macarthy* in *Antijacobin Review* 55 (Feb. 1819), 509–21; *British Review* 13 (May 1819): 482-94; *Edinburgh Monthly Review* 1 (Jun. 1819): 655–62; *New Monthly Magazine* 10 (Jan. 1819): 529–33.

37 On the frescoes in the Camera di San Paolo, see David Ekserdjian, *Correggio* (New Haven: Yale University Press, 1998).

38 In Morgan's suggestive phrase, she says she she "found a niche" for the Abbess of Parma in her novel, *Boudoir*, II: 210.

39 Morgan, *The O'Briens and the O'Flahertys*, 498.

40 As Hofkosh has pointed out, not all interiors attached to women in the period signify innerness (*Sexual Politics*, chap. 6), but it remains the primary coding of female interiors in eighteenth and nineteenth-century novels.

41 See Deidre Lynch, *The Economy of Character: Novels, Market Culture, and the Business of Inner Meaning* (Chicago and London: University of Chicago Press, 1998). See also Andrea K. Henderson, *Romantic Identities: Varieties of Subjectivity, 1774–1830* (Cambridge: Cambridge University Press, 1996).

42 Morgan, *France*, 233.

43 *Ibid.*

44 The nun's chamber may thus be added to the overlooked scenes of female writing in the period described by Joel Haefner, "The Romantic Scene(s) of Writing," *Re-Visioning Romanticism: British Women Writers, 1776-1837*, ed. Carol Shiner Wilson and Joel Haefner (Philadelphia: University of Pennsylvania Press, 1994), 256–73.

45 On the spread of sodalities and confraternities in early nineteenth-century Ireland, see S. J. Connolly, "Mass Politics and Sectarian Conflict, 1823–30," in Vaughan (ed.), *A New History of Ireland*, vol. v: *Ireland Under the Union, I (1801–70)*, 74–76.

46 [Mortimer O'Sullivan], review of *Eighth Report of the Commissioners of Irish Education Inquiry*, *Quarterly Review* 37 (Mar. 1828): 483, 484.

47 On More and philanthropy, see in particular Keane, *Women Writers and the English Nation*, chap. 6, and Mellor, *Mothers of the Nation*, chap. 1.

48 Morgan makes few references to Wollstonecraft, but one of the most significant appears in a long note on sexual difference appended to vol. I of *Woman and Her Master*. Morgan argues that foregrounding difference has historically worked to the disadvantage of women, but Wollstonecraft's reverse tactic of denying difference has produced a conclusion "equally false, if not equally injurious." For Morgan, "common humanity" outweighs any sexual difference and underpins the claim to equal rights for both genders, but she resists the elision of sexual difference altogether, *Woman and Her Master*, I: 215–17.

49 A notable instance is Tobias Smollett's statement in Letter XXVII of his *Travels* that the "confrairies" of Italy "may be compared to the Free-Masons, Gregoreans, and Antigallicans of England," *Travels Through France and Italy*, ed. Frank Felsenstein (Oxford: Oxford University Press, 1981), 221.

50 Cf. Morgan's comment in her diary, following the mock-complaint of a conservative acquaintance (Lady Chapman) that Morgan had turned her sons into liberals: "It is thus we women, the secret tribunal of society can mine and countermine" (*Memoirs*, II: 378). This sense of secret female agency becomes a more prominent thread in her later work, especially in *Woman and Her Master*, which takes a special pleasure in drawing attention to figures like the wife of Jeroboam, who acted as a secret agent, and Laena, who was fatally involved in a conspiracy to free Athens (95, 159).

51 Simmel, *Sociology*, 330.

52 *Ibid.*, 347.

53 *Ibid.*, 375.

54 Willa Murphy, "Maria Edgeworth and the Aesthetics of Secrecy," in Foley and Ryder (eds.), *Ideology and Ireland in the Nineteenth Century*, 46, 47.

4 THE SHUDDER OF HISTORY: IRISH GOTHIC AND RUIN WRITING

1 While Maturin is generally seen as a pioneer of Irish Gothic, *The Milesian Chief* itself has received little recognition as an inaugural text of the genre, most critics concentrating on his later *Melmoth the Wanderer* (1820). Margot Gayle Backus's recent *The Gothic Family Romance: Heterosexuality, Child Sacrifice, and the Anglo-Irish Colonial Order* (Durham, N.C. and London: Duke University Press, 1999) makes no mention of *The Milesian Chief*, while Julian Moynahan makes only a brief reference in his discussion of Irish Gothic in *Anglo-Irish: The Literary Imagination in a Hyphenated Culture* (Princeton: Princeton University Press, 1995), chap. 6. Eagleton dismisses the novel, along with *The Wild Irish Boy*, as "lurid parodies of Lady Morgan" before moving on to *Melmoth* as exemplary of Protestant Gothic, *Heathcliff and the Great Hunger*, 187. Trumpener, however, gives prominence to *The Milesian Chief* as an important

transitional text between the national tale and the historical novel, *Bardic Nationalism*, 147–48.

2 Charles Robert Maturin, *The Milesian Chief: A Romance*, 4 vols. (London, 1812), I: iv–v.

3 Maturin evidenced a marked preference for privatives, apparent as early as the Dedicatory Letter to his first novel, *The Wild Irish Boy*, where he defines himself as follows: "I am an Irishman, unnoticed and unknown," *The Wild Irish Boy*, vi.

4 For a suggestive reading of *Corinne* as a ruin text, see Marie-Claire Vallois, "Old Idols New Subjects: Germaine de Staël and Romanticism," in *Germaine de Stael: Crossing the Borders*, ed. Madelyn Gutwirth, Avriel Goldberger, and Karyna Szmurlo (New Brunswick: Rutgers University Press, 1991), 82–97.

5 Stael, *Corinne*, 65.

6 *Ibid.*, 73.

7 Review of *Melmoth the Wanderer*, *Eclectic Review*, n.s., 14 (Dec. 1820): 548. The reviewer links Maturin specifically to "the corrupt and exaggerated sensibility of the German school." At the same time, however, he also strikes one of the other keynotes in the contemporary reception of Maturin when he allows that within the "whole chaos of absurdity, we have been frequently struck with conceptions of the greatest force and splendour" (548). Walter Scott first struck this particular note in his important early notice of Maturin's *Fatal Revenge* for the *Quarterly Review*: "In truth, we rose from his strange chaotic novelromance [*sic*] as from a confused and feverish dream, unrefreshed, and unamused, yet strongly impressed by many of the ideas which had been so vaguely and wildly presented to our imagination," *Quarterly Review* 3 (May 1810): 347.

8 "On the Writings of Mr. Maturin, and More Particularly His 'Melmoth'," [Baldwin's] *London Magazine* 3 (May 1821): 515.

9 Eagleton, *Heathcliff*, 187. On Irish Gothic and Protestant landlord anxiety, see also Kilfeather, "'Strangers at Home'," chap. 4, and Moynahan, *Anglo-Irish*, chap. 6.

10 On *The Milesian Chief* itself as a tale of usurpation, for example, see Fiona Robertson, *Legitimate Histories*, 214–25.

11 *Childe Harold's Pilgrimage* Canto IV: cvii in *Byron: Poetical Works*, rev. edn., ed. John Jump (London: Oxford University Press, 1970).

12 Jean Starobinski, *The Invention of Liberty, 1700–1789*, trans. Bernard C. Swift (Geneva: Editions D'Art Albert Skira, 1964), 180.

13 On ruin landscapes, see Louis Hawes, *Presences of Nature: British Landscape 1780–1830* (New Haven: Yale Center for British Art, 1982), 35–48.

14 *The Lay of the Last Minstrel* (2: lines 1–2), *Sir Walter Scott: Selected Poems*, ed. Thomas Crawford (Oxford: Clarendon Press, 1972). Maturin quotes these lines in *The Milesian Chief*, I: 179.

15 Ann Bermingham stresses the pessimism of the picturesque in her analysis of its aesthetics and politics, *Landscape and Ideology: The English Rustic Tradition, 1740–1860* (Berkeley: University of California Press, 1986), chap. 2. See also

Malcolm Andrews, *The Search for the Picturesque: Landscape Aesthetics and Tourism in Britain, 1760–1800* (Stanford: Stanford University Press, 1989). Andrews has usefully collected a substantial number of key period documents in *The Picturesque: Literary Sources and Documents*, 3 vols. (Mountfield: Helm Information, 1994).

16 Bermingham, *Landscape and Ideology*, 85.

17 Starobinski, *Invention of Liberty*, 180.

18 Walter Scott, *Waverley*, ed. Claire Lamont (Oxford: Oxford University Press, 1986), 340.

19 For an account of how ruins helped establish a naturalized imperial British identity, see Anne Janowitz, *England's Ruins: Poetic Purpose and the National Landscape* (Oxford: Blackwell, 1990).

20 Stael, *Corinne*, 72.

21 Constantin François de Chasseboeuf Volney, *The Ruins; or, a Survey of the Revolutions of Empires* (London: Edwards, Brown, n.d.), vii.

22 *Georg Simmel, 1858–1918: A Collection of Essays, with Translations and a Bibliography*, ed. Kurt H. Wolff (Columbus: The Ohio State University Press, 1959), 259.

23 *Wordsworth: Poetical Works*, rev. edn., ed. Ernest De Selincourt and Thomas Hutchinson (Oxford: Oxford University Press, 1969), lines 131–35.

24 Friedrich Schiller, *On the Naive and Sentimental in Literature*, trans. Helen Watanabe-O'Kelly (Manchester: Carcanet New Press, 1981), 21.

25 Luke Gibbons, *Transformations in Irish Culture* (Notre Dame: University of Notre Dame Press, 1996), 159–60. In her classic twentieth-century ruin text, Rose Macaulay describes the ubiquity of ruins in Ireland in this way: "It is a fact that one cannot travel more than a few miles in Ireland without passing some broken abbey or church; they lie strewn along coast and river, hill and plain, island and lake-side, in ruinous profusion. Destroyed by Danes, by Normans, by Englishmen, by decay, by time, by poverty, vandalism and dissolution, their crumbling arches and portals and fragments of wall stand in reproachful witness to the passing of a murdered culture," *Pleasure of Ruins*, ed. Constance Babington Smith; interpreted in photographs by Roloff Beny (1953; rev. edn. London: Thames & Hudson, 1977), 133.

26 T. Crofton Croker, *Researches in the South of Ireland* (1824; rpt., New York: Barnes and Noble, 1968), 22.

27 For a reading of the ruin debate as staged by Morgan, see Trumpener, *Bardic Nationalism*, 143–45.

28 Michael Banim, *The Croppy: A Tale of the Irish Rebellion of 1798*, 3 vols. (1828; rpt., New York: Garland, 1978), III: 227.

29 Morgan, *The O'Briens and the O'Flahertys*, 534–44, 552.

30 *Journal of Thomas Moore*, ed. Wilfred S. Dowden, 5 vols. (Newark: University of Delaware Press, 1983), II: 659.

31 See Luke Gibbons, "Between Captain Rock and a Hard Place: Art and Agrarian Insurgency," 31–32.

32 Thomas Moore, *Memoirs of Captain Rock, the Celebrate Irish Chieftain, with Some Account of His Ancestors*. Written by Himself (London, 1824), iv. Moore refers

to *Captain Rock* in his journal as "my Irish Tour" when he begins writing the volume, *Journal*, II: 667.

33 Schiller, *On the Naive and Sentimental*, 22

34 *Ibid.*, 49

35 *Ibid.*

36 Dominick LaCapra, "Trauma, Absence, Loss," *Critical Inquiry* 25 (Summer 1999): 696–727.

37 I am drawing loosely on the notion of history as insistence in Geraldine Friedman, *The Insistence of History: Revolution in Burke, Wordsworth, Keats, and Baudelaire* (Stanford: Stanford University Press, 1996).

38 Ian Duncan, *Modern Romance and Transformations of the Novel: The Gothic, Scott, Dickens* (Cambridge: Cambridge University Press, 1992), 24.

39 Starobinski, *Invention of Liberty*, 188.

40 On the spectralization of time in domestic gothic, see Terry Castle, "The Spectralization of the Other in *The Mysteries of Udolpho*," *The New Eighteenth Century: Theory, Politics, English Literature*, ed. Felicity Nussbaum and Laura Brown (New York and London: Methuen, 1987), 231–53.

41 Rose Macaulay, however, combines haunting and hovering when she observes that even though old ruins muffle the kind of anger stirred by modern war ruins, "the haunting gods hover about with reproachful sighs: one cannot forget," *Pleasure of Ruins*, 134.

42 Stael, *Corinne*, 72.

43 Laurence Goldstein, *Ruins and Empire: The Evolution of a Theme in Augustan and Romantic Literature* (Pittsburgh: University of Pittsburgh Press, 1977), 10.

44 Stael, *Corinne*, 286. Christopher Woodward points out that the early nineteenth century witnessed a marked increase in literary and visual images of proleptic ruin, "Scenes from the Future," *Visions of Ruin: Architectural Fantasies and Designs for Garden Follies* (London: Sir John Soane's Museum, 1999), 15–17. My thanks to David Skilton for alerting me to this intriguing collection of ruin commentary.

45 *The Works of Anna Laetitia Barbauld*, ed. Lucy Aikin (London, 1825), lines 47–50.

46 *The Standard Edition of the Complete Psychological Works of Sigmund Freud*, ed. James Strachey and Anna Freud, 24 vols. (London: Hogarth, 1975), XXIV: 39. Suggestively, the references to recent Irish history Maturin appends to *Melmoth the Wanderer* in footnotes tend to highlight unnatural deaths. Vol. III, chap. 12, for instance, aligns its depiction of a mob lynching with, on the one hand, the murder of the antiquarian Dr. Hamilton in Donegal in 1797 and, on the other, the killing of Lord Kilwarden during Robert Emmet's 1803 insurrection, *Melmoth the Wanderer*, ed. Douglas Grant (Oxford: Oxford University Press, 1989), 256 n, 257 n.

47 Joep Leerssen reads this scene rather differently as exemplifying the "ahistoricity of Gaelic Ireland" in early nineteenth-century Irish fiction, *Remembrance and Imagination*, 50–51.

48 Croker, *Researches*, 347.

49 Friedrich Nietzsche, *On the Advantage and Disadvantage of History for Life*, trans. Peter Preuss (Indianapolis: Hackett Publishing, 1980), 10.

50 *Ibid.*

51 Maturin himself is often understood as an "internal migrant"or "homeless" soul (e.g., Deane, *Short History*, 100; Moynahan, *Anglo-Irish*, chap. 6).

5 AGITATED BODIES: THE EMANCIPATION DEBATE AND NOVELS OF INSURGENCY IN THE 1820s

1 Review of Moore, *Memoirs of Captain Rock*, *Literary Chronicle* (17 Apr. 1824): 241.

2 Catholic agitation – indeed, the Emancipation debate in general – has not received a great deal of attention from literary historians of the Romantic period, although it was arguably (as Wendy Hinde puts it) "the most controversial and intractable issue in English politics" in the first three decades of the nineteenth century, *Catholic Emancipation: A Shake to Men's Minds* (Oxford: Blackwell, 1992), 1. Among political historians, the role of O'Connell and the Catholic Association, along with the implications of the Roman Catholic Relief Act of 1829, remains a subject of some controversy. S. J. Connolly, while not discounting the larger political importance of the agitation, finds it largely "irrelevant" to the parliamentary debate, while Thomas Bartlett stresses the importance of a politicized Catholic peasantry (formed in part by O'Connell's agitation) in forcing the government's hand after the Waterford election. See Connolly, "The Union Government, 1812–32," in *New History of Ireland*, volume V: *Ireland Under the Union, I* 67; Bartlett, *The Fall and Rise of the Irish Nation*, 340. See also Brian Jenkins, *Era of Emancipation: British Government of Ireland, 1812–1830* (Kingston and Montreal: McGill-Queen's University Press, 1988) and Fergus O'Ferrall, *Catholic Emancipation: Daniel O'Connell and the Birth of Irish Democracy 1820–30* (Dublin: Gill and Macmillan, 1985). O'Ferrall provides a useful appendix on the status of Catholics after the Relief Act of 1829 (318–23).

3 Lord Anglesey was appointed Lord Lieutenant of Ireland in 1827. By 1828 his advice was somewhat redundant, the agitation campaign having been under way on all fronts since at least the founding of the Catholic Association in 1823.

4 Žižek, *A Leftist Plea*, 989.

5 *Ibid.*

6 *The Select Speeches of Daniel O'Connell, M.P*, ed. John O'Connell, 2nd ser. (Dublin: James Duffy, 1872), II: 109.

7 "Dr Milner and Others on the Catholics of Ireland," *Edinburgh Review* 14 (Apr. 1809): 64. The author may be Sydney Smith.

8 William Lecky, *Leaders of Public Opinion in Ireland: Swift – Flood – Grattan – O'Connell*, rev. edn. (London, 1871), 232, 233. Seamus Deane includes O'Connell in a suggestive discussion of the political resonances of Irish speech and accent in the period, *Strange Country*, 63–65.

9 *The Correspondence of Daniel O'Connell,1829–1832*, ed. Maurice R. O'Connell, vol. IV (Dublin: Stationery Office,1977), 96.

10 Morgan, *The O'Briens and the O'Flahertys*, 63. Morgan and O'Connell were linked in the popular imagination, as is evident in a comic verse of the period on Dublin town:

> Och, Dublin city, there's no doubtin'
> Bates every city upon the say;
> Tis there you'll hear O'Connell spoutin'
> And Lady Morgan making tay;
> For 'tis the capital of the finest nation,
> Wid charming pisantry on a fruitful sod,
> Fighting like divils for conciliation
> And hating each other for the love of God.
> (quoted in Mary Campbell, *Lady Morgan*, 196).

Morgan herself, while supporting O'Connell's campaign, disliked and distrusted him as a person, telling an interlocutor at the end of 1833 that "[t]he eel is a lump of lead compared with O'Connell, he has no one fixed principle; the end, with him, consecrates the means, and *that* end is – O'Connell, the beginning and end of all things," *Lady Morgan's Memoirs*, II: 378.

11 Belanger finds the 1820s "the most productive decade for the novel concerned with Ireland" in the period between Union and Emancipation, "Some Preliminary Remarks on the Production and Reception of Fiction Relating to Ireland 1800–1829."

12 Review of *The Anglo-Irish of the Nineteenth Century*, *Athenaeum* 8 (Oct. 1828): 788.

13 Deane, *Strange Country*, 68. On Thomas Moore in the 1820s and *Memoirs of Captain Rock*, see also Leerssen, *Remembrance and Imagination*, 79–88.

14 Moore, *Captain Rock*, xiii.

15 "Works on Ireland," *Blackwood's Edinburgh Magazine* 15 (May 1824): 550.

16 "Works on Ireland," 550; "Ireland," *British Review* 22 (Nov. 1824): 446; "Ireland, and Captain Rock," *British Critic* 21 (Apr. 1824): 433.

17 [Sydney Smith], "*Memoirs of Captain Rock*," *Edinburgh Review* 41 (Oct. 1824): 143, 152.

18 "Irish Writers in Ireland," *Ghost of the Rushlight* 1 (1826): 8.

19 *Sir Walter Scott's Journal 1829–32*, ed. John Guthrie Tait (Edinburgh: Oliver & Boyd, 1946), 31, 33. My thanks to Judith Wilt for pointing me to this reference.

20 [F.D. Maurice], "National Tales of Ireland," *Westminster Review* 9 (Apr. 1828): 440.

21 [William Empson], "The Last of the Catholic Question – Its Principle, History, and Effects," *Edinburgh Review* 49 (Mar. 1829), 268.

22 The rapidity of the move into representation can be seen in the fact that as early as September 1798 the *Monthly Review* noticed a publication titled *The Causes of the Rebellion in Ireland Disclosed* in an article on "Affairs of Ireland," *Monthly Review* 27 (Sep. 1798): 94–97. Personal memoirs also appeared very quickly, the *Analytical Review* noticing in the following month *A Narrative of the Sufferings and Escapes of Charles Jackson, late Resident at Wexford in Ireland,*

"Jackson's *Sufferings and Escape from Wexford*," *Analytical Review* 28 (Oct. 1798): 429. Richard Musgrave's notorious Ascendancy reading, *Memoirs of the Different Rebellions in Ireland*, appeared in 1801, and went through several editions in a few years. For the debate in the immediate aftermath of the rising, see Kevin Whelan's chapter, "'98 After '98" in *Tree of Liberty*.

23 On 1798 as a discomfiting subject avoided or displaced by the first Irish novelists, see Tom Dunne, "Representations of Rebellion: 1798 in Literature," in *Ireland, England, and Australia: Essays in Honour of Oliver MacDonagh*, ed. F.B. Smith (Canberra: Australian National University, 1990), 14–40; and Vivian Mercier, "English Readers: Three Historical Moments." Mitzi Myers contests Dunne's argument by extending and regendering the idea of what constitutes a rebellion narrative in "'Like the Pictures in a Magic Lantern': Gender, History, and Edgeworth's Rebellion Narratives." Myers' notion of "wartime words" offers an important corrective to Dunne's reading of the early Irish novels, although it remains the case that 1798 did not become a direct subject of fiction until the 1820s.

24 Eyre Evans Crowe, "The Northerns of Ninety-Eight," in vol. II of his *Yesterday in Ireland*, 3 vols. (London: 1829).

25 I have discussed this point at some length in *The Achievement of Literary Authority*, chap. 3.

26 James McHenry, *O'Halloran, or the Insurgent Chief: A Tale of the United Irishmen* (Belfast, 1847), 7. I cite the later edition of the novel, which altered the original subtitle, replacing the date 1798 to name the United Irishmen. It also included an appendix identifying places and names in the narrative.

27 *Ibid.*, 7–8.

28 *Waverley; or 'Tis Sixty Years Since*, ed. Claire Lamont (Oxford: Oxford University Press, 1986), 340.

29 Moore, *Captain Rock*, ix.

30 Dunne, "Representations of Rebellion," 34.

31 [Maurice], "National Tales of Ireland," 438. There is an ever-expanding literature on 1798 and on the United Irishmen. For a useful introduction, see the essays in *The Mighty Wave: The 1798 Rebellion in Wexford*, ed. Dáire Keogh and Nicholas Furlong (Dublin: Four Courts Press, 1996) and the important work by, among others, Nancy J. Curtin, *The United Irishmen: Popular Politics in Ulster and Dublin, 1791–1798* (Oxford: Clarendon Press, 1994), Marianne Elliott, *Partners in Revolution*, and Kevin Whelan, *The Tree of Liberty*. See also Bartlett, *The Fall and Rise of the Irish Nation*.

32 Whelan, "Reinterpreting the 1798 Rebellion in County Wexford," in Keogh and Furlong (eds.), *The Mighty Wave*, 23.

33 Moore's comment appears in the postscript to a letter to Major-General Johnson, which Cornwallis enclosed in his dispatch of June 22, rpt. in "Intelligence of Importance From the London Gazette," *Gentlemen's Magazine* 68 (Aug. 1798): 714.

34 Reported in "Interesting Intelligence from Ireland," *Gentlemen's Magazine* 69 (Jan. 1799): 72. In a related point, R. B. McDowell concludes that "the very incohesiveness of the rising made its complete suppression a difficult task,"

Ireland in the Age of Imperialism and Revolution 1760–1801 (Oxford: Clarendon Press, 1979), 633.

35 "Interesting Intelligence," 71.

36 "Review of Public Affairs: Ireland," *Critical Review* 25 (Apr. 1799): 577.

37 Banim, *The Croppy*, III: 316.

38 [Francis Jeffrey], "O'Driscol's *History of Ireland*," *Edinburgh Review* 46 (Oct. 1827): 433.

39 *Ibid.*

40 In his landmark article on early nineteenth-century Irish historiography, Donald MacCartney emphasizes the degree to which it was shaped by contemporary political debates, "The Writing of History in Ireland 1800–30," *Irish Historical Studies* 10 (Sep. 1957): 347–62.

41 [Jeffrey], "O'Driscol's *History*," 433.

42 Preface to the second edition of *Lyrical Ballads*, *Wordsworth: Poetical Works*, 740.

43 I draw loosely on Søren Kierkegaard, *Repetition*, trans. Walter Lowrie (Princeton: Princeton University Press, 1941), 3–4.

44 "Ireland, and Captain Rock," 435.

45 The last phrase comes from Christian Isobel Johnstone, "Florence O'Brien: An Irish Tale," *Tait's Magazine* 7 (Jan.–Jun. 1836): 264.

46 Leerssen, *Remembrance and Imagination*, 9. Luke Gibbons similarly refers to "unfinished business" in *Transformations in Irish Culture*, 157.

47 Quoted in Donald MacCartney, "The Writing of History," 362. History in this mode thus emphatically belongs to what Marshall Brown calls "history-for," "Rethinking the Scale of Literary History," *Rethinking Literary History*, ed. Mario Valdes and Linda Hutcheon (Oxford: Oxford University Press, 2002).

48 "Reid's *Travels in Ireland*," *Monthly Review* n.s. 2, vol. 101 (Jul. 1823), 245.

49 The 1841 census recorded a population of 8,175,124, and there are no reliable figures for before that date, although there seems to be a consensus among modern historians that at the turn of the nineteenth century the Irish population was around five million. In the 1820s, figures of six or seven million were routinely invoked, and O'Connell proposed a figure of some eight million (see *Select Speeches*, 277). The crucial point is not so much absolute numbers as the rate of growth. In the century between 1740 and 1840, Ireland's population quadrupled (England's population, meanwhile, doubled in the same period), and Ireland's annual growth rate from 1750 to 1821 (it started slowing in the 1820s) is estimated somewhere between 1.3 and 1.6 percent, making it the highest growth rate in Europe. For an overview see Cormac Ó Gráda,, "Poverty, Population, and Agriculture, 1801–45,"*A New History of Ireland*, volume V: *Ireland Under the Union, 1* . For a more detailed economic analysis, see Joel Mokyr and Cormac Ó Gráda, "New Developments in Irish Population History, 1700–1850," *Economic History Review* 27 (1984): 473–88.

50 O'Connell, *Select Speeches*, 8.

51 "Dr. Milner and Others," 64.

52 [Empson], "The Last of the Catholic Question," 262.

53 [John Banim], *The Anglo-Irish of the Nineteenth Century: A Novel*, 3 vols. (London: 1828), III: 130–31.

54 Linda Colley notes that the 1831 census showed around 580,000 Irish in Britain, representing an enormous increase in the post-Union period. She usefully lists the anti-emancipation petitions received from the mainland cities where they clustered, *Britons: Forging the Nation 1707–1837* (New Haven and London: Yale University Press, 1992), 329–30.

55 "Ireland: Its Evils and Remedies," *Quarterly Review* 38 (Jul. 1828): 66.

56 [William Johnston], "Ireland As It Is: In 1828," *Blackwood's Magazine* 24 (Oct. 1828): 453. The articles ran in volumes 24 and 25 from October 1828 to February 1829.

57 Johnston's contributions to *Blackwood's* on the Irish question also include a story of failed interdenominational romance set in 1798, "The Irish Yeoman. – A Tale of the Year Ninety-Eight" (May 1828), along with a travel series, "Sketches on the Road in Ireland," which ran from April to August 1829. On his career, see Maurice Milne, "A Neglected Paternalist: William Johnston of *Blackwood's Magazine*," *Victorian Periodicals Review* 28 (Spring 1995): 11–26. Milne points out that Johnston was erroneously spelled Johnstone in the original *Wellesley Index to Victorian Periodicals*, so that much of his periodical production was initially overlooked.

58 [Johnston], "Ireland As It Is," 556.

59 This phrase appears in a slightly earlier article on "The Clare Election," *Blackwood's Magazine* 24 (Aug. 1828): 224.

60 Thomas Carlyle, "Repeal of the Union," *The Examiner*, 29 Apr. 1848, 275. On the typing of Irish immigrants in British discourse of the midcentury, see Corbett, *Allegories of Union*, chap.3.

61 [Johnston], "Ireland As It Is," vol. 24: 551, 555, 556.

62 Steven Goldsmith, "Blake's Agitation," in *Rhetorical and Cultural Dissolution in Romanticism*, ed. Thomas Pfau and Rhonda Ray Keresmar (Durham, N.C. and London: Duke University Press, 1996), 766.

63 Hazlitt, *Complete Works*, XII: 264.

64 Lucy Newlyn, *Reading, Writing, and Romanticism: The Anxiety of Reception* (Oxford: Oxford University Press, 2000), chap. 9.

65 Stanley Cavell's important meditation on the language of philosophy, which has a special interest in figures of Romantic thought, stresses philosophy's desire to eliminate "voice" and "interest" in order to remove its transcendent ambitions from the contingency and instability of the person. See in particular *Conditions Handsome and Unhandsome: The Constitution of Emersonian Perfectionism* (Chicago and London: University of Chicago Press, 1990). For an excellent account of Cavell's intersection with British Romanticism, see Edward Duffy, "The Romantic Calling of Thinking: Stanley Cavell on the Line with Wordsworth," *Studies in Romanticism* 17 (1998): 615–45.

66 See his review of Morgan's *Life and Times of Salvator Rosa*, "Lady Morgan's Life of Salvator," *Edinburgh Review* 40 (Jul. 1824): 316–49.

67 Bartlett, *Fall and Rise*, 345.

68 O'Connell, *Select Speeches*, 270.

69 Quoted Oliver MacDonagh, in *The Hereditary Bondsman: Daniel O'Connell 1775–1829* (London: Weidenfeld and Nicolson, 1988), 214.
70 *Ibid.*, 255.
71 Lecky, *Leaders of Public Opinion*, 249.
72 Morgan, *Memoirs*, II: 319.
73 See also Felicia Hemans' account of an O'Connellite procession she saw in Dublin in 1833 as "a very remarkable I might say *portentous* scene," Henry F. Chorley, *Memorials of Mrs. Hemans, With Illustrations of Her Literary Character From Her Private Correspondence* (Philadelphia, 1836) 244. My thanks to Gary Kelly for this reference.
74 Morgan, *Memoirs*, II: 276.
75 Žižek, "A Leftist Plea," 990 n.
76 Although Banim's novel is mostly seen as a rewriting of Edgeworth's *The Absentee*, the novel itself tends to foreground its connection to Morgan. Its trio of heroines comes directly out of Morgan's later national tale, while references to *The Wild Irish Girl* appear early in the text, with Morgan being explicitly named in a memorable scene featuring John Wilson Croker and the *Quarterly*, *Anglo-Irish*, I: 120–21. On *Anglo-Irish* and *The Absentee*, see Barry Sloan, *The Pioneers of Anglo-Irish Fiction 1800–1860* (Gerrards Cross: Colin Smythe, 1986), 98; and Robert Tracy, *The Unappeasable Host*, 46. For Banim as national novelist, see also Tom Dunne, "The Insecure Voice: A Catholic Novelist in Support of Emancipation," *Culture et Pratiques Politiques en France et en Irlande XVI–XVIIIe Siècle* (Paris: Centre De Recherches Historiques, 1988), 213–33.
77 On the novel as a political *Bildungsroman*, see Terry Eagleton, *Crazy John and the Bishop and Other Essays on Irish Culture* (Notre Dame: University of Notre Dame Press, 1998), 219.
78 Introductory Letter, *The Boyne Water* (London, 1826), xxiii-iv.
79 Banim is intensifying the well-established motif of unstable Anglo-Irish identity that shaped the national tale from the start. As Mitzi Myers points out, Edgeworth in particular evidences an early and decided sense that "Anglo-Irish identities are always problematic, papering over the colonialist indeterminacy of origins," "Goring John Bull: Maria Edgeworth's Hibernian High Jinks versus the Imperialist Imaginary," in *Cutting Edges: Postmodern Critical Edges in Eighteenth-Century Satire*, ed. James E. Gill (Knoxville: University of Tennessee Press, 1995), 371.
80 The national nomenclature also underlines the surfacing in the 1820s of a new racial inflection in discussions of nationality, although that inflection would not become fully racialized until later in the century. The racial note goes hand-in-hand with the expulsion of the Anglo-Irish as a "mongrel" colonial class, as in references to "mongrel legislators, neither Irish nor English" (*The Croppy*, II: 38) or to the "yoke of the Anglo-Irish Creoles" (Crowe, "Northerns of Ninety-Eight," III: 176).
81 Eagleton, *Heathcliff*, 176.
82 Morgan, *Book of the Boudoir*, I: vii.
83 Morgan, "Prefatory Address," *Wild Irish Girl*, 262.

Bibliography

PRIMARY SOURCES

[Adams, Jane]. "A Private Narrative of the Rebellion of 1798." Appendix to T. Crofton Croker. *Researches in the South of Ireland*. London: 1824.

"Affairs of Ireland." *Monthly Review* 27 (Sep. 1798): 94–97.

[Banim, John]. *The Anglo-Irish of the Nineteenth Century: A Novel*. 3 vols. London: 1828.

The Boyne Water, A Tale, By the O'Hara Family. London: 1826.

Banim, Michael. *The Croppy: A Tale of the Irish Rebellion of 1798*. 3 vols. (1828). New York: Garland, 1978.

Barbauld, Anna Laetitia. *The Works of Anna Laetitia Barbauld*. Ed. Lucy Aikin. London: 1825.

[Blake family]. *Letters From the Irish Highlands*. London: 1825.

[Brougham, Henry]. "Porter's *Travels in Russia and Sweden*." *Edinburgh Review* 14 (Apr. 1809): 170–87.

Byron, Lord George Gordon. *Byron: Poetical Works*. Rev. edn. Ed. John Jump. London: Oxford University Press, 1970.

The Complete Miscellaneous Prose. Ed. Andrew Nicholson. Oxford: Clarendon Press, 1991.

Lord Byron's Selected Letters and Journals. Ed. Leslie A. Marchand. Cambridge, Mass.: Belknap Press, 1982.

[Campbell, Thomas.] *A Philosophical Survey of the South of Ireland, In a Series of Letters to John Watkinson, M.D.* London: 1777.

Carlyle, Thomas. "Repeal of the Union." *The Examiner* no. 2100 (29 Apr. 1848): 275–76.

Carr, John. *The Stranger in Ireland; or a Tour in the Southern and Western Parts of that Country in the Year 1805*. London: 1806.

"Carr's *Tour in Holland and Germany*." *Edinburgh Review* 10 (Jul. 1907): 271–83.

Chorley, Henry F. *Memorials of Mrs. Hemans, With Illustrations of Her Literary Character From Her Private Correspondence*. Philadelphia: 1836.

Coleridge, Samuel Taylor. *The Collected Works of Samuel Taylor Coleridge*. Vol. III: *Essays on His Times in the Morning Post and the Courier, I*. Ed. David V. Erdman. Princeton: Princeton University Press, 1978.

Cooper, George. *Letters on the Irish Nation: Written During a Visit to That Kingdom in the Autumn of the Year 1799*. London: 1800.

[Croker, John Wilson]. Review of John Carr *Descriptive Travels in the Southern and Eastern parts of Spain and the Balearic Isles, in the Year 1809, Quarterly Review* 7 (Jun. 1812): 408–11.

"Mason's *Statistical Account of Ireland.*" *Quarterly Review* 13 (Apr. 1815): 76–82.

[Croker, John Wilson and William Gifford]. "France, by Lady Morgan." *Quarterly Review* 17 (Apr. 1817): 260–86.

Croker, T. Crofton. *Researches in the South of Ireland Illustrative of the Scenery, Architectural Remains and the Manners and Superstititions of the Peasantry with an Appendix containing a Private Narrative of the Rebellion of 1798*. London: 1824. Rpt., Barnes and Noble, 1968.

Crowe, Eyre Evans. *Yesterday in Ireland.* 3 vols. London: 1829.

Curwen, J. C. *Observations on the State of Ireland, Principally Directed to its Agriculture and Rural Population; In a Series of Letters, Written on a Tour Through That Country.* 2 vols. London: 1818.

Dewar, Daniel. *Observations on the Character, Customs, and Superstitions of the Irish; And on Some of the Causes Which Have Retarded the Moral and Political Improvement of Ireland.* London: 1812.

"Domestic Literature." *New Annual Register* 27 (1806): 289–373.

"Dr. Milner and Others on the Catholics of Ireland." *Edinburgh Review* 14 (Apr. 1809): 60–64.

Dubois, Edward. *My Pocket Book; or, Hints for "A Ryghte Merrie and Conceitede" Tour, in Quarto: To be Called "The Stranger in Ireland," in 1805*. London: 1807.

Edgeworth, Frances, ed. *Memoir of Maria Edgeworth with a Selection from her Letters* (privately printed, 1867).

Edgeworth, Maria. *The Absentee* (1812). Eds. W. J. McCormack and Kim Walker. Oxford: Oxford University Press, 1988.

Castle Rackrent and Ennui (1800; 1809). Ed. Marilyn Butler. London: Penguin, 1992.

Ormond (1817). Ed. Claire Connolly. London: Penguin, 2000.

Tour in Connemara and the Martins of Ballinahinch. Ed. Harold Edgeworth Butler. London: Constable & Co., 1950.

The Works of Maria Edgeworth. 12 vols. Ed. Marilyn Butler and Mitzi Myers. London: Pickering & Chatto, 1999/2000.

[Edgeworth, Maria, and Richard Lovell Edgeworth]. "Carr's *Stranger in Ireland.*" *Edinburgh Review* 10 (Apr. 1807): 40–60.

[Empson, William]. "The Last of the Catholic Question – Its Principle, History, and Effects." *Edinburgh Review* 49 (Mar. 1829): 218–72.

Erlington, the Rev. Thomas. *A Sketch of the State of Ireland, Past and Present.* Dublin: 1808.

[Fitzsimon, Ellen O'Connell]. "Irish Novels and Irish Novelists." *Dublin Review* 4 (Apr. 1838): 495–543.

Gamble, John. *A View of Society and Manners, in the North of Ireland, in the Summer and Autumn of 1812*. London: 1813.

Glassford, James. *Notes of Three Tours in Ireland, In 1824 and 1826*. Bristol: 1832.

[Gough, John]. *A Tour in Ireland, In 1813 & 1814; With an Appendix, Written in 1816, on another visit to that Island*. By an Englishman. Dublin [1817].

Grenville, Lord William Wyndham, 1st baron. *Letter from the Right Honourable Lord Grenville to the Earl of Fingall*. London: 1810.

Grimes, Seamus, ed. *Ireland in 1804*. Dublin: Four Courts Press, 1980.

Hall, James. *Tour Through Ireland; Particularly the Interior & Least Known Parts: Containing an Accurate View of the Parties, Politics, and Improvements, in the Different Provinces; With Reflections and Observations on the Union of Britain and Ireland; the Practicability and Advantages of A Telegraphic Commnication Between the Two Countries, and Other Matters of Importance*. 2 vols. London: 1813.

Hazlitt, William. *The Complete Works of William Hazlitt*. 21 vols. Ed. P. P. Howe. London: Dent, 1930–34.

"Lady Morgan's Life of Salvator." *Edinburgh Review* 40 (Jul. 1824): 316–49.

Hoare, Sir Richard Colt, Bart. *Journal of A Tour In Ireland, A.D. 1806*. London: 1807.

Hume, David. *A Treatise of Human Nature*. Ed. L. A. Selby-Bigge. Oxford: Clarendon Press, 1973.

"Intelligence of Importance From the London Gazette." *Gentlemen's Magazine* 68 (Aug. 1798): 709–15.

"Interesting Intelligence from Ireland." *Gentlemen's Magazine* 69 (Jan. 1799): 71–72.

"Ireland." *British Review* 22 (Nov. 1824): 412–46.

"Ireland, and Captain Rock." *British Critic* 21 (Apr. 1824): 421–45.

"Ireland: Its Evils and Remedies." *Quarterly Review* 38 (Jul. 1828): 53–84.

"Irish Writers in Ireland." *Ghost of the Rushlight* 1 (1826): 6–9.

"Jackson's *Sufferings and Escape from Wexford*." *Analytical Review* 28 (Oct. 1798): 429.

[Jeffrey, Francis]. "O'Driscol's *History of Ireland*." *Edinburgh Review* 46 (Oct. 1827): 433–70.

"Pamphlets on the Catholic Question." *Edinburgh Review* 11 (Oct. 1807): 116–44.

[Johnston, William]. "Ireland As It Is: In 1828." *Blackwood's Magazine* 24 and 25 (Oct. 1828–Feb. 1829): vol. 24: 453–61, 530–57, 752–62; vol. 25: 72–80, 193–200.

"The Clare Election." *Blackwood's Magazine* 24 (Aug. 1828): 223–25.

[Johnstone, Christian Isobel]. "Florence O'Brien: An Irish Tale." *Tait's Magazine* 7 (Jan.–Jun. 1836): 46–58, 89–102, 262–71, 361–82.

"Lady Morgan's Princess." *Tait's Edinburgh Magazine*, n.s., 2 (Feb. 1835): 85–114.

Kavanagh, Julia. *English Women of Letters: Biographical Sketches*. 2 vols. London: 1863.

"Lady Morgan–Her Publisher, &c.." *Literary Gazette*, (6 Oct. 1821): 639–40.

Lecky, William Edward Hartpole. *Leaders of Public Opinion in Ireland: Swift–Flood–Grattan–O'Connell*. Rev. edn. London: 1971.

[Lister, T. H.]. "Novels Descriptive of Irish Life." *Edinburgh Review* 52 (1831): 410–31.

McHenry, James. *O'Halloran, or The Insurgent Chief: A Tale of the United Irishmen. To Which is Added an Appendix, Containing Biographical Memoirs of the Principal Characters, and Descriptive of the Scenery of the Work.* Belfast: 1847.

[MacIntosh, James]. "Wakefield's *Ireland.*" *Edinburgh Review* 20 (Nov. 1812): 346–69.

[Malthus, T. R.]. "Newenham and Others on the State of Ireland." *Edinburgh Review* 12 (Jul. 1808): 336–55.

Occasional Papers of T. R. Malthus on Ireland, Population, and Political Economy. Ed. Bernard Semmel. New York: Burt Franklin, 1963.

[Mason, William Shaw]. *Bibliotheca Hibernicana: Or A Descriptive Catalogue of a Select Irish Library Collected For the Right Hon. Robert Peel* (1823). Shannon: Irish University Press, 1970.

Maturin, Charles Robert. *Melmoth the Wanderer* (1820). Ed. Douglas Grant. Oxford: Oxford University Press, 1989.

The Milesian Chief: A Romance. 4 vols. London: 1812.

The Wild Irish Boy. London: 1808.

[Maurice, F. D.?]. "National Tales of Ireland." *Westminster Review* 9 (Apr. 1828): 422–40.

[Mill, James]. "State of Ireland." *Edinburgh Review* 21 (Jul. 1813): 340–64.

Moore, Thomas. "Irish Novels." *Edinburgh Review* 43 (Feb. 1826): 356–72.

Journal of Thomas Moore. 5 vols. Ed. Wilfred S. Dowden. Newark: University of Delaware Press, 1983.

Memoirs of Captain Rock, the Celebrated Irish Chieftain, with Some Account of His Ancestors. Written By Himself. London: 1824.

Morgan, Sydney Owenson (Lady). *Absenteeism.* London: 1825.

The Book of the Boudoir. 2 vols. London: 1829.

Book Without a Name. London: 1841.

Florence Macarthy: An Irish Tale. 4 vols. London: 1818.

France. London: 1817.

Lady Morgan's Memoirs: Autobiography, Diaries, Correspondence. 2 vols. Ed. W. Hepworth Dixon and Geraldine Jewsbury. London: 1862.

Letter to the Reviewers of "Italy;" Including an Answer to a Pamphlet entitled "Observations Upon the Calumnies and Misrepresentations in Lady Morgan's Italy". London: 1821.

The Missionary (1811). Ed. Julia M. Wright. Peterborough, Ont.: Broadview Press, 2002.

The O'Briens and the O'Flahertys (1827). London: Pandora, 1988.

O'Donnel: A National Tale. London: 1814. Rpt., New York: Garland, 1979.

O'Donnel rev. edn. London: 1835.

Patriotic Sketches of Ireland, Written in Connaught. London: 1807.

The Princess; or the Beguine. 3 vols. London: 1835.

Twelve Original Hibernian Melodies, with English Words, Imitated and Translated, from the Works of the Ancient Irish Bards. London: 1805.

The Wild Irish Girl: A National Tale (1806). Ed. Claire Connolly and Stephen Copley. London: Pickering and Chatto, 2000.

The Wild Irish Girl. Rev. edn. London: 1846.

Woman and Her Master (1840). Westport, Conn.: Hyperion Press, 1976.

Murray, Patrick Joseph. *The Life of John Banim* (1857). New York and London: Garland Publishing, 1978.

"Newenham's *View of the Circumstances of Ireland*." *Monthly Review* 67–68 (Apr.–May 1812): 355–72; 191–202.

O'Connell, Daniel. *The Correspondence of Daniel O'Connell: Volume 4 (1829–1832)*. Ed. Maurice R. O'Connell. Dublin: Stationery Office, 1977.

The Select Speeches of Daniel O'Connell, MP. 2 vols. Ed. John O'Connell. Second series. Dublin: James Duffy, 1872.

"On the Writings of Mr. Maturin, and More Particularly His 'Melmoth'." [Baldwin's] *London Magazine* 3 (May 1821): 514–24.

[O'Sullivan, Mortimer]. Review of *Eighth Report of the Commissioners of Irish Education Inquiry*. *Quarterly Review* 37 (Mar. 1828): 459–84.

Plumptre, Anne. *Narrative of a Residence in Ireland During the Summer of 1814, and That of 1815*. London: 1817.

Reid, Thomas. *Travels in Ireland in the Year 1822, Exhibiting Brief Sketches of the Moral, Physical, and Political State of the Country: With Reflections on the Best Means of Improving its Condition*. London: 1823.

"Reid's *Travels in Ireland*." *Monthly Review*, n.s., 2, vol. 101 (Jul. 1823): 239–46.

Review of Banim, *The Anglo-Irish of the Nineteenth Century*. *Athenaeum* (8 Oct. 1828): 788–90.

Review of Curwen, *Observations on the State of Ireland*. *British Review* 12 (Aug. 1818): 71–89.

Review of Gamble, *A View of Society and Manners in the North of Ireland*. *Gentleman's Magazine* 89 (Jul. 1819): 51–54.

Review of Maturin, *Melmoth the Wanderer*. *Eclectic Review*, n.s., 14 (Dec. 1820): 547–58.

Review of Moore, *Memoirs of Captain Rock*. *Literary Chronicle* (17 Apr. 1824): 241–44.

Review of Morgan, *Ida of Athens*. *Annual Review* 7 (1809): 588–94.

British Critic 33 (May 1809): 525.

Review of Morgan, *Florence Macarthy*. *Antijacobin Review* 55 (Feb. 1819): 509–21.

British Review 13 (May 1819): 482–94.

Edinburgh Monthly Review 1 (Jun. 1819): 655–62.

Monthly Magazine 46 (Jan. 1819): 531.

New Monthly Magazine 10 (Jan. 1819): 529–33.

Review of Morgan, *The O'Briens and the O'Flahertys*. *Literary Gazette* (3 Nov. 1827): 707–09.

New Monthly Magazine 20 (Dec. 1827): 497–505.

"Review of Public Affairs: Ireland." *Critical Review* 25 (Apr. 1799): 577–79.

Rousseau, Jean-Jacques, and Johann Gottfried Herder. *On the Origin of Language*. Trans. John H. Moran and Alexander Gode. Chicago and London: University of Chicago Press, 1966.

Schiller, Friedrich. *On the Naive and Sentimental in Literature.* Trans. Helen Watanabe-O'Kelly. Manchester: Carcanet New Press, 1981.

[Scott, Walter, with William Gifford]. "Carr's *Caledonian Sketches.*" *Quarterly Review* 1 (Feb. 1809): 178–93.

Scott, Walter. Review of Maturin, *Fatal Revenge. Quarterly Review* 3 (May 1810): 339–47.

Sir Walter Scott; Selected Poems. Ed. Thomas Crawford. Oxford: Clarendon Press, 1972.

Sir Walter Scott's Journal 1829–32. Ed. John Guthrie Tait. Edinburgh: Oliver & Boyd, 1946.

Waverley. Ed. Claire Lamont. Oxford: Oxford University Press, 1986.

Shelley, Percy. *The Complete Works of Percy Bysshe Shelley.* 10 vols. Ed. Roger Ingpen and Walter E. Peck. New York: Gordian Press, 1965.

The Letters of Percy Bysshe Shelley. 2 vols. Ed. Frederick I. Jones. Oxford: Clarendon Press, 1964.

Smith, Adam. *The Theory of Moral Sentiments.* Eds. D. D. Raphael and A. L. Macfie. Indianapolis: Liberty Fund, 1982.

[Smith, Sydney]. "Heude's *Voyage and Travels.*" *Edinburgh Review* 32 (Jul. 1819): 111–18.

"*Memoirs of Captain Rock.*" *Edinburgh Review* 41 (Oct. 1824): 143–53.

"Parnell's *History of Irish Popery Laws.*" *Edinburgh Review* 13 (Oct. 1808): 77–82.

Smollett, Tobias. *Travels Through France and Italy* (1766). Ed. Frank Felsenstein. Oxford: Oxford University Press, 1981.

Stael, Germaine de. *Corinne, or Italy.* Trans. Avriel H. Goldberger. New Brunswick: Rutgers University Press, 1987.

Major Writings of Germaine de Stael. Ed. Vivian Folkenflik. New York: Columbia University Press, 1987.

Sullivan, Denis. *A Picturesque Tour Through Ireland, Illustrated With Numerous Coloured Views of the Most Interesting Scenery.* London: 1824.

[Talfourd, T. N.]. "Irish Romance–New Tales of the O'Hara Family." *New Monthly Magazine* 19 (Jun. 1827): 21–25.

[Townsend, Horatio]. Review of *Tales of the O'Hara Family. Blackwood's Edinburgh Magazine* 24 (Oct. 1828): 469–74.

"Trimmer on the State of Agriculture in Ireland." *Monthly Review* 68 (May 1812): 310–15.

Trotter, John Bernard. *Walks Through Ireland, in the Years 1812, 1814, and 1817; Described in a Series of Letters to An English Gentleman.* London: 1819.

Volney, Constantin François de Chasseboeuf (Comte de). *The Ruins; or, a Survey of the Revolutions of Empires.* London: Edwards, Brown, n.d.

Wakefield, Edward. *An Account of Ireland, Statistical and Political.* 2 vols. London: 1812.

"Wakefield's *Account of Ireland.*" *Monthly Review* 71 (May and Jun. 1813): 1–18.

Wordsworth, William. *Wordsworth: Poetical Works.* Eds. Thomas Hutchinson and Ernest De Selincourt. London: Oxford University Press, 1969.

"Works on Ireland." *Blackwood's Edinburgh Magazine* 15 (May 1824): 544–50.

Young, Arthur. *A Tour in Ireland 1776–1779*. 2 vols. Ed. A.W. Hutton. Shannon: Irish University Press, 1970.

SECONDARY SOURCES

Anderson, Benedict. *Imagined Communities: Reflections on the Origin and Spread of Nationalism*. Rev. edn. London: Verso, 1991.

Andrews, J. H. "Land and People, c. 1780." In Moody and Vaughan (eds.), *A New History of Ireland* IV: 236–64.

Andrews, Malcolm. *The Picturesque: Literary Sources and Documents*. 3 vols. Mountfield: Helm Information, 1994.

The Search for the Picturesque: Landscape Aesthetics and Tourism in Britain, 1760–1800. Stanford: Stanford University Press, 1989.

Arendt, Hannah. *On Revolution*. New York: Penguin, 1965.

Backus, Margo Gayle. *The Gothic Family Romance: Heterosexuality, Child Sacrifice, and the Anglo-Irish Colonial Order*. Durham, N.C. and London: Duke University Press, 1999.

Bakhtin, Mikhail. *The Dialogic Imagination: Four Essays*. Trans. Caryl Emerson and Michael Holquist. Ed. Michael Holquist. Austin: University of Texas Press, 1981.

Speech Genres & Other Late Essays. Trans. Vern W. McGee. Eds. Caryl Emerson and Michael Holquist. Austin: University of Texas Press, 1986.

Bakhtin, Mikhail, and P. N. Medvedev. *The Formal Method in Literary Scholarship: A Critical Introduction to Sociological Poetics*. Trans. Albert J. Wehrle. Cambridge, Mass.: Harvard University Press, 1985.

Bartkowski, Frances. *Travelers, Immigrants, Inmates: Essays in Estrangement*. Minneapolis: University of Minnesota Press, 1995.

Bartlett, Thomas. *The Fall and Rise of the Irish Nation: The Catholic Question 1690–1830*. Dublin: Gill and Macmillan, 1992.

Belanger, Jacqueline. "Some Preliminary Remarks on the Production and Reception of Fiction Relating to Ireland 1800–1829." *Cardiff Corvey: Reading the Romantic Text* 4 (May 2000), <http://www.cf.ac.uk/encap/corvey/articles/cc04_n02.html>.

Bermingham, Ann. *Landscape and Ideology: The English Rustic Tradition, 1740–1680*. Berkeley: University of California Press, 1986.

Bhabha, Homi K. *The Location of Culture*. London and New York: Routledge, 1994.

Bhabha, Homi K., ed. *Nation and Narration*. London and New York: Routledge, 1990.

Bolton, G. C. *The Passing of the Irish Act of Union: a Study in Parliamentary Politics*. London and Oxford: Oxford University Press, 1966.

Bourdieu, Pierre. *In Other Words: Essays Towards a Reflexive Sociology*. Trans. Matthew Adamson. Stanford: Stanford University Press, 1990.

Budick, Sanford, and Wolfgang Iser, eds. *The Translatability of Cultures: Figurations of the Space Between*. Stanford: Stanford University Press, 1996.

Burgess, Miranda J. *British Fiction and the Production of Social Order 1740–1830*. Cambridge: Cambridge University Press, 2000.

"Violent Translations: Allegory, Gender, and Cultural Nationalism in Ireland, 1796–1806." *Modern Language Quarterly* 59 (1998): 33–70.

Butler, Marilyn. "Distinction in the Early Nineteenth-Century Novel." *Modern Language Quarterly* 58 (Dec. 1997): 475–95.

Introduction. *Castle Rackren and Ennui*, 1–54. London: Penguin, 1992.

Maria Edgeworth: A Literary Biography. Oxford: Clarendon Press, 1972.

Buzard, James. *The Beaten Track: European Tourism, Literature, and the Ways to Culture, 1800–1918*. Oxford: Clarendon Press, 1993.

Cameron, Kenneth Neill. *The Young Shelley: Genesis of a Radical*. New York: Macmillan, 1950.

Campbell, Mary. *Lady Morgan: The Life and Times of Sydney Owenson*. London: Pandora, 1988.

Castle, Terry. "The Spectralization of the Other in *The Mysteries of Udolpho*." In *The New 18th Century: Theory, Politics, English Literature*, ed. Felicity Nussbaum and Laura Brown, 231–53. New York and London: Methuen, 1987.

Cavell, Stanley. *Conditions Handsome and Unhandsome: The Constitution of Emersonian Perfectionism*. Chicago and London: University of Chicago Press, 1990.

Certeau, Michel de. *Culture in the Plural*. Trans. Tom Conley. Ed. Luce Giard. Minneapolis: University of Minnesota Press, 1997.

The Practice of Everyday Life. Trans. Steven Randall. Berkeley: University of California Press, 1984.

The Writing of History. Trans. Tom Conley. New York: Columbia University Press, 1988.

Chambers, Ross. *Room for Maneuver: Reading the Oppositional in Narrative*. Chicago and London: University of Chicago Press, 1991.

Chandler, James. *England in 1819: The Politics of Literary Culture and the Case of Romantic Historicism*. Chicago and London: University of Chicago Press, 1998.

Clifford, James. "Traveling Cultures." In *Cultural Studies*, ed. Lawrence Grossberg, Cary Nelson, and Paula Treichler, 96–116. New York: Routledge, 1992.

Clifford, James, and George E. Marcus, eds. *Writing Culture: The Poetics and Politics of Ethnography*. Berkeley: University of California Press, 1986.

Colley, Linda. *Britons: Forging the Nation 1707–1837*. New Haven: Yale University Press, 1992.

Connolly, Claire. Introduction. *The Wild Irish Girl*, xv–lvi. London: Pickering and Chatto, 2000.

"'I accuse Miss Owenson': *The Wild Irish Girl* as Media Event." *Colby Quarterly* 36 (2000): 98–115.

Connolly, S. J. "Mass Politics and Sectarian Conflict, 1823–30." In Vaughan (ed.), *A New History of Ireland*, v: 74–107.

"The Union Government, 1812–32." In Vaughan (ed.), *A New History of Ireland*, v: 48–73.

Copley, Stephen, and Peter Garside, eds. *The Politics of the Picturesque*. Cambridge: Cambridge University Press, 1994.

Corbett, Mary Jean. *Allegories of Union in Irish and English Writing, 1790–1870*. Cambridge: Cambridge University Press, 2000.

Corkery, Daniel. *Synge and Anglo-Irish Literature: A Study*. Cork: Cork University Press, 1931.

Cronin, Michael. *Translating Ireland: Translation, Languages, Cultures*. Cork: Cork University Press, 1996.

Curtin, Nancy J. *The United Irishmen: Popular Politics in Ulster and Dublin, 1791–1798*. Oxford: Clarendon Press, 1994.

Davis, Leith. *Acts of Union: Scotland and the Literary Negotiation of the British Nation 1707–1830*. Stanford: Stanford University Press, 1998.

Deane, Seamus. "Irish National Character 1790–1900." In Dunne, *The Writer as Witness*, 90–103.

"The Production of Cultural Space in Irish Writing." *boundary 2* 21 (Fall 1994): 117–44.

A Short History of Irish Literature. Notre Dame: University of Notre Dame Press, 1986.

Strange Country: Modernity and Nationhood in Irish Writing Since 1790. Oxford: Clarendon Press, 1997.

"Virtue, Travel and the Enlightenment." In *Nations and Nationalisms: France, Britain, Ireland and the Eighteenth-Century Context*, ed. Michael O'Dea and Kevin Whelan, 275–95. Oxford: Voltaire Foundation, 1995.

Dennis, Ian. *Nationalism and Desire in Early Historical Fiction*. London: Macmillan, 1997.

Donoghue, Frank. *The Fame Machine: Book Reviewing and Eighteenth-Century Literary Careers*. Stanford: Stanford University Press, 1996.

Duffy, Edward. "The Romantic Calling of Thinking: Stanley Cavell on the Line with Wordsworth." *Studies in Romanticism* 17 (1998): 615–45.

Duncan, Ian. *Modern Romance and Transformations of the Novel: The Gothic, Scott, Dickens*. Cambridge: Cambridge University Press, 1992.

Dunne, Tom. "'Fiction as the Best History of Nations': Lady Morgan's Irish Novels." In Dunne, *The Writer as Witness*, 133–59.

"Haunted by History: Irish Romantic Writing 1800–50." In *Romanticism in National Context*, ed. Roy Porter and Mikulás Teich, 68–91. Cambridge: Cambridge University Press, 1988.

"The Insecure Voice: A Catholic Novelist in Support of Emancipation." In *Culture et Pratiques Politiques en France et en Irlande XVI–XVIIIe Siècle*, 213–33. Paris: Centre De Recherches Historiques, 1988.

"Representations of Rebellion: 1798 in Literature." In *Ireland, England, and Australia: Essays in Honour of Oliver MacDonagh*, ed. F. B. Smith, 14–40. Canberra: Australian National University, 1990.

Dunne, Tom, ed. *The Writer as Witness: Literature as Historical Evidence*. Cork: Cork University Press, 1987.

Eagleton, Terry. *Heathcliff and the Great Hunger: Studies in Irish Culture*. London: Verso, 1995.

Crazy John and the Bishop and Other Essays on Irish Culture. Notre Dame: Notre Dame Press, 1998.

Eger, Elizabeth, Charlotte Grant, Clíona Ó Gallchoir, and Penny Warburton, eds. *Women, Writing and the Public Sphere 1700–1830*. Cambridge: Cambridge University Press, 2001.

Ekserdjian, David. *Correggio*. New Haven: Yale University Press, 1998.

Elliott, Marianne. *Partners in Revolution: The United Irishmen and France*. New Haven: Yale University Press, 1982.

Fabian, Johannes. "Remembering the Other: Knowledge and Recognition in the Exploration of Central Africa." *Critical Inquiry* 26 (1999): 49–69.

Time and the Other: How Anthropology Makes Its Object. New York: Columbia University Press, 1983.

Ferris, Ina. *The Achievement of Literary Authority: Gender, History and the Waverley Novels*. Ithaca: Cornell University Press, 1991.

"Mobile Words: Romantic Travels and Print Anxiety." *Modern Language Quarterly* 60 (Dec. 1999): 451–68.

"The Question of Ideological Form: Arthur Young, the Agricultural Tour, and Ireland." In *Ideology and Form in Eighteenth-Century Literature*, ed. David H. Richter, 129–45. Lubbock: Texas Tech University Press, 1999.

Flanagan, Thomas. *The Irish Novelists 1800–1850*. New York: Columbia University Press, 1958.

Fogarty, Anne. "Imperfect Concord: Spectres of History in the Irish Novels of Maria Edgeworth and Lady Morgan." In Kelleher and Murphy, *Gender Perspectives in Nineteenth-Century Ireland*, 116–26.

Foley, Tadhg, and Seán Ryder, eds. *Ideology and Ireland in the Nineteenth Century*. Dublin: Four Courts Press, 1998.

Freud, Sigmund. *The Standard Edition of the Complete Psychological Works of Sigmund Freud*. Eds. James Strachey and Anna Freud. London: Hogarth, 1975.

Friedman, Geraldine. *The Insistence of History: Revolution in Burke, Wordsworth, Keats, and Baudelaire*. Stanford: Stanford University Press, 1996.

Fulford, Tim, and Peter J. Kitson, eds. *Romanticism and Colonialism: Writing and Empire, 1780–1830*. Cambridge: Cambridge University Press, 1998. 35–47.

Gellner, Ernest. *Nations and Nationalism*. Ithaca: Cornell University Press, 1983.

Gibbons, Luke. "Between Captain Rock and a Hard Place: Art and Agrarian Insurgency." In Foley and Ryder, *Ideology and Ireland in the Nineteenth Century*, 23–44.

"Romanticism, Realism and Irish Cinema." In *Cinema in Ireland*, ed. Kevin Rockett, Luke Gibbons, and John Hill. London: Croom Helm, 1987.

Transformations in Irish Culture. Notre Dame: University of Notre Dame Press, 1996.

Goldsmith, Steven. "Blake's Agitation." In *Rhetorical and Cultural Dissolution in Romanticism*, ed. Thomas Pfau and Rhonda Ray Keresmar, 753–96. Durham, N.C. and London: Duke University Press, 1996.

Goldstein, Laurence. *Ruins and Empire: The Evolution of a Theme in Augustan and Romantic Literature*. Pittsburgh: University of Pittsburgh Press, 1977.

Guest, Harriet. *Small Change: Women, Learning, Patriotism, 1750–1810*. Chicago and London: University of Chicago Press, 2000.

Habermas, Jürgen. *The Structural Transformation of the Public Sphere*. Trans. Thomas Burger. Cambridge, Mass.: MIT Press, 1989.

Hadfield, Andrew, and John McVeagh, eds. *Strangers To That Land: British Perceptions of Ireland From the Reformation to the Famine*. Gerrards Cross: Colin Smythe, 1994.

Haefner, Joel. "The Romantic Scene(s) of Writing." In *Re-Visioning Romanticism: British Women Writers, 1776–1837*, ed. Carol Shiner Wilson and Joel Haefner, 256–73. Philadelphia: University of Pennsylvania Press, 1994.

Harrington, John P., comp. and ed. *The English Traveller in Ireland: Accounts of Ireland and the Irish Through Five Centuries*. Dublin: Wolfhound Press, 1991.

Hawes, Louis. *Presences of Nature: British Landscape 1780–1830*. New Haven: Yale Center for British Art, 1982.

Henderson, Andrea K. *Romantic Identities: Varieties of Subjectivity, 1774–1830*. Cambridge: Cambridge University Press, 1996.

Hinde, Wendy. *Catholic Emancipation: A Shake to Men's Minds*, Oxford: Blackwell, 1992.

Hofkosh, Sonia. *Sexual Politics and the Romantic Author*. Cambridge: Cambridge University Press, 1998.

Hollingworth, Brian. *Maria Edgeworth's Irish Writing: Language, History, Politics*. New York: St. Martin's Press, 1999.

Holmes, Richard. *Shelley: The Pursuit*. London: Penguin, 1987.

Hooper, Glenn. "Anne Plumptre: An Independent Traveller." In Kelleher and Murphy, *Gender Perspectives in Nineteenth-Century Ireland*, 129–39.

"Stranger in Ireland: The Problematics of the Post-Union Travelogue." *Mosaic* 21 (Mar. 1995): 25–47.

Hooper, Glen, ed. *The Tourist's Gaze: Travellers to Ireland, 1800–2000*. Cork: Cork University Press, 2001.

Idman, Niilo. *Charles Robert Maturin: His Life and Works*. Helsingfors: Helsingfors Centraltryckeri, 1923.

Irigaray, Luce. *This Sex Which Is Not One*. Trans. Catherine Porter. Ithaca: Cornell University Press, 1985.

Iser, Wolfgang. "Representation: A Performative Act." In *The Aims of Representation: Subject/Text/History*, ed. Murray Kreiger, 217–32. New York: Columbia University Press, 1987.

Janowitz, Anne. *England's Ruins: Poetic Purpose and the National Landscape*. Oxford: Blackwell, 1990.

Jenkins, Brian. *Era of Emancipation: British Government of Ireland, 1812–1830*. Kingston and Montreal: McGill-Queen's University Press, 1988.

Jones, Vivien. "'The Coquetry of Nature': Politics and the Picturesque in Women's Fiction." In Copley and Garside, *The Politics of the Picturesque*, 120–44.

Kakfa, Franz. *Tagebücher*. Ed. Max Brod. New York: Shocken Books, 1948.

Keane, Angela. *Women Writers and the English Nation in the 1790s*. Cambridge: Cambridge University Press, 2000.

Kelleher, Margaret, and James H. Murphy, eds. *Gender Perspectives in Nineteenth-Century Ireland: Public and Private Spheres*. Dublin: Irish Academic Press, 1997.

Kelly, Gary. *Women, Writing, and Revolution 1790–1827*. Oxford: Clarendon Press, 1993.

English Fiction of the Romantic Period 1789–1830. London: Longmans, 1989.

Keogh, Dáire, and Nicholas Furlong, eds. *The Mighty Wave: The 1798 Rebellion in Wexford*. Dublin: Four Courts Press, 1996.

Kiberd, Declan. *Inventing Ireland: The Literature of the Modern Nation*. Cambridge, Mass.: Harvard University Press, 1995.

Kierkegaard, Søren. *Repetition*. Trans. Walter Lowrie. Princeton: Princeton University Press, 1941.

Kilfeather, Siobhán Marie. "'Strangers at Home': Political Fictions by Women in Eighteenth-Century Ireland." Ph.D. diss., Princeton University Press, 1989.

Klancher, Jon. *The Making of English Reading Audiences, 1790–1832*. Madison: University of Wisconsin Press, 1987.

Kowaleski-Wallace, Elizabeth. *Their Fathers' Daughters: Hannah More, Maria Edgeworth and Patriarchal Complicity*. New York: Oxford University Press, 1991.

Kreilkamp, Vera. *The Anglo-Irish Novel and the Big House*. Syracuse: Syracuse University Press, 1998.

Kristeva, Julia. *Powers of Horror: An Essay on Abjection*. Trans. Leon S. Roudiez. New York: Columbia University Press, 1982.

Strangers to Ourselves. Trans. Leon S. Roudiez. New York: Columbia University Press, 1991.

LaCapra, Dominick. "Trauma, Absence, Loss." *Critical Inquiry* 25 (Summer 1999): 696–727.

Leerssen, Joep. "How *The Wild Irish Girl* Made Ireland Romantic." *Dutch Quarterly Review of Anglo-American Letters* 18 (1988): 209–27.

Mere Irish & Fior-Ghael: Studies in the Idea of Irish Nationality, its Development and Literary Expression Prior to the Nineteenth Century. Amsterdam: John Benjamins Publishing Company, 1986.

"On the Treatment of Irishness in Romantic Anglo-Irish Fiction." *Irish University Review* 20 (1990): 251–63.

Remembrance and Imagination: Patterns in the Historical and Literary Representation of Ireland in the Nineteenth Century. Notre Dame: University of Notre Dame Press, 1997.

Lew, Joseph W. "Sidney Owenson and the Fate of Empire." *Keats–Shelley Journal* 39 (1990): 39–65.

Lloyd, David. *Anomalous States: Irish Writing and the Post-Colonial Moment.* Durham, N.C.: Duke University Press, 1993.

Nationalism and Minor Literature: James Clarence Mangan and the Emergence of Irish Cultural Nationalism. Berkeley: University of California Press, 1987.

Lynch, Deidre. "The (Dis)Locations of Romantic Nationalism: Shelley, Staël, and the Home Schooling of Monsters." In *The Literary Channel: The Inter-National Invention of the Novel*, ed. Margaret Cohen and Carolyn Dever, 194–224. Princeton: Princeton University Press, 2002.

"Domesticating Fictions and Nationalizing Women: Edmund Burke, Property, and the Reproduction of Englishness." In *Romanticism, Race and Imperial Culture, 1780–1834*, ed. Alan Richardson and Sonia Hofkosh, 40–61. Bloomington and Indianapolis: Indiana University Press, 1996.

The Economy of Character: Novels, Market Culture, and the Business of Inner Meaning. Chicago and London: University of Chicago Press, 1998.

Lyotard, Jean-François. *The Lyotard Reader.* Ed. Andrew Benjamin. Oxford: Blackwell, 1989.

Macaulay, Rose. *Pleasure of Ruins.* Ed. Constance Babington Smith. Interpreted in photographs by Roloff Beny. Rev. edn. London: Thames & Hudson, 1977.

MacCartney, Donald. "The Writing of History in Ireland 1800–30." *Irish Historical Studies* 10 (Sep. 1957): 347–62.

McCormack, W. J. *Ascendancy and Tradition in Anglo-Irish Literary History from 1789 to 1939.* Oxford: Clarendon Press, 1985.

The Pamphlet Debate on the Union Between Great Britain and Ireland, 1797–1800. Dublin: Irish Academic Press, 1996.

McCormack, W. J. and Kim Walker. Introduction to *The Absentee*, by Maria Edgeworth, pp. ix–xlii.

MacDonagh, Oliver. *The Hereditary Bondsman: Daniel O'Connell 1775–1829.* London: Weidenfeld and Nicolson, 1988.

Ireland: The Union and its Aftermath. Rev. edn. London: Allen & Unwin, 1977.

McDowell, R. B. *Ireland in the Age of Imperialism and Revolution 1760–1801*. Oxford: Clarendon Press, 1979.

McKeon, Michael. "The Pastoral Revolution." In *Refiguring Revolutions: Aesthetics and Politics From the English Revolution to the Romantic Revolution*, ed. Kevin Sharpe and Steven N. Zwicker, 267–89. Berkeley: University of California Press, 1998.

McLeod, Deborah. Introduction to *Something New: Or, Adventures at Campbell-House*, by Anne Plumptre. Peterborough, Ont.: Broadview Press, 1996.

Magnuson, Paul. *Reading Public Romanticism.* Princeton: Princeton University Press, 1998.

Manning, Peter J. *Reading Romantics: Text and Context.* New York: Oxford University Press, 1990.

Maxwell, Constantia, ed. *The Stranger in Ireland: From the Reign of Elizabeth to the Great Famine.* London: Cape, 1954.

Mellor, Anne K. *Romanticism and Gender.* New York and London: Routledge, 1993.

Mothers of the Nation: Women's Political Writing in England 1780–1830. Bloomington and Indianapolis: Indiana University Press, 2000.

Mercier, Vivian. "English Readers: Three Historical Moments." In *Irish Writers and Politics*, ed. Okifumi Komesu and Masaru Sekine, 3–35. Gerrards Cross: Colin Smythe, 1990.

Merleau-Ponty, Maurice. *The Prose of the World.* Trans. John O'Neil. Ed. Claude Lefort. Evanston: Northwestern University Press, 1973.

Michasiw, Kim Ian. "Nine Revisionist Theses on the Picturesque." *Representations* 38 (1992): 76–100.

Milne, Maurice. "A Neglected Paternalist: William Johnston of *Blackwood's Magazine.*" *Victorian Periodicals Review* 28 (Spring 1995): 11, 26.

Moers, Ellen. *Literary Women: The Great Writers.* New York: Oxford University Press, 1976.

Mokyr, Joel, and Cormac Ó Gráda. "New Developments in Irish Population History, 1700–1850." *Economic History Review* 27 (1984): 473–88.

Moody, T. W. and W. E. Vaughan, eds. *A New History of Ireland.* Vol. IV: *Eighteenth-Century Ireland.* Oxford: Clarendon Press, 1986.

Morash, Christopher. *Writing the Irish Famine.* Oxford: Clarendon Press, 1995.

Moskal, Jeanne. "Gender, Nationality, and Textual Authority in Lady Morgan's Travel Books." In *Romantic Women Writers: Voices and Countervoices*, ed. Paula R. Feldman and Theresa M. Kelley, 170–93. Hanover: University Press of New England, 1995.

Moynahan, Julian. *Anglo-Irish: the Literary Imagination in a Hyphenated Culture.* Princeton: Princeton University Press, 1995.

Mullan, John. *Sentiment and Sociability: The Language of Feeling in the Eighteenth Century.* Oxford: Clarendon Press, 1988.

Murphy, Willa. "Maria Edgeworth and the Aesthetics of Secrecy." In Foley and Ryder, *Ideology and Ireland in the Nineteenth Century*, 45–54.

Myers, Mitzi. "'Completing the Union': Critical *Ennui*, the Politics of Narrative, and the Reformation of Irish Cultural Identity." *Prose Studies* 18 (1995): 41–77.

"Goring John Bull: Maria Edgeworth's Hibernian High Jinks versus the Imperialist Imaginary." In *Cutting Edges: Postmodern Critical Edges in Eighteenth-Century Satire*, ed. James E. Gill, 367–94. Knoxville: University of Tennessee Press, 1995.

"'Like the Pictures in a Magic Lantern': Gender, History, and Edgeworth's Rebellion Narratives." *Nineteenth-Century Contexts* 19 (1996): 373–412.

Newlyn, Lucy. *Reading, Writing, and Romanticism: The Anxiety of Reception.* Oxford: Oxford University Press, 2000.

Nietzsche, Friedrich. *On the Advantage and Disadvantage of History for Life.* Trans. Peter Preuss. Indianapolis: Hackett Publishing, 1980.

O'Farrell, Patrick J. *Ireland's English Question: Anglo-Irish Relations 1534–1970.* London: B. T. Batsford, 1971.

O'Ferrall, Fergus. *Catholic Emancipation: Daniel O'Connell and the Birth of Irish Democracy 1820–30*. Dublin: Gill and Macmillan, 1985.

Ó Gráda, Cormac. "Poverty, Population, and Agriculture, 1801–45." In Vaughan (ed.), *A New History of Ireland*, v: 108–32.

Ozouf, Mona. *Les Mots Des Femmes: Essai Sur La Singularité Française*. Paris: Fayard, 1995.

Pinch, Adela. *Strange Fits of Passion: Epistemologies of Emotion, Hume to Austen*. Stanford: Stanford University Press, 1996.

Poovey, Mary. *A History of the Modern Fact: Problems of Knowledge in the Sciences of Wealth and Society*. Chicago and London: University of Chicago Press, 1998.

Porter, Dennis. *Haunted Journeys: Desire and Transgression in European Travel Writing*. Princeton: Princeton University Press, 1991.

Pratt, Mary Louise. *Imperial Eyes: Travel Writing and Transculturation*. London and New York: Routledge, 1992.

Rafroidi, Patrick. *Irish Literature in English: The Romantic Period (1789–1850)*. 2 vols. Gerrards Cross: Colin Smythe, 1980.

Robertson, Fiona. *Legitimate Histories: Scott, Gothic, and the Authorities of Fiction*. Oxford: Clarendon Press, 1994.

Russett, Margaret. *De Quincey's Romanticism: Canonical Minority and the Forms of Transmission*. Cambridge: Cambridge University Press, 1997.

Sherman, Stuart. *Telling Time: Clocks, Diaries, and English Diurnal Form, 1660–1785*. Chicago and London: University of Chicago Press, 1996.

Simmel, Georg. *Georg Simmel, 1858–1918: A Collection of Essays, with Translations and a Bibliography*. Ed. Kurt H. Wolff. Columbus: The Ohio State University Press, 1959.

The Sociology of George Simmel. Trans. and ed. Kurt H. Wolff. Illinois: The Free Press, 1950.

Siskin, Clifford. *The Work of Writing: Literature and Social Change in Britain 1700–1830*. Baltimore: Johns Hopkins University Press, 1998.

Sloan, Barry. *The Pioneers of Anglo-Irish Fiction 1800–1860*. Gerrards Cross: Colin Smythe, 1986.

Smyth, William J. "A Plurality of Irelands: Regions, Societies and Mentalities." In *In Search of Ireland: A Cultural Geography*, ed. Brian Graham, 19–42. London: Routledge, 1997.

Spender, Dale, ed. *Living By the Pen: Early British Women Writers*. New York: Teachers College Press, 1992.

Stallybrass, Peter, and Allon White. *The Politics and Poetics of Transgression*. Ithaca: Cornell University Press, 1986.

Starobinski, Jean. *The Invention of Liberty, 1700–1789*. Trans. Bernard C. Swift. Geneva: Editions d'Art Albert Skira, 1964.

Stewart, Susan. *Crimes of Writing: Problems in the Containment of Representation*. New York: Oxford University Press, 1991; Durham, N.C.: Duke University Press, 1994.

Thom, Martin. *Republics, Nations, and Tribes*. London: Verso, 1995.

Tracy, Robert. "Maria Edgeworth and Lady Morgan." *Nineteenth-Century Fiction* 40 (1985): 1–22.

The Unappeasable Host: Studies in Irish Identities. Dublin: University College Dublin Press, 1998.

Trumpener, Katie. *Bardic Nationalism: The Romantic Novel and the British Empire.* Princeton: Princeton University Press, 1997.

Tymoczko, Maria. "Two Traditions of Translating Early Irish Literature." *Target* 3:2 (1991): 207–24.

Vallois, Marie-Claire. "Old Idols New Subjects: Germaine de Staël and Romanticism." In *Germaine de Stael: Crossing the Borders*, ed. Madelyn Gutwirth, Avriel Goldberger, and Karyna Szmurlo, 82–97. New Brunswick: Rutgers University Press, 1991.

Vaughan, W. E., ed. *A New History of Ireland.* Volume V: *Ireland Under the Union, I (1801–1870).* Oxford: Clarendon Press, 1989.

Venuti, Lawrence, ed. *Rethinking Translation: Discourse, Subjectivity, Ideology.* New York: Routledge, 1992.

Watson, Nicola. *Revolution and the Form of the British Novel, 1790–1825: Intercepted Letters, Interrupted Seductions.* Oxford: Clarendon Press, 1994.

Weekes, Ann Owens. *Irish Women Writers: An Uncharted Tradition.* Kentucky: The University Press of Kentucky, 1990.

Welsh, Alexander. *Strong Representations: Narrative and Circumstantial Evidence in England.* Baltimore and London: Johns Hopkins University Press, 1992.

Whelan, Kevin. *The Tree of Liberty: Radicalism, Catholicism and the Construction of Irish Identity 1760–1830.* Notre Dame: University of Notre Dame Press, 1996.

Woods, C. J. "The Authorship of *A Tour in Ireland in 1813 & 1814.*" *Notes and Queries* 34 (1987): 481–82.

"Irish Travel Writings as Source Material." *Irish Historical Studies* 28 (1992): 171–83.

Woodward, Christopher. "Scenes From the Future." In *Visions of Ruin: Architectural Fantasies and Designs for Garden Follies*, 15–17. London: Sir John Soane's Museum, 1999.

Wright, Julia. "'The Nation Begins to Form': Competing Nationalisms in Morgan's *The O'Briens and the O'Flahertys.*" *ELH* 66 (1999): 939–63.

Young, Robert. J. C. *Colonial Desire: Hybridity in Theory, Culture, and Race.* New York: Routledge, 1995.

Žižek, Slavoj. "A Leftist Plea for 'Eurocentrism'." *Critical Inquiry* 24 (Summer 1998): 988–1009.

Index

CAMBRIDGE STUDIES IN ROMANTICISM

GENERAL EDITORS
MARILYN BUTLER, *University of Oxford*
JAMES CHANDLER, *University of Chicago*

1. MARY A. FAVRET
Romantic Correspondence: Women, Politics and the Fiction of Letters

2. NIGEL LEASK
British Romantic Writers and the East: Anxieties of Empire

3. TOM FURNISS
Edmund Burke's Aesthetic Ideology
Language, Gender and Political Economy in Revolution

4. PETER MURPHY
Poetry as an Occupation and an Art in Britain, 1760–1830

5. JULIE A. CARLSON
In the Theatre of Romanticism: Coleridge, Nationalism, Women

6. ANDREW BENNETT
Keats, Narrative and Audience

7. DAVID DUFF
Romance and Revolution: Shelley and the Politics of a Genre

8. ALAN RICHARDSON
Literature, Education, and Romanticism: Reading as Social Practice, 1780–1832

9. EDWARD COPELAND
Women Writing about Money: Women's Fiction in England, 1790–1820

10. TIMOTHY MORTON
Shelley and the Revolution in Taste: The Body and the Natural World

11. LEONORA NATTRASS
William Cobbett: The Politics of Style

12. E.J. CLERY
The Rise of Supernatural Fiction, 1762–1800

13. ELIZABETH A. BOHLS
Women Travel Writers and the Language of Aesthetics, 1716–1818

14. SIMON BAINBRIDGE
Napoleon and English Romanticism

15. CELESTE LANGAN
Romantic Vagrancy: Wordsworth and the Simulation of Freedom

16. JOHN WYATT
Wordsworth and the Geologists

17. ROBERT J. GRIFFIN
Wordsworth's Pope: A Study in Literary Historiography

18. MARKMAN ELLIS
The Politics of Sensibility
Race, Gender and Commerce in the Sentimental Novel

19. CAROLINE GONDA
Reading Daughters' Fictions, 1709–1834
Novels and Society from Manley to Edgeworth

20. ANDREA K. HENDERSON
Romantic Identities: Varieties of Subjectivity, 1774–1830

21. KEVIN GILMARTIN
Print Politics: The Press and Radical Opposition
in Early Nineteenth-Century England

22. THERESA M. KELLEY
Reinventing Allegory

23. GARY DYER
British Satire and the Politics of Style, 1789–1832

24. ROBERT M. RYAN
The Romantic Reformation
Religious politics in English Literature, 1789–1824

25. MARGARET RUSSETT
De Quincey's Romanticism
Canonical Minority and the Forms of Transmission

26. JENNIFER FORD
Coleridge on Dreaming
Romanticism, Dreams and the Medical Imagination

27. SAREE MAKDISI
Romantic Imperialism: Universal Empire and
the Culture of Modernity

28. NICHOLAS M. WILLIAMS
Ideology and Utopia in the Poetry of William Blake

29. SONIA HOFKOSH
Sexual Politics and the Romantic Author

30. ANNE JANOWITZ
Lyric and Labour in the Romantic Tradition

31. JEFFREY N. COX
Poetry and Politics in the Cockney School
Keats, Shelley, Hunt and their Circle

32. GREGORY DART
Rousseau, Robespierre and English Romanticism

33. JAMES WATT
Contesting the Gothic
Fiction, Genre and Cultural Conflict, 1764–1832

34. DAVID ARAM KAISER
Romanticism, Aesthetics, and Nationalism

35. ANDREW BENNETT
Romantic Poets and the Culture of Posterity

36. PAUL KEEN
The Crisis of Literature in the 1790s
Print Culture and the Public Sphere

37. MARTIN PRIESTMAN
Romantic Atheism: Poetry and Freethought, 1780–1830

38. HELEN THOMAS
Romanticism and Slave Narratives
Transatlantic Testimonies

39. JOHN WHALE
Imagination Under Pressure, 1789–1832
Aesthetics, Politics, and Utility

40. MICHAEL GAMER
Romanticism and the Gothic
Genre, Reception, and Canon Formation, 1790–1820

41. MAUREEN N. McLANE
Romanticism and the Human Sciences
Poetry, Population, and the Discourse of the Species

42. TIMOTHY MORTON
The Poetics of Spice
Romantic Consumerism and the Exotic

43. MIRANDA J. BURGESS
British Fiction and the Production of Social Order, 1740–1830

44. ANGELA KEANE
Women Writers and the English Nation in the 1790s

45. MARK PARKER
Literary Magazines and British Romanticism

46. BETSY BOLTON
Women, Nationalism and the Romantic Stage
Theatre and Politics in Britain, 1780–1800

47. ALAN RICHARDSON
British Romanticism and the Science of the Mind

48. M.O. GRENBY
The Anti-Jacobin Novel: British Conservatism and the French Revolution

49. CLARA TUITE
Romantic Austen
Sexual Politics and the Literary Canon

50. JEROME J. McGANN ED. JAMES SODERHOLM
Byron and Romanticism

51. INA FERRIS
The Romantic National Tale and the Question of Ireland